Glynn Christian's
DELICATESSEN
COOKBOOK

Other books by Glynn Christian

Cheese and Cheese-making
Bread and Yeast Cookery
The Delicatessen Food Handbook
Glynn Christian's Radio and TV Cookbook
Get Fresh with Glynn Christian
Wonderful World of Food

Biography
Fragile Paradise – The Discovery of
Fletcher Christian

Glynn Christian's
DELICATESSEN COOKBOOK

MACDONALD & CO
London & Sydney

For PL who often had to sing for our supper

Acknowledgements

A special thanks is due to my friends, old and new, amongst the food writing establishment, who have welcomed me so generously. I am most grateful to John Tovey and Prue Leith, Claudia Roden, Paul Levy, Kathie Webber, Michael Smith, Lady Harlech, Lyn Hall, Lady Arabella Boxer, Brian Taylor, Katie Stapleton, Sue Fleming, Rosie Stark and the late, loved Marika Hanbury Tenison who all played some part in this book. My thanks also to OVER 21, to BBC TV Breakfast Time, and to Gloria Hunniford of Radio 2 for allowing me to use recipes created for them.

A MACDONALD BOOK
© Glynn Christian 1984

First published in Great Britain in 1984
by Macdonald & Co (Publishers) Ltd
London & Sydney

A member of BPCC plc

ISBN 0 356 09743 9

Filmset by Cylinder Typesetting Ltd, London
Printed and bound in Great Britain by
Hazell, Watson & Viney Limited,
Members of the BPCC Group,
Aylesbury, Bucks

Macdonald & Co (Publishers) Ltd
Maxwell House
74 Worship Street
London EC2A 2EN

Contents

Introduction

No other part of the food industry in Great Britain is expanding as fast as delicatessen foods. Even the mighty supermarkets are taking note of a growing public demand for variety and personal service and putting delicatessen counters into their shops. To me, a deli counter in a supermarket is the closest we can get to having our old-fashioned corner shops back. Yet deli counters are also where the newer idea of fast food really began.

But the personal service, and greater variety now sold at specialist counters and shops, is no guarantee of old-fashioned quality, standards or flavours. Many a modern pâté enthusiast has never eaten proper pâté, for what he spreads on his bread or toast has been made weeks before, in huge factories, and is packed with expanders and preservatives to help it last its chequered career. There are cheese enthusiasts who have never eaten a proper Cheddar cheese, bean people who wouldn't recognize real baked beans . . . and almost no one now knows what a quiche should be.

This book will help solve some of those problems. It may not be quite what you expect, unless you expected something idiosyncratic, a little unbalanced and very surprising. It is all those things, yes, but it also performs two other functions.

First, the recipes expand considerably the ideas found in my *Delicatessen Food Handbook*. Most are original, many of them created for BBC TV *Breakfast Time*, or for *Pebble Mill at One*, and all will help you make really fine food with delicatessen products.

Second, the book will be a help to those who own delicatessens but who are unable always to get the products they want or to those who don't have access to a delicatessen. Here there are pâté and cheesecake recipes, pickling and baking recipes, alternatives to the soggy quiche, ways to cure your own salmon –

even a method to smoke food in your kitchen without damaging your health or your house.

You won't find a recipe for absolutely everything, no exhaustive treatise on every bean, grain, herb or spice you have ever heard about or read of in my previous books. Instead, I have simply chosen the recipes I enjoyed creating and eating most during the past few years. Enjoyment – yours and mine – and some regard for the way things should be were my two criteria.

One more surprise. The book is four or five times as long as it seems. That's because most recipes end with a series of *Options*, my suggestions for alternative ingredients and flavour combinations. Indeed, once the manuscript was finished, I found some of the best ideas of all were amongst these options. Harvest these as well as the main recipes, and I think you will be well pleased.

Enjoy eating my words. I've enjoyed writing them.

Glynn Christian

1 Pâtés and Terrines

A decent pâté or terrine should be enough to keep anyone down on the farm. Essentially a way of preserving pork or game in the days before refrigeration, they are first cousins to meat loaf, but have a higher fat content. The growth of interest in, and availability of, pâtés is perhaps the most easily noticed part of the phenomenal growth in delicatessen foods this last ten years.

Little else is as satisfying as the rich, full flavour of a well made and aged pâté, smooth or chunky, garlicky, gamey or herbed. I've eaten excellent types made with only four or five ingredients. Yet, because most of the pâtés available in delicatessens have been imported, they are stuffed with a catalogue of extenders, preservatives, emulsifiers, anti-oxidants and extra flavouring and are as far away from real pâté as can be imagined.

I developed many of these pâtés for my delicatessen in sheer frustration at not being able to buy what I wanted. Eventually I had a small industry on my hands supplying a range of unadulterated, honest pâtés to shops all over London, including Harrods. They spawned dozens of competitive companies, most of whom no longer exist, although a couple continue with people who left my kitchen!

Modern refrigeration techniques and the wide choice of goods today mean the humble pâté has been elevated into far grander realms than imagined by the farmer's wife of earlier this century. Now we can make them from vegetables and fish and such delicacies as sweetbreads. You will find examples of all those here and, if you've made pâtés before, you may well find some of my techniques unorthodox; but you will also find those techniques give a more honest and satisfying representation of the flavours of your ingredients.

In particular, my methods of making game pâtés differ from the norm, in which the animal or bird's flesh is roasted to some predetermined degree and then layered in a forcemeat. To me these constructions rarely taste of the game for which they are named – it really is asking too much for some ready-cooked pheasant breast to flavour a pork forcemeat and also to retain some savour for itself. Therefore I hit upon the plan of simmering game in wine or in a marinade, which extracts all possible flavour from the bones, skin and fat. The flesh is then combined with a forcemeat and the much-reduced cooking liquid; chicken livers are used as the major binder. I also use quite a lot of bacon, for the saltpetre used in its curing adds a welcome pinkness to the finished product, as do the chicken livers.

First, some basic recipes, and then a variety of game pâtés employing my techniques. Don't forget that the flavour will develop considerably over 5-6 days after cooking; and it certainly will not do your pâté – or you – much credit if you cut into one less than 24 hours after it has been cooked.

Once you do serve your pâtés, please give a thought to doing so without toast. Pâté eaten with a knife and fork is much easier to serve, eliminating the fuss of making toast at the last minute. A couple of special relishes or sauces, a leaf or two of an unusual salad ingredient and suddenly pâté is interesting again. On the Orient Express I found it served atop a blanched leaf of Savoy cabbage, which was a wondrous electric green. The pâté had been moistened with a little dressing, which included walnut oil, and then scattered with the tiniest imaginable cubes of raw beetroot and turnip.

REALLY GOOD BASIC PÂTÉ

Once you have made this pâté a couple of times, you will have the confidence to adjust it to become absolutely your own. It is vital that you do not stint on the herbs and spices – remember the meat you are flavouring is quite bland and that everything cooks together a long time. If you like a pâté that is slightly squashy and spreads, leave out the breadcrumbs – they are, in any case, somewhat unorthodox, but for catering, buffets and picnics it is sometimes easier to have a pâté that cuts and serves precisely.

For about 3 lb/1.3 kg weight

1 lb/450 g *belly of pork, trimmed*	½ tsp *ground allspice*
12 oz/350 g *fatty bacon*	½ tsp *black pepper*
1 lb/450 g *liver (see below)*	2-3 tbsp *brandy, red or white wine*
8 oz/225 g *onions*	1½ oz/40 g *dry, white*
2-3 *garlic cloves*	*breadcrumbs*
1 tsp *dried thyme*	4 oz/115 g *streaky bacon, sliced*
½ tsp *ground nutmeg*	

Mince or cut the belly of pork into quite coarse pieces. The fatty bacon should be very much finer. Mix together well.

Make a purée of the liver, onions, garlic, thyme, spices and alcohol. (You can use pig's liver, but I think chicken livers give a much nicer flavour and colour to the cooked pâté.) Mix this well-flavoured purée with the pork and bacon, then stir in the breadcrumbs.

Pile neatly into a bowl or loaf tin of 3 pint/1.7 litre capacity then arrange the strips of streaky bacon over the top, digging the ends well down the sides of the container. Stand in a pan of boiling water then bake for 1¼ hours in a preheated 350°F/180°C/Gas 4 oven.

Do not press when the pâté comes from the oven as this expresses the delicious juices, which are much more useful inside the pâté than outside.

Options   To vary this recipe, apart from leaving out the breadcrumbs and using different livers or mixtures of livers, change the texture of the pork and/or bacon to give a rougher or smoother finish. Four or five juniper berries added to the liver purée would give a gamey flavour and this is always better if accompanied by some grated orange rind (say 1-2 teaspoons). A few pinches of ground cloves are always a good addition to any pork dish. You might use rosemary instead of thyme or use a combination of the two as well.

The flavour of dried mushrooms which have been reconstituted in red wine (and that liquid reduced to a few tablespoons and used in the mixture) is preferable to fresh ones. If you would like a bit more texture, reconstitute some dried chestnuts in red wine with a cinnamon stick and a bay leaf or two, and add them with the strained, reduced liquid; for the best effect, keep the chestnuts in as big pieces as possible.

BASIC CHICKEN LIVER PÂTÉ

Makes about 2 lb/900 g weight

12 oz/350 g *fatty bacon, smoked or green*
4 oz/115 g *butter*
4 oz/115 g *onions, sliced*
¼-½ tsp *dried rosemary*
½-1 tsp *dried thyme*
1 lb/450 g *chicken livers*
3-4 tbsp *medium sherry or brandy*
Black pepper, to taste

The fattest bacon of all, which is also the cheapest, is flank and sometimes that can be bought in whole pieces. Ordinary streaky bacon is also suitable for this recipe and you do not have to cut off the rind as it will be well cooked and then chopped fine or liquidized.

Cut or chop the bacon finely and put it into a covered saucepan over medium heat until most of the fat has started to run, but do not let the bacon crispen. Add the butter and onions and herbs and continue to cook until the onions are really soft.

The variation in herb content is based on the enormous difference in types of dried herbs, often dependent on how long you have kept them. Use less of fresher ones, more of older ones – or increase one or the other simply because you like the flavour.

Once the onions are really well cooked, add the whole chicken livers and turn up the heat. Keep turning the mixture to ensure even cooking. As soon as the livers are cooked, but while their juices are still pink, place everything from the pan into a liquidizer or food processor and process until it is the texture you prefer.

For something only slightly textured, first divide the cooked mixture in half. Process the first half until really smooth and put to one side. Process the second half until medium to fine then mix the two together.

Flavour with medium sherry or brandy and add pepper to taste. Put into a container and when cold cover with melted butter.

An excellent spreading pâté, but one which will cut neatly, too. Serve scooped onto some interesting salad leaves and eat with a knife and fork. Here are some of the variations possible.

Chicken and Walnut
Add a dessertspoon or more of walnut oil to the finished pâté plus 2-4 oz/50-115 g of walnuts in as large or small pieces as you prefer. To enhance the contrast of texture, toast the walnuts lightly.

Chicken and Green Peppercorns
Add at least 2 teaspoons of green peppercorns to the mixture just before you add the chicken livers. Walnuts are also nice with this mixture.

Chicken and Hazelnuts
Add toasted, coarsely crushed hazelnuts. Serve with a little hazelnut oil or with a small salad of chicken breast dressed with hazelnut oil-flavoured mayonnaise.

Chicken and Olive
Blanch 6 oz/175 g green or black olives, stone them and cut neatly in half. Add a third to the mixture before puréeing and stir the remainder into the finished mixture. Dress with olive oil.

CHICKEN TERRINE WITH NO LIVER

There are a number of people who simply cannot get on with the flavour or idea of eating liver, and to them most of the wonderful world of pâtés is quite lost; as it is to those not able to eat pork.

This baked terrine contains neither liver nor pork, but isn't quite the mundane chicken meat loaf. The recipe, from Denver, uses burghul wheat and ground almonds as part of the binding mixture, but you could use breadcrumbs instead, as explained overleaf.

For a 3 lb/1.3 kg loaf tin

1¾-2 lb/800-900 g *boned,
   skinned chicken flesh*
2 oz/50 g *burghul wheat*
4 oz/115 g *watercress*
4 oz/115 g *onions*
1 level tsp *ground mace*
1 level tsp *ground coriander*
1 tsp *sea salt*

1 tsp *black pepper, finely ground*
2 *eggs*
4 oz/115 g *ground almonds*
½ pt/300 ml *double or soured
   cream*
Vine leaves (optional)
4 tbsp *brandy (optional)*

The chicken meat may be all white or a mixture of white and dark. For the former you will need at least four large breasts; for the latter a chicken weighing over 3½ lb/1.6 kg dressed.

Cover the burghul with water and soak for 20 minutes. Take a whole chicken breast, remove the long supreme from underneath in one piece, then divide the rest of the breast into three long strips, which should be about the same size as the supreme. Keep these to one side.

You will need two bunches of watercress; weigh them then trim the stalks until you have the required amount. Reserve a palmful.

Chop the onions and watercress finely in a food processor together with the mace, coriander, salt and pepper. Blend in the eggs.

Drain the burghul, squeeze gently. Add with the almonds. Keep the processor running then slowly add the chicken flesh (except the reserved strips) until all is smooth. Add the cream or soured cream, scraping down the bowl several times to ensure an evenly textured mixture.

Pale coloured terrines can be discoloured during baking, even in a pottery container, so I think it best to line whatever you use with vine leaves, shiny side out. Spoon in just over half the mixture. Salt and pepper the reserved chicken strips generously. Chop the reserved watercress coarsely and roll the strips in that; arrange in two lines the length of the terrine. Spoon on the brandy if you are using it. Add the rest of the chicken mixture. Smooth well, ensuring the corners are tightly filled. Cover with vine leaves and weave them in with those from the side.

Seal the tin with a dome of aluminium foil then stand that in a roasting tin of boiling water which comes halfway up the sides of the terrine. Bake for 1¼-1½ hours at 350°F/180°C/Gas 4. Let cool in the pan, then chill well before turning out and serving in slices

A well-reduced tomato sauce with chopped watercress in it would be nice and colourful, and could be heightened with the merest dash or Tabasco or a chili sauce.

If you are really stuck for ideas, this terrine would be a sensational hot starter providing you had the time to make it on the day and the oven were free.

Options You could replace both the burghul and the almonds – or just one of them – with an equal weight of fresh wholemeal or rye breadcrumbs. Coarsely chopped pistachios would give luxury to either version.

PHEASANT PÂTÉ

Makes about 3 lb/1.3 kg weight

1 *well-hung pheasant*
12 oz/350 g *streaky bacon, cut in strips or cubes*
1 pt/575 ml *strong red wine*
4 oz/115 g *onions*
2-3 *garlic cloves*
24 *black peppercorns*
8 *juniper berries*
2 *mace blades*
4 *fresh bay leaves*
2 dessertsp *brandy, whisky or gin*
12 oz/350 g *chicken livers*
1 tbsp *flour*
6 oz/175 g *belly of pork*
1 tsp *dried thyme*

First remove as many as possible of any remaining feathers from the bird, then cut in quarters and put into a saucepan with the bacon strips or cubes, wine, onions, garlic, peppercorns, juniper, mace and bay. Simmer gently until the meat is tender and comes easily from the bones.

Take the pieces of pheasant out and wait until they are cool enough to handle. Remove the breasts, put to one side and pour over the brandy, whisky or gin. Take all the other flesh, skin, fat, etc. off the bones and put into a liquidizer or food processor. Add all the solids from the cooking stock, plus the chicken livers. Process until really smooth. Add the plain flour and mix well. Turn into a bowl.

Cut the belly of pork into quite small pieces or chop in a food processor. Add these to the mixture.

Add dried thyme (or half thyme, half rosemary) to the stock and reduce until it is somewhere between ¼ and ½ pint/150-300 ml. Mix ¼ pint/150 ml into the pâté mixture. Take a bowl or loaf tin of 3 pint/1.7 litre capacity and add two-thirds of the pâté. Cut the marinated breast meat into long, thick strips and arrange on top, sprinkling over any alcohol that has not been absorbed. Spread on the rest of the pâté and pour over the remaining stock.

Stand the bowl or the tin in a roasting tray and pour in boiling water to a depth of 2-3 in/5-7.5 cm and bake in a 350°F/180°C/Gas 4 oven for 1¼ hours or until the cooking juices are no longer tinted with pink. Let cool thoroughly, then cover and chill well. If you plan to store it for some time there is a definite advantage in sealing the top with butter or with a mixture of butter and lard. To make that edible as well as practical, flavour it somewhat with the alcohol used for marinating.

This will make a firm but slightly crumbly pâté suitable for spreading or slicing very carefully. For something firmer, you might add up to 1 oz/25 g dry breadcrumbs, which is a better technique than pressing under a weight.

Option   Use two grouse instead of the pheasant and substitute rosemary for the thyme and whisky for the brandy.

VENISON PÂTÉ

Makes about 3 lb/1.3 kg weight

1 lb/450 g *stewing venison, lean*	2 tsp *ground cinnamon*
½ pt/300 ml *strong red wine*	½ tsp *ground nutmeg*
4 oz/115 g *onions*	12 oz/350 g *streaky bacon*
2-4 *garlic cloves, chopped*	½ tsp *ground rosemary*
4 oz/115 g *whole orange, in pieces*	1 tsp *dried thyme*
8 *juniper berries*	1 lb/450 g *chicken livers*
12 *black peppercorns*	8 oz/225 g *belly of pork*
3 *fresh bay leaves*	3 dessertsp *whisky*
2 *mace blades*	2 oz/50 g *ground almonds*

Cube the venison, then place in a bowl with the wine, onions, garlic, orange (take out the pips), juniper, peppercorns, bay, mace, cinnamon and nutmeg. Marinate for 24 hours.

Cut the bacon into strips or cubes and add that too. Put the mixture in a pan, cover and cook gently until the venison is tender and the bacon has started to melt. Drain the marinade into a separate pan, add the rosemary and thyme and put to reduce over gentle heat down to just under ¼ pint/150 ml.

Meanwhile, liquidize all the contents of the original saucepan, but leave some texture. Separately, purée the chicken livers, then fold the two together. Chop the belly of pork as coarsely or finely as you like and mix that in thoroughly as well. Mix in the reduced liquid plus the whisky and almonds.

For a firm, strong pâté, stir up to 1 oz/25 g of dry breadcrumbs into the mixture before baking.

This is now the basis of an excellent venison pâté and could be just covered with strips of bacon and baked in a loaf tin as it is for about an hour in a 350°F/180°C/Gas 4 oven. But for more important occasions, wrap it in vine leaves and for absolutely momentous occasions, continue as follows.

Options   Have ready 1 lb/450 g of lambs' sweetbreads. To prepare them you must soak them in at least three changes of water over 3 or 4 hours to remove all blood, then blanch them for a few minutes in boiling water which will firm them up nicely. Carefully remove any traces of fat, gristle or membrane, trying to keep the sweetbreads as whole as possible. While they wait their turn, let them rest in a helping of whisky or brandy, or even a medium sherry (Amontillado) would do.

Once the venison mixture is ready, line a large oiled loaf tin with vine leaves. If bought commercially, soak them in hot water for 5 minutes before using; if from your garden, wilt them in hot water for about the same time. Ensure the shiny side of each leaf is towards the outside of the tin. Put two-thirds of the venison pâté carefully into the tin, then arrange the sweet-breads in parallel lines along the length of the tin. Sprinkle on any remaining alcohol, then top up with the remaining pâté. Cover with leaves and fold over those from the sides of the tin. Cover the tin with a dome of aluminium foil – seal tightly around the edges but leave 3-4 in/7.5-10 cm free above the mixture – stand in a tray of boiling water and bake 1¼ hours at 350°F/180°C/Gas 4.

Chill very well before serving in thin slices with a variety of sharp jellies and mustards. A jelly of rowan berries, a few raspberries and a creamy horseradish sauce are all excellent.

If you can buy shelled pistachios, blanch 1 oz/25 g for a couple of minutes, remove their skins, and stir into the basic mixture before putting into the tin. Or chop some roughly and scatter them over each serving.

PÂTÉ OF LAMBS' SWEETBREADS AND PERNOD

Although a bit of a fiddle, this is a most worthwhile exercise, and on a hot summer's day makes the most tantalizing and stimulating start to any meal. Yet it is also very grand and can well take its place at the most sophisticated dinner table any time of the year, particularly in the second version. The technique of setting with butter and cream is the same as for the Smoked Salmon Pâté later on in this chapter.

Serves 6-8

1 lb/450 g *lambs' sweetbreads*	1 *egg*
1 level tsp *onion, chopped*	*Salt*
½ level tsp *garlic, chopped*	1½ tsp *Pernod*
2 tsp *lemon juice*	6 oz/175 g *butter, melted*
2 *egg whites*	¼ pt/150 ml *double cream, chilled*

Soak the sweetbreads in three changes of water over 4 hours to ensure all blood is dissolved away. Plunge into boiling water and simmer for 2 minutes until nicely firmed, then drain and cool under cold running water. Remove extraneous fat, membrane and gristle. Place in liquidizer or food processor with the onion, garlic, lemon juice, egg whites, whole egg and salt. Process until really smooth then pass through a sieve. Put this purée into an ovenproof dish, cover with foil, stand in boiling water and bake gently at 350°F/180°C/Gas 4 until just set (about 30 minutes). Do not let it brown.

Once this is cool, beat it smooth with the Pernod and melted butter, which should be only just warm. Whip the chilled cream then fold them together. Turn into a pretty dish to set and make a decorative pattern on top with a fork or knife tip.

This pâté could be accompanied by very good wholemeal bread or even with toast, if the bread used was not presliced. Serve in scoops on a plate which has been covered with crisp, fresh, raw spinach leaves, lightly dressed. Scatter very thin slices of crisp endive or incredibly thin circles of raw leek over all and dribble tiny cubes of raw or cooked beetroot onto the pâté. A couple of beautiful prawns completes the picture.

Options Both sweetbreads and Pernod go extremely well with seafood and there are many ways you can take advantage of this by utilizing the excellent range of seafood in cans. The simplest is just to serve the pâté with prawns, mussels, smoked clams, clams, crab or whatever.

Otherwise, drain a can of Danish mussels, then dress them with a tiny portion of lemon juice and olive oil (just enough to moisten them). Mix some mayonnaise with powdered saffron. Fold in the mussels then add a lot of chopped parsley so the mixture is quite firm. Put into the base of a lightly oiled ring mould or loaf tin then lightly pile the pâté mixture atop them. When unmoulded the rugged topping will give a marvellous effect and make the dish much more substantial.

A more unorthodox approach is to use the outstanding Norwegian brands of dried seafood soups and to follow their directions for making sauces. With the addition of brandy and cream the mixed seafood, lobster and crab versions are amazingly good. (Don't be tempted to use any canned soup as the seafood versions always taste of starch somehow.) Let the sauce cool and serve your sweetbread pâté in a pool of it. Add some choice pieces of prawn, poached monkfish or whatever you can get your hands on.

VEGETABLE PATCH PÂTÉ

The much vaunted terrines of vegetable presented as the star turn of many a modern chef have always disappointed me. Somehow it seemed a swizz to call them terrines of vegetable when the vegetables were held together with a mousse of ham or tongue or some other part of an animal. I therefore determined to make a terrine entirely of vegetables and used the techniques behind my savoury flans as the basis.

This recipe makes a large party pâté, so you might halve the quantity to make something for a dinner party; it will keep in the refrigerator for over a week.

Serves 15-20

2 lb/900 g *parsnips*	8 *eggs*
¾ pt/425 ml *milk or single cream*	4 tbsp *lemon juice*
2 oz/50 g *butter*	2 lb/900 g *vegetables, in thin strips*
8 oz/225 g *curd or cream cheese*	*Vine leaves, as required*

Scrub the parsnips well and cut them up roughly, but do not peel them. Poach until tender in creamy milk or single cream, together with the butter. Liquidize and strain, then let cool before beating in the cheese, eggs and lemon juice. If you do this when the parsnip purée is hot you will deflate the cheese, and the mixture will not be able to support the patchwork of vegetables

The variety of vegetables with which you dramatize the basic pâté should be chosen for a contrast of colour, texture and taste, and three or four will be enough. None needs to be precooked but all must be in long strips or cubes and each must be independently seasoned. Green beans (I use frozen haricot beans), strips of carrot or of turnip can be smothered in finely chopped parsley or sprinkled well with nutmeg. Equally, the beans or celeriac or fennel could be drenched in garlic, the turnip could be smeared in mustard, sliced artichoke bottoms bathed in tarragon vinegar or tossed in chopped fresh mint, thyme or rosemary. Peas can be avoided.

Once you have your purée ready and your vegetables prepared, liberally oil a 3 pint/1.7 litre loaf tin then line with overlapping vine leaves, shiny sides outermost, leaving a border hanging over the top of the tin.

Pour in a shallow layer of parsnip then arrange your heaviest vegetable in lines lengthwise along the tin. Add more purée and then another vegetable and so on until everything is used up and the tin is filled. Top with vine leaves and interweave those with the excess from the sides to make a neat parcel. Stand in boiling water in a roasting tray and cover the pâté with a dome of foil tightly sealed around the loaf tin's edges. Bake 1¼ hours in a preheated oven at 350°F/180°C/Gas 4. Let stand 15 minutes then invert on to a large platter, simply to check it will emerge. If not you will have to do a little scalpel work, but remember it is only the vine leaves you are dissecting. Then line the loaf tin with clingfilm or foil and replace the pâté so it stays firmly in shape whilst it is cooling. Place in a refrigerator so it chills thoroughly.

Options   Instead of parsnips you might choose to use celeriac or carrot, but ensure the latter is well flavoured – it would be a waste of effort to use sweet new carrots. If you have a garden full of herbs, then scatter through a layer of chopped mixed herbs. For greater variety and individuality, you could mix some cream cheese with herbs, add 1 egg per ¼ pint/150 ml of mixture and have a herb cheese layer somewhere in the construction; or to avoid any question of being mistaken for a vegetarian, you might employ strips or cubes of tongue, ham or cooked chicken.

Those with a specially artistic bent would achieve a great coup by soft-boiling and shelling some quails' eggs and arranging them in strips along the pâté.

BLOODY MARY SAUCE

Any cold herby tomato-based sauce would be good with the above pâté – it certainly needs some sauce, if only for the sake of presentation – but none will be better than this, which I call

Bloody Mary Sauce for various reasons, and which makes six small tasty servings.

14-16 oz/400-450 g *canned plum tomatoes*	1 tsp *Worcestershire sauce*
1 tbsp *vodka*	2 tsp *lemon juice*
	Celery salt

Reduce the canned plum tomatoes in their own juice until just a few tablespoons of pulp are left at the bottom of the pan. Use great care and a low heat or you will caramelize the tomatoes. Sieve this to remove the pips and any skin, then mix in the vodka, Worcestershire sauce, lemon juice and, with great care, a very few sprinkles of celery salt. This should be served ice-cold.

NO-BAKE FISH TERRINE

So many people are now interested in reducing their intake of cholesterol that I felt obliged to create this recipe when I was designing a wedding buffet for BBC TV's *Breakfast Time*. Although I specify white fish like cod or whiting, you could use salmon or trout, or be luxurious and employ monkfish to suggest the flavour and texture of lobster.

For a 1½ lb/675 g terrine

14-16 oz/400-450 g *boneless white fish*	1 oz/25 g *onion, chopped*
7-8 oz/200-225 g *boneless smoked fish*	½ oz/15 g *parsley, stalks only*
	3 strips *lemon peel*
4 oz/115 g *cooked, drained spinach*	2 *fresh bay leaves*
	10 *black peppercorns, crushed*
Salt, pepper, nutmeg, to taste	2 *egg whites*
½ pt/300 ml *dry white wine*	1 envelope *gelatine*
	Lemon juice (optional)

Carefully bone, skin and trim both the plain and smoked fish. Ideally, do not use 'golden' fillets as the colour in these will drain out; a small properly smoked haddock is excellent, perhaps the best, but you could also use mackerel, provided that, too, has been naturally smoked. Kipper is another good choice but the fine bones are difficult to remove and those that remain make it difficult to slice the finished terrine. Prepare the spinach, ensuring it really is nice and dry. Season it with salt, pepper and nutmeg.

Put the wine with the onion, parsley stalks, lemon, bay and peppercorns into a shallow pan, bring slowly to the boil then add the white fish and cook gently until done. Remove the fish. In the same stock, gently poach the smoked fish, remove, then strain the cooking liquid and measure. It should be ¼ pint/ 150 ml – either reduce back to this level by heating or add a little white wine to make it up.

Make a purée of the white fish, the spinach and egg whites. Dissolve the gelatine powder in a little of the strained stock, then mix well with the balance of stock. Blend this into the fish and spinach mixture, too. Taste and season with salt, pepper and nutmeg and perhaps a little lemon juice.

The terrine can be made in a lightly oiled container, or, to be absolutely sure it will turn out, you might carefully line such a container with clingfilm, ensuring you have it as smooth as possible, or you will get a wrinkled and aged-looking result. Otherwise, line the terrine with vine leaves, which will look terrific, but because they are uncooked will not be all that edible; you could gently simmer them for 20-30 minutes before use which would help. Whatever you choose, prepare the container then carefully spoon in about two-thirds of the fish and spinach mixture. Pull the smoked fish into long pieces and lay them lengthwise along the mixture, in one layer or in rows. Add the remaining mixture, smooth the surface and then chill thoroughly for at least 4 hours – overnight is better as this allows the flavours to develop more fully.

Serve in slices with a salad.

Options   The basic mixture may be used as a carrier for a number of other ingredients that are happy with fish; for instance, you might replace the smoked fish with some quails' eggs, or prawns, cooked mussels or clams. Or you could make a fish and vegetable terrine, layering the spinach and fish mixture with crisp, precooked vegetables or, say, with flakes of pink salmon, sticks of green baby asparagus and bright new carrots.

If for some reason the terrine is a bit broken or the clingfilm has set it into furrows, smother it with parsley chopped finely with lemon peel and garlic, a useful mixture called gremolata that properly belongs atop shin of veal – Osso Bucco. If you can stand a little cholesterol, smear it thickly with soured cream, or soured cream and cream cheese, given savour with horseradish. Gremolata would also look and taste terrific with that.

SMOKED SALMON PÂTÉ

Many delicatessens will sell you the skins of smoked salmon, or leftover pieces of the flesh at cheap rates, and these are a good basis for a pâté – or should be.

I don't think I've tasted any as good as that made with my recipe; the problem with most others is that they cook the mixture which naturally reduces the fish's flavour. This pâté relies on butter to set it and lets the flavour of the fish shine through. It is a simple matter to halve or to double this recipe.

Serves 6-8

8 oz/225 g *smoked salmon*	*A capful of white vermouth or*
4-6 oz/115-175 g *butter*	*brandy*
Lemon juice, to taste	¼ pt/150 ml *double or whipping*
White pepper, to taste	*cream*

If the fish is not entirely fresh and has gone a little oily it is necessary to treat it slightly. Cut it up into pieces, put into a saucepan and barely cover with water. Put over medium heat and watch it until it just starts to simmer which is enough to have melted any surface oil. Carefully pour the water off the fish – do not tip it all into a strainer as this will leave the oil on the fish. The trick is to siphon it off, as you would fat from a roasting pan.

Melt the butter, but do not have it too hot, and combine with the salmon in a liquidizer or food processor and process until very smooth. Carefully add lemon juice, a little white pepper and about a capful of brandy or white vermouth. Put into a bowl and allow to cool to room temperature but do not let it set. Whip the cream then fold the mixtures together. Put into individual ramekins or one pretty bowl and, when set, cover with more melted butter. Dill goes well, either in or with this.

MR CHRISTIAN'S PRAWN MOUSSE

Most pâtés using prawns or other shellfish often dilute the delicate flavour far too much. This one does not.

The use of cottage cheese reduces the cholesterol level somewhat but, if you are sensible about the overall balance in your diet, you could leave it out and double the amount of cream used.

Remember to let the prawns defrost overnight in the refrigerator, the only way to guarantee that they stay succulent and flavourful.

Makes 1½-2 lb/675-900 g and can be halved

1 lb/450 g *prawns, defrosted*
6 oz/175 g *butter, melted, warm*
1 *lemon*
White pepper, to taste
4 oz/115 g *cottage cheese*

¼ pt/150 ml *double or whipping cream*
Brandy or white vermouth
Extra butter and dill for decoration

Make a purée of the prawns in a food processor or liquidizer. Add the melted butter and juice only of the lemon. Flavour with a little finely ground white pepper. Leave to cool but do not let it set firmly.

Sieve the cottage cheese to remove the lumps. Whip cream until stiff but not dry and fold together with the cheese. Fold the cheese/cream mixture into the cool prawn purée and finish the flavour with a little brandy or white vermouth – the latter giving the most subtle and interesting flavour.

Put into individual ramekins or one or two larger bowls. Chill then seal with warm (not hot) melted butter. You might decorate with chopped fresh dill or dried dill or with a few reserved prawns.

For extra interest and texture some coarsely chopped prawns, rolled in dill, could be folded through the mixture before it is potted. For instance, you could make a pâté of prawns using just half the above quantities and then fold 8 oz/225 g of prawns into that.

As this dish is not set with gelatine it will soften when left in a warm place and thus should be served almost directly from the refrigerator. Try to dissuade your guests from drenching it with lemon juice.

2 Chinese Tea-Smoking

Smoked foods are amongst the most fascinating, delicious and rewarding goods found on a delicatessen counter. Or can be. Smoked salmon is expensive, smoked sturgeon is rare, smoked oysters are in filthy oil and smoked mackerel is most often 'smoked' by being painted with artificial flavour and colour.

I always thought the alternative was a smoke house in the backyard, if you had a backyard, or a portable smoker; both options seemed a lot of hassle and money. Then suddenly I discovered tea-smoking, a Chinese trick, that can be done in a saucepan or wok, the latter being infinitely better because it's broader and thus more capacious.

The technique and equipment required are beyond nobody, yet the difference a little smoking can make to ready-cooked, shop-bought food is phenomenal. If you go one step further and combine the smoking with the cooking, an entirely new world opens before you.

I have now made many experiments and the only problem I have found is in the use of thin-bottomed saucepans. They will buckle and curve in emulation of a wok. Unless you have a really thick-bottomed saucepan, do not attempt this variation, but nip out and buy a wok set, ensuring it includes a steaming rack.

BASIC TEA-SMOKING

First line the entire inside, and the lid, of your wok or your saucepan with heavy-duty cooking foil. Second, mix up the smoking ingredients.

4 oz/115 g *rice, barley, wheat or*   4 oz/115 g *sugar*
    rye grains   *(brown gives more pungency)*
                                 2 oz/50 g *dry black tea leaves*

Rice is always used by the Chinese, but then that is all they have. Any of the others is perfectly adequate, for the function is less that of flavouring and more that of aerating the mixture, at least that is the way it seems. This mixture is spread over the foil and the smoking (steaming) rack or trivet is placed upon it.

The food to be smoked is arranged evenly on the rack, the lid is put on then firmly sealed with one or two damp towels or tea towels.

SMOKING COOKED FOODS

To smoke very lightly food that is already cooked and which has a delicate flavour, such as hard-boiled eggs, poached chicken and so forth, turn the flame beneath the saucepan or wok to a medium heat – with a wok the flame's tip should be touching the surface of the vessel. Leave for 5 minutes, then reduce the heat to low – if you put your ear carefully to the lid you should hear the mixture *just* hissing and sizzling a little. Leave 10 minutes.

Turn the heat off and wait 5 minutes which allows the smoke to settle.

If the food to be smoked already has a strong flavour, such as a garlic sausage, of if you prefer a strong smokiness, then keep the heat at medium setting for 10 minutes and reduce it to low for 5 minutes; leave another 5 minutes before opening the smoker.

Leave the smoked food longer if you like – it will stay warm if not hot and the flavour will not be affected. Because of the tight seal, little moisture is lost even from naturally dry foods.

The variety of foods that can be reflavoured with tea smoke is as wide as your imagination. Remember it adds a wondrous glow, so there is a cosmetic advantage too. Thus pale chicken or fish, sausages like bratwurst or weisswurst, can all be made to look good: see Chinese Salted Duck and Four-Day Salted Chicken. Even food that already has a golden colour, such as cooked whole chickens, are enhanced by the smoke tones.

Frankfurters can have their skin flavour improved and even the great British banger becomes special with a smoke coat.

The prettiest trick comes, wouldn't you know it, from the Chinese, who smoke everything – including tea. When there is a little spare space in your smoker, add some hard-boiled but shelled eggs. The colour and flavour will be truly stunning, particularly if you have added herbs to the smoking mixture (see below).

SPECIAL EFFECTS DEPARTMENT

There are two major variations on the above techniques. The first is to add extra flavour to precooked foods by adding a savoury herb to the smoking mixture; the second is to marinate fish before it is smoked from raw.

Simple sharp flavours are best for both these variations but the resinous herbs certainly give better results. Rosemary is superb, but juniper is equally good. To check if a dried herb or spice is worth incorporating in your smoking mixture put a teaspoonful or so in to a hot nonstick pan and wait for the smoke to form. If it smells like grass or just another smoke, it won't be worth the effort.

A heaped dessertspoonful of dried rosemary is enough to give an elusive and unique tang to hard-boiled, shelled eggs, and the colour is sublime. Use the same amount of juniper berries, slightly crushed and twice the amount of black peppercorns, which add a rather amazing coffee-like sharpness to the smoke.

In broad terms, rosemary is probably the better choice for lighter flesh and fishy things, whereas juniper acts more excitingly with pork products. Of course, there is always the exception and Juniper-smoked Salmon is one of them.

HOT-SMOKED RAW FISH

Hot-smoked salmon is a great favourite in the USA and in Scandinavia. The fish is smoked close enough to the fire to cook it at the same time and I realized during my experiments that enough heat was probably generated in my wok to cook most fish.

It worked; and I think gave me some of the greatest flavour

thrills of this entire book. Even the simplest fish cooked over the basic smoking mixture is a revelation in flavour, moistness and texture. Honestly, you will never have had it so good; you will be hard put to recognize the resultant sweet and succulent flesh of the mackerel as in any way connected with the drear chewing gum usually served as smoked mackerel, hot or cold.

At its simplest it is dead simple. Ensure the fish is at room temperature rather than directly from the refrigerator (prawns excepted). Add only a judicious sprinkling of an excellent sea salt and a small squeeze of lemon juice.

The well-sealed atmosphere means that variations of cooking times or of thickness of flesh can largely be ignored, and I've never overcooked anything beyond redemption. Traditionally smoked foods are often dry, and that can be used as your excuse if an experiment fails, but I doubt it will.

To ensure the fish is cooked through turn the heat up to medium for 10 minutes, reduce to low for 5 minutes then leave an additional 10 minutes before unsealing.

The only problem I found was that too great a quantity of fish made so much juice the smoking was inhibited. Try not to cover more than half the rack with prepared fish, but see recipe for Rosemary-Smoked Trout for a way to help.

Here are a few ideas to get you started:

Mackerel
Fillets are best – salt only the exposed flesh and lay them skin side down on the rack.

Trout
Can be filleted but are more stunning if you sit two or three of them upright on the rack by spreading the cleaned body cavity. It won't matter if the thin flesh of the belly overlaps from fish to fish.

Salmon
Choose darnes or cutlets of 4-6 oz/115-175 g in weight. Compensate for their leanness by adding a touch of butter.

Smoke anything that comes to hand – really spectacular are prawns, but choose them big or you will dry them out.

I have sometimes found that when cooking fish from raw, the juices they emit stop the smoking mixture getting hot enough to draw the oils from juniper, rosemary or orange peel. The best precautions are to put at least half the herbs or orange directly onto the aluminium foil before adding the smoking mixture, which will ensure they get maximum heat well before anything dribbles down to put out their fires. Also, ensure there is plenty of your chosen addition to be seen around the edge of the top of the smoking mixture, for they are most likely to be out of the way of any escaping liquid and will be closest to the hot metal.

This is not a problem when smoking ready-cooked food – at least it hasn't been so far.

TEA-SMOKED BELLY OF PORK

This recipe perfectly illustrates how tea-smoking gives a final polish to a dish which, although intrinsically delicious, looks a little boring. Don't be shy about taking the wok with the smoked meat to the table before you serve it . . . when I first did this I actually showed them the before and the after!

Serves 6

3 lb/1.3 kg net *lean belly of pork*	2 *cinnamon sticks*
1 *onion, sliced*	4 *cloves*
2 *bay leaves*	4-6 *dried red chillies*
2 tsp *black peppercorns*	4-6 *whole garlic cloves*
3 *star anise*	

The belly of pork must be trimmed of bone and other extraneous inedible bits and pieces and can be in one or two pieces. The skin should be deeply scored. Put all the remaining ingredients into a large saucepan and add enough water to cover the meat – you'll have to guess a little. Bring this to the boil very slowly then pop in the meat. Add boiling water if more is needed to cover the meat. Simmer gently until meltingly tender – perhaps 1½-2 hours – but do not boil it ragged. If you find the cooking liquid seems a little tame, add a little more flavouring.

Remove the meat and let cool and drain. It will look pale and very uninteresting but taste pretty good.

Prepare a smoking mixture and place the pork pieces on a rack over this. Seal the wok in the usual way and smoke for 10 minutes over a high heat, 5 at medium. Turn off heat and leave another 5 minutes before opening. Slice and serve.

Options   If you have some sesame oil, a little of this might be brushed over the meat when it comes out of the wok. You might also want to sprinkle thin slices or sticks of green ginger root onto the skin of the meat before smoking.

ROSEMARY-SMOKED TROUT

Serves 4

4 × 6 oz/175 g *trout fillets*	6 sprigs *fresh rosemary*
1 tsp *creamed horseradish*	4 dessertsp *soured cream*
1 tsp *parsley, chopped*	*Beetroot, finely chopped*
1 *basic smoking mixture*	

First take the trouble to excavate gently the fine bones left in the trout fillets. Then slide a very sharp knife between the flesh and skin at the tail end of each fillet. Work knife in a sawing action to detach the skin in one piece until about 2 in/5 cm from the other end of the fillet. Leave skin attached.

Spread the horseradish and parsley evenly on the upper side of each fillet then roll firmly from the tail end. Wrap the skin around the roll of fish.

Prepare the wok and the smoking mixture and lay the rosemary on top of the mixture; if you have no fresh rosemary a dessertspoon of dried can be sprinkled over the top instead.

Cover the wok and seal, then smoke at medium heat for 10 minutes, low for 5 minutes. Turn off the heat and wait another 10 minutes before opening to serve.

The cooked fish should be unrolled to expose the cooked flesh, which will be smoked golden at both exposed ends. Then fold back the skin to show the beautiful smoked effect on that. Add a spoonful of soured cream to each plate and scatter with very finely chopped beetroot. A sprig of dill or fennel looks nice on the plate too. Serve warm rather than hot.

Option   For grand occasions, smoke one or two cooked, shelled quails' eggs per person at the same time.

JUNIPER-SMOKED SALMON

The resinous flavour of juniper is a good if surprising accompaniment to salmon – I presume because they both come from the same sort of countryside. I found this improved if the salmon was lightly coated with a sweet herb like basil; parsley would be equally effective.

Serves 4

4 × 8 oz/225 g *salmon cutlets, raw*
4 dessertsp *olive oil*
2 dessertsp *lemon juice*
½ dessertsp *salt*

4 dessertsp *fresh basil or parsley, chopped*
1 *basic smoking mixture*
At least 1 dessertsp *juniper berries*

Anoint the salmon cutlets with the oil, lemon juice and salt then roll in the coarsely chopped herbs. (Use just 1 teaspoon of dried basil but never use dried parsley.)

Leave to marinate for 2 hours in a cool place or for 4 hours in a refrigerator, ensuring you bring the latter version back to room temperature before cooking and smoking.

Make the smoking mixture, place in the smoker and mix in the juniper berries; I think it helps to crush them slightly before use but the difference may not be marked. Put the salmon on the rack, cover and seal, then smoke at medium temperature for 10 minutes, then low for 5-10 minutes – the longer time if the steaks are small but thick or if they weigh more than 8 oz/225 g each. Turn off the heat and leave an extra 10 minutes before eating.

Plain mashed potatoes and a green vegetable would be quite enough accompaniment; or a simple salad with a dressing that is not too sharp.

Option   Use some gin in the marinade to heighten the juniper effect.

Note   Do not try to cook more than four cutlets at once or the amount of juice will prevent any smoke being formed.

3 Sausages, Spiced and Salted Meats

Salted (or pickled) meats have slowly disappeared as the introduction of refrigeration meant that this method of preservation was no longer a common necessity. Apart from bacon or the odd meal of salt beef, only hams remain on our table; and, sad to say, the majority of people presented with a traditionally salted and dried ham turn up their noses, saying it is too dry or too salty. They prefer the modern, sweet, soft hams, which are artificially high in liquid content and obtain their texture only through a process that first shreds and pulls the salted meat and then presses and steams it back into shape.

Salting and drying a whole ham or large pieces of meat is fraught with difficulty for the amateur, especially in houses that do not have cool larders; the drying process is particularly dangerous. But the salt-pickling of meat that is to be cooked immediately is well within the scope of the smallest household and adds excellent mild flavour to cheap cuts of meat.

BASIC BRINE

The basic contents of a brine are salt to keep the meat fresh, sugar to balance the flavour and toughening effect of the salt, and saltpetre, which will turn the flesh an attractive pink colour and further act as a most reliable germicide. Note that although salt will prevent most nasties growing, there are other organisms that thrive in a brine without oxygen – it is these that give the unique flavour to salted meats, not the presence of salt itself. But there are exceptionally poisonous organisms that also thrive in those conditions and saltpetre, even in minuscule amounts, protects you from them.

There are a few other caveats about using a brine, which I'd better tell you before you begin. First, all your containers must be well rinsed out with a boiling solution of soda crystals and water, rinsed again and dried. This will ensure that no taints, smells or fats that would affect your brine remain. Plastic buckets or washing-up bowls are adequate if closed carefully; otherwise use stoneware and *not* the more porous earthenware. Second, each time you remove a piece of meat from the brine you are weakening the concentration. Taking a few small pieces won't matter much, but taking a large piece out or removing a lot of small pieces will seriously diminish the ability of the brine to continue preserving your meat, as the salt level will have fallen. Each time you make a large difference to the contents of your brine, therefore, you should add extra brine, but allowing for the salt that has been taken, it should be twice as strong as the first one you made. Actually, unless you make a complicated brine, it is as well to remove all the remaining meat, clean out the container as above, make a new brine and rest assured.

To avoid all these problems I have eschewed the rather romantic idea of having a brine bath continuously on the go. Instead, I plan ahead for a time I know I will be using extra meat – for parties or more especially over Christmas and New Year, when I will empty the brine in a few days. Then a brine bath filled with goodies frees space in the refrigerator and gives fascinating alternatives to holiday meals. After rich festive fare it is terrific to have a simple piece of boiled salt pork, to use some salted belly of pork to make your own sausages or, even better, to use the same as the basis for a home-made pâté.

Brisket or silverside of beef can also go into brines, and so, for a short time, can duck or chicken.

Meat put into brine overnight can still be grilled or roasted. But the salt will have toughened the flesh if left longer than that, hence the practice of boiling salted meats. As Elizabeth David suggests in *Spices, Salt and Aromatics in the English Kitchen*, salt beef (and pork) is improved if you add a tumblerful of wine or, especially, of cider, to the cooking liquid, for this then makes the resultant stock even more useful for making robust wintery soups.

Old recipes call for far higher proportions of salt than would be acceptable to most of today's palates, anything up to 2 lb/900 g per gallon/4.5 litres of water. But that was necessary to ensure meat would remain edible over very long periods. Nowadays the following proportions are probably right for both the customs and tastes of the day.

1-1½ lb/450-675 g *sea salt*   3 oz/85 g *saltpetre*
1-1½ lb/450-675 g *sugar*   1 gallon/4.5 litres *water*
  (demerara or golden
  granulated)

Put sea salt and the same amount of sugar into a large pan with the saltpetre. Then add the cold water. Bring to the boil very slowly, stirring it when you remember to do so, and let it simmer for 5 minutes. Once thoroughly cooled your brine is ready.

To add extra flavour to the brine, you can tie herbs and spices in a piece of cloth and let them boil with the brine, or simply throw them in and strain them out. The proportions used in the next recipe are a guide, and you will see there why I advocate rather more spices than most people. The only time you might use fewer is when your meats will only be brined for 24 hours and then grilled or roasted.

The meats you put into your brine must be right under the surface, or, if not, must be turned at least once a day.

Belly of pork is wonderful for salting as it has so many uses – boiled and baked, as sausages, as a pâté base and so on. But trotters, a spring of pork (the fore-quarter shoulder really) and spare-rib steaks are equally marvellous.

RATHER SPECIAL SPICED BRINE

This is a combination of ideas culled from the writings of Elizabeth David and Jane Grigson, plus the experiments of the late Marika Hanbury Tenison and myself. The use of wine in a brine seemingly comes from Italy – the flavour of the wine is naturally welcome, the alcohol also helps preserve the meat, and I have used far more spices than usual. If the meat is to be boiled in water, the flavours of the brine and its contents will be diluted by the liquid and diminished by the very process of cooking. Therefore you *must* overcompensate in the beginning or simply use the basic brine above.

Of course, such a well-flavoured brine as this is doubly excellent for the times you just wish to dip something in overnight like belly of pork for sausages or a piece of pork for boiling or baking.

Makes about 1 gallon/4.5 litres

5 pt/2.8 litres *fresh, cold water*	2 tsp *allspice berries*
1¼ lb/575 g *sea salt*	2 tsp *black peppercorns*
1¼ lb/575 g *demerara sugar*	2 *cinnamon sticks*
3 oz/85 g *saltpetre*	16 *cloves*
1 oz/25 g *pickling spices*	6 *fresh bay leaves*
2 tsp *juniper berries*	3 pt/1.7 litres *dry white wine*

Put all the ingredients except the wine into a preserving pan or large saucepan and bring very slowly to the boil. Keep some sort of cover over the liquid or you will lose so much by evaporation you will change the proportions of the brine. Once it comes to the boil, let it simmer very gently for just a few minutes, then take the pan from the heat and pour in the wine. If you buy one of the big 1.5 litre bottles of dry Italian wine you will have to make it up to 3 pints/1.7 litres with a little water. Stir well and leave to cool thoroughly. You must not add the wine on the heat or heat it once the wine is added or the alcohol will evaporate.

Once cool, strain through a sieve lined with a couple of layers of very clean muslin directly into your brining container which should be clean, sweet and dry as outlined in the introduction.

PRUE LEITH'S SIMPLE SAUSAGE . . .

This recipe kindly given by Prue Leith is indeed simple, and encouraged me to go on to the ideas that follow.

Serves 6-8

2 lb/1.3 kg *belly of pork*	1 tsp *black pepper coarsely ground*
3 tbsp *fresh white breadcrumbs*	2 tsp *dried sage*
2 *egg yolks*	4 *juniper berries crushed*
2 tsp *coarse sea salt*	

The belly of pork should be minced quite finely – on a medium blade at the absolute most. Mix everything together evenly then fry a teaspoon or so to check that you like the flavour. You could add more salt or pepper or a little of another herb or spice, especially ground allspice or dried thyme.

Then roll portions of the meat into sausage shapes, ensuring they do not taper towards the end but are straight-sided. Fry or bake slowly until evenly brown and firm to the touch. If you use lightly brined belly of pork, go easy on extra salt.

... AND SIMPLE TOMATO SAUCE

8 oz/225 g *canned plum tomatoes*	1 *thyme sprig*
1 tbsp *tomato purée*	1 *bay leaf*
½ tsp *sugar*	1 *small onion, sliced*
1 *garlic clove*	1 *celery stalk*
1 tbsp *fresh marjoram*	*Salt, to taste*

Simmer together the tomatoes and juice with the tomato purée, sugar, crushed garlic, marjoram (or oregano, 1 teaspoon if dried), thyme, bay leaf, onion and celery. When well reduced and mushy, push through a sieve using the back of a soup ladle. Serve hot or cold. Do not salt until after you have made the final purée as you may find you need none at all.

CAMARGUE SAUSAGES

Readers of my *Delicatessen Food Handbook* who have looked up Toulouse sausages will recall that I encountered on the beach of Aigues-Mortes a 4-year-old girl, who walked over to hand me some of the sausages her parents were cooking. Chewy and chunky, pink, herby and garlicky – they were quite simply the best I have ever tasted. This recipe goes a long way to recreating their flavour, and the experience of making them has convinced me that thyme is a far better friend to pork than sage ever was.

Serves 6-8

3 lb/1.3 kg *fatty belly or shoulder pork (see below)*	2-3 tsp *fresh thyme leaves*
	10 *juniper berries*
3 *garlic cloves, new*	2 tsp *ground nutmeg*
2 tsp *sea salt*	3 pinches *saltpetre*
1 tsp *black peppercorns*	

The meat should be minced on medium grinding blades. It is

better to mince than to chop for the sausage will then stick together without the necessity of bindings or skins. If you spy only very lean belly of pork at the butchers, buy just 2 lb/900 g of that plus 1 lb/450 g of back fat and combine those. (Remember, these weights are net of bone and skin.)

Gather together your seasonings. If the garlic cloves are not newly harvested, then just two of the stronger older ones might be enough. If you have fresh thyme, strip it from its twigs; about 1½ teaspoons is enough of the dried stuff. Saltpetre is not essential but it will give the finished sausages a healthier look.

Chop up the garlic somewhat and then put all the flavouring ingredients into a mortar and pound them until you have made something like a paste. Ensure that all the black peppercorns and juniper berries are crushed, for although it looks lovely to see them in large pieces it can be a shock to the palate. Still, perhaps you like that.

Now mix this into the meat. I find that the best way is to have both hands in the bowl and to open and close my hands with outstretched fingers. The squishing actually helps the final texture, for softening the fat and smaller pieces of meat means they are more likely to stick together. Be firm but gentle, and be resolute about making the mixture even. Leave it for a day, or overnight if you can, to let the flavours develop and the saltpetre penetrate. You might immediately like to fry a little amount to test the flavourings, but it will not be that much of a guide (to tell the truth it is delicious cooked at once, but so much better the next day – if you are a small family, you can do both, cooking some fresh and some the next day).

If you got a butcher to mince the pork, see if he will also put the sausage into casings but this may be as much trouble as doing it yourself. I found the mixture behaved perfectly well by being floured and rolled into rolls or patted into patties. Cook in a nonstick pan with no added fat or, even better, bake slowly in the oven.

Options   The same amount of meat brined overnight, before mincing, in the Rather Special Brine turned out to be fantastic, needing not a spot of extra flavouring. If you have to chop your meat or like it really chunky but can't or won't put it in skins, then add 3-4 oz/85-115 g of fresh breadcrumbs and a couple of eggs to the mixture. Fry up a small amount to find if you then wish to add a little flavouring, but I would be surprised if you do.

This mixture, brined or not, is the right sort of thing for baking in brioche (see Chapter 8).

PAPRIKA SAUSAGES

These sausages are somewhat like the chorizos of Spain and the gyulas of Hungary, but even the French make paprika sausages, so perhaps they can simply be thought of as European. It is worth taking time to test when you make these, so you can judge both the proportion of hot to sweet paprika and the overall amount. You could make some with just hot paprika and some with all sweet if you like, but the mixture is better, I think.

Serves 6-8

3 lb/1.3 kg *fatty belly of pork*	1 tsp *ground black pepper*
1 *large onion*	1-2 tsp *salt*
2 *garlic cloves*	4-6 *fresh parsley sprigs, chopped*
2 tsp *hot paprika*	¼-½ tsp *ground allspice*
3 tsp *sweet paprika*	

Have the pork minced quite finely; the onion and the garlic must be particularly finely minced. Remember that onion sours quickly and so if you include it the sausages should be eaten within a couple of days. Mix in the other ingredients using, say, about three-quarters of the mixed paprikas then fry up a tea-spoonful to see how you like it.

When you shape these into sausages, you might like to brush them with beaten egg and roll them in fine fresh white bread-crumbs before frying. Very good with cabbage dishes.

I once used such a mixture as a stuffing under the skin of a turkey and it worked extremely well.

HOME-MADE SAUSAGES IN BEER

You can use any style of beer for this, from a light ale or lager up to something as rich as Guinness. I reckon the hopped flavour of beers and ales works better than the unhopped lager.

Serves 2 or 3

4-6 *skinless sausages*	1 or 2 *bay leaves*
At least ½ oz/15 g *butter*	*Black pepper, coarsely ground*
1 *onion, thinly sliced*	At least 1 pt/575 ml *beer*

First you must stiffen the sausages by covering them with boiling water for 2 minutes. Drain and dry them, then put into a pan with the butter, onion and bay leaves. Brown and seal the sausages, flavour well with the pepper and pour in half the beer. Turn the heat up high and let the beer reduce by at least half its volume. Then add the remaining beer, or as much as is needed just to cover the sausages. Bring back to the boil, put a lid on the pan, then simmer gently for 15 minutes.

Serve the sausages and thin sauce directly onto a bed of mashed potatoes, or thicken the sauce with about 1 tablespoon of potato flour, cornflour or arrowroot.

HOME-MADE SAUSAGES WITH SOURED CREAM

Serves 2 or 3

4-6 *large skinless sausages*	5 fl oz/142 ml *soured cream*
½ oz/15 g *butter*	At least 1 tsp *mustard*
1 *onion, thinly sliced*	*Salt and pepper, to taste*

Fry the sausages with butter and sliced onion until nicely browned then remove from the pan and slice thickly. If they tend to fall apart, leave as they are.

Take a small carton of soured cream (if the contents are a little different from the amounts mentioned above it won't matter) and turn it into the pan together with mustard. Stir well then add salt and pepper according to your taste and that of the sausages. Return the sausage slices to the pan and heat through gently in the sauce. Serve sprinkled with parsley and a little hot or sweet paprika accompanied, inevitably but deliciously, by mashed or boiled potatoes.

SIMPLE SPICED SALT BEEF

Here is an interesting way to enjoy spiced beef, which was long traditional at Christmas time, without first having to brine the meat yourself. Allow about 4 days before you cook it, and a couple more before you eat it if you can.

To serve 6, generously

3 oz/85 g *brown sugar*	1 tsp *ground coriander*
2 tsp *black peppercorns*	½ tsp *ground cloves*
1 tsp *ground mace*	6 *dried bay leaves*
1 tsp *ground nutmeg*	3-6 *garlic cloves (optional)*
1 tsp *mustard powder*	4-5 lb/1.8-2.2 kg *lean salt beef*

Pound the sugar with the black peppercorns then mix in the spices. Crumble in the bay leaves then crush and mix in the garlic if you are using it.

Stand the meat on a substantial plate or dish and press the spice mixture firmly into as much of the surface as possible. Then cover the plate tightly with aluminium foil – perhaps using two layers to ensure the garlic and other scents do not escape to invade other goodies. Refrigerate for 4-6 days.

Put the meat into a saucepan and cover it with cold water. To the water add whatever you like in the way of flavourings – onion, juniper berries, carrots, parsnips, turnips, etc. – or cook just as it is. Simmer gently for 4 hours or longer if it needs it to be really tender, but don't boil it ragged.

It may be served hot but is perfectly marvellous if left to cool in the liquid and served the next day. The vegetables used in the cooking liquid will, unfortunately, be useless.

FOUR-DAY-SALTED CHICKEN

One of the major uses of the Chinese tea-smoking technique in Chapter 2 is to add colour and skin flavour to duck that has been salted for 3 days and then steamed. Unquestionably delicious. But duck is so expensive in comparison to chicken, I thought I would see if the idea might be applied to the latter. I don't pretend that it is authentic Chinese, but I promise you will probably not have tasted a better chicken.

Like salt-cured duck, this chicken is best eaten cold if unsmoked, and warm or cold if smoked. It can be a main course for 4-6 or a buffet or appetizer course for rather more.

1 *large roasting chicken*	4 *whole cloves*
1 heaped tsp *coarse sea salt*	6 *whole allspice berries*
crystals	2 in/5 cm *fresh ginger root*
1 dessertsp *black peppercorns*	*Soya sauce (optional)*

Trim the chicken, taking off the tail and excess neck skin, and also pulling out any interior fat. Then press down firmly on the breast until the ribs crack either side and the carcass is flattened.

Put the salt, peppercorns, cloves and allspice berries into a nonstick pan and stir over medium heat until the spices are smoking a little and the salt appears to have browned somewhat (5-7 minutes). Turn out of the pan and pound or crush well. Peel and slice the ginger root very finely.

Gently lift the skin from the breast of the chicken and slide the slices of ginger between the skin and the flesh. Continue your interior excavation and lift also the skin of the legs to insert ginger slices there. Pat dry the chicken of any excess moisture and gently rub the salt and spice mixture into the skin and into the cavity. Put the carcass onto a flat dish with sides, cover and leave in the refrigerator for 3-4 days. A liquid will slowly form and the bird *must* be turned a couple of times a day.

When you are ready to cook the bird you must assemble a steamer if you do not have a large wok. You cannot roast a salted bird. The salting will have made the flesh too tough for anything but steaming or boiling. An adequate steamer can be made by standing a cake rack in a deep roasting dish and making a dome of heavy aluminium foil for the pan. Cook on the hob, topping up with boiling water as required.

The chicken must be drained of the brine then placed in a clean dish, standing on the rack in your wok or steamer. Contrary to much belief and practice it is quite wrong to steam anything – fish, fowl or vegetable – without standing it in or on a plate. Otherwise, the steam dissolves the goodness of the food and it drips away into the water below – you may as well boil it! I often use a 1 in/2.5 cm deep metal pie dish for steaming, as its rim makes it simple to handle when hot.

It is optional but there is definite flavour and aesthetic

advantage in now rubbing a little soya sauce all over the skin of the bird and waiting until it has been absorbed. Don't overdo it. If in doubt, a little demerara sugar could be mixed with the soya, too.

Now steam the chicken over medium heat for at least 90 minutes. Pour off the juices that have collected, and reserve them for flavouring vegetables or as the base for a stock for cooking noodles and rice. Let the chicken cool and then slice and joint it or, if you know about such things, chop it into pieces the way the Orientals do. You see – even though it takes 4 days, you have almost nothing to do.

Options   Once cooked and cold the chicken can be tea-smoked, which will give it an extra golden glow and extra flavour. If you want to smoke your salted chicken, there is no need to use soya sauce – but you may. Sesame oil would also add extra delicious flavour to the skin.

CHINESE SALTED DUCK

Serves 4 as a main course; 8 as a starter

4-5 lb/1.8-2.2 kg *duck, dressed weight*	1 tsp *peppercorns (see below)*
2½ tbsp *sea salt*	1 in/2.5 cm *ginger root, peeled*
	2 *spring onions*

Cut the tail piece from the duck, trim off excess neck skin and remove all fat from inside the cavity. Press down on the breast-bone and flatten the duck.

Mix the salt and peppercorns; ideally, you should use seeded Szechuan peppercorns available only from Chinese super-markets. Put the mixture into a dry small pan and heat over medium heat, stirring all the time, for about 5 minutes by which time the salt will look slightly brown and the peppers will start smoking and emitting a delicious, slightly coffee-like smell. Let cool, then crush coarsely.

Rub this mixture all over the duck and inside the cavity. Put the duck into a dish, cover with foil or cling film and leave in the refrigerator for 3 days, turning once a day in the liquid that will form.

The duck must then be steamed. Chop the ginger and spring

onions, and put half the mixture inside the duck, half on top. Steam in your wok for 1½ hours, ensuring the water level is kept up. Remove the onion and ginger, pour off any juice then chill the duck thoroughly before cutting up.

For a real sensation smoke the duck over tea leaves as explained in Chapter 2 using the 5-10-5 minute system. Brush the duck lightly with sesame oil and serve hot or cold. It will be quite firm of texture, but is exceedingly delicious and can be served in very small amounts.

BRAWN

Also known as head cheese or fromage de tête, brawn is remarkably delicious if care is taken to ensure the jelly is well flavoured. Like bread, it is also far simpler to make than you imagine, for although the process takes a whole day, you are only employed for 20-30 minutes.

You start with half a pig's head, and although not essential, there is a great improvement in colour and flavour if you are able to put the head in brine for 3 or 4 days first. Your butcher might do it for you, otherwise I recommend you go for the Rather Special Spiced Brine, which gives you noticeably better results in my opinion.

In my version of brawn I add parsley and fresh herbs to the finished dish, rather in the style of Burgundian ham. It looks much nicer and is fresher and more summery on the tongue than to have it on the outside, which is more usual.

Half a pig's head will make a nice big bowl or loaf tin of brawn and will cost you very little indeed. If it has been brined basically longer than a couple of days, put it into cold water and bring slowly to the boil. Discard that water, then start all over again. (If you've used my gentler brine, you won't need to do this.) Make sure the water covers the head well (it is a good idea to ask your butcher to divide it into 3 or 4 pieces), then add flavoursome ingredients – a couple of onions and carrots, lots of parsley stalks, 2 or 3 sticks of celery, some bay and garlic. Be generous, for the long cooking means that most of their savour will vanish. Bring the saucepan very slowly to the boil then leave to simmer. It should barely plop from time to time. The slower and longer the cooking the better the result, so keep going until the meat is falling from the bones – I find it is usually at least 6 hours and, although some do it in an oven, I like to be able to watch it more easily.

Now take out the pieces of pork, then measure 1½ pints/ 850 ml of the strained cooking liquid. Put this to boil gently until it has reduced to about ¾ pint/425 ml. Then add ½ pint/ 300 ml red or white wine and reduce to ¾ pint/425 ml again. Adjust the seasoning and freshen the flavour with grated lemon peel plus a teaspoon or so of wine vinegar or lemon juice (I prefer the former).

To check the seasoning, which should be strong, dip a piece of the hot head meat into the sauce, but remember that when it is cold it won't taste half as strong.

While the sauce was reducing, you should have picked all the meat from the bones and cut into pieces, large or small, including the ear, skin and fat. (If in doubt, make your pieces big rather than small – it looks better.) Some people leave the tongue whole but, whatever you prefer, skin it.

This meat needs extra flavour too, traditionally done with allspice, nutmeg and cloves. I like quite a lot of allspice, followed by about half as much nutmeg and the merest pinch of ground cloves. Start with something less than a level teaspoon of ground allspice and go on from there.

Then add the spiced meat to the well-flavoured stock and simmer for another 20 minutes until the liquid is level with the top of the meat or just a little below it. Remove from the heat and stir in a good handful of chopped parsley and other sweet, fresh herbs – marjoram, thyme and the like – favouring the parsley heavily. Leave to cool and as it does, keep tasting and correcting the seasoning little by little. Once it is cool turn the lot into a loaf tin or a bowl and let it set firmly in the refrigerator.

Brawn can be cut directly from its container but looks very nice turned out and coated with lightly toasted white bread-crumbs. Keep it well refrigerated.

I have avoided giving many specific amounts for making brawn on purpose; everything depends on the amount of time you need to cook and the freshness of your herbs and spices, and as the savour cooks away you must compensate. To follow a strict recipe for something like this would be an absolute waste of time and a swizz by any writer who suggested it was possible.

4 Fish and Shellfish

The fishy content of a delicatessen is one of the most important for the harassed entertainer. Whether in cans or from the cold counter, fish will give you starters, main courses, light meals, picnic food and savouries. If you fancy trying your hand at marinating, pickling or smoking you will then become your own delicatessen counter and increase your choice dramatically.

Shellfish in cans are almost universally good, provided you drain away the horrid cottonseed oil in which some smoked varieties are packed; otherwise the broth or light brine in which they are commonly canned should be kept for use in stocks and sauces. Remember that all canned shellfish (and many fresh ones) are fully cooked and so need be only warmed through in any sauce or dish. Anything more and they will toughen and shrink. My *Radio and TV Cookbook* contains a recipe for a Smoked Oyster and Artichoke Ring Mould which is unsurpassably good.

Canned fish is not so reliable, for there are extraordinary variations of quality in both content and packing technique. Generally you should be certain of higher quality in a specialist delicatessen but with so many new brands of almost everything on the market it is not always easy for a proprietor to know. Tuna is a prime example of traps for the unwary. Look for succulent white tuna, chicken of the sea, but treat cheap tuna with great suspicion. If it comes from somewhere east it may be the coarse variety known as horse mackerel. Also be wary of buying fish pâtés and soups in tins, particularly the former, unless you are prepared to lash out on brandy and cream and other flavourings. Few of the pâtés are much better than low-quality pastes, tasting highly farinaceous rather than fishy; basically they have too many ingredients and suffer further by being cooked at the high temperatures needed for safety in canning. You'll find my fish pâté recipes in the first chapter offer you ways to retain as much true savour as possible.

I suppose you know smoked foods, like everything else, are supposed to be bad for us because of the carcinogens in the preservative smoke? Therefore, such food often isn't smoked at all but artificially given the flavour and colour associated. The upshot is that these products may not last as well as properly smoked foods. It is best to treat all smoked foods as fresh these days – get them refrigerated and keep them refrigerated. Safest bet of all is to smoke fish yourself as you need it and my ideas on Chinese tea-smoking earlier in this book will show you how simple this is to achieve.

It has not proved possible to keep all fish recipes in this part of the book. As well as the separate pâté and terrines mentioned, there are seafood salads and sauces elsewhere, easily spotted in the index.

SEAFOOD PILAFF

This simple supper meal is more filling than it looks and proof that great tastes do not require hours spent in the kitchen.

Serves 4

1 oz/25 g *butter*	*shellfish in brine:*
2 sachets *powdered saffron*	*mussels, cockles, clams*
8 oz/225 g *Arborio rice*	*(drained weight)*
8-12 oz/225-350 g *canned*	1 *bay leaf*

Melt the butter in a heavy saucepan. Add saffron then gently sauté the rice until it is opaque.

Meanwhile open the cans of seafood and drain, keeping the liquid. Measure the liquid and make up to just over 1 pint/575 ml with water or good chicken stock. Add to saucepan with a big bay leaf and stir just once. Cook over good heat until water is same level as rice and bubbling holes appear.

Layer shellfish on rice, cover saucepan with clean tea towel, seal tightly with saucepan lid and leave over very low heat for 7 minutes. Gently toss rice and seafood together and serve quickly, remembering it is as yet unsalted.

The short fat grains of Italian Arborio rice are by far the best for this sort of dish. If you cannot get them, the fragrant thin grains of Basmatti are excellent. And if neither of these, then any long-grain rice will do, I suppose.

SEAFOOD EGGS

Stuffed eggs can go and get precisely that in most cases. They are predictable, usually mealy in the mouth and often over-flavoured with mustard or with cheap curry powder. This version is prettier, tastier, easier and, yes, more expensive. But it tastes good and could start off a dinner party with style.

Serves 6

6 *eggs*
5-7 oz/150-200 g *mixed seafood*
Celery leaves or fresh dill or fennel,
    to taste
Lemon juice, to taste

1 tsp *brandy*
1 *small garlic clove*
¼ pt/150 ml *mayonnaise or*
    soured cream

Hard-boil the eggs by placing in cold water, bringing slowly to the boil then simmering for 5 minutes. Immediately put into running cold water until absolutely cold, cracking the shells slightly. Shell the eggs and cut in half lengthwise, trimming a little off each rounded side so the white will sit flat. Carefully remove the yolks and reserve.

Choose almost any mixture of seafood that appeals to you, but definitely include something pink – prawns or crab, salmon or smoked salmon. Chop up a few teaspoons of celery leaf or fresh dill or fennel. Toss the seafood in the herbs, sprinkle with a little lemon juice and brandy, then add the finely chopped garlic. Mix that gently into mayonnaise or soured cream (or a little of each) then pile nicely into the egg whites.

Force the egg yolks through a sieve and sprinkle them over. Serve chilled topped with mayonnaise or soured cream.

If it is time for showing off, mount each bateau of stuffed egg on a thin piece of cold, buttered toast on which you have spread black mock caviare. Around the plate, scatter tiny pieces of barely poached cucumber.

SOUFFLÉD BABY CLAMS

I first ate these in Bangkok, but believe the idea is from the pretty fishing settlements of New England. It is an extraordinary idea but memorably delicious with a salad for lunch or as a stunning starter.

Makes 12

7-8 oz/200-225 g *smoked baby clams, drained*
1 *lemon*
4 tbsp *mayonnaise*
¼ tsp *hot paprika*

Salt and pepper, to taste
6-12 *slices of brown or white bread (see method)*
3 *egg whites*

Drain the clams well if they are in oil then rinse with about half the juice of the lemon and pat dry. If you can't get smoked baby clams, plain ones will do but these will not need to be rinsed after draining.

Combine your clams with the grated rind of half the lemon and another teaspoon of its juice, the mayonnaise, paprika, salt and pepper. Leave in a cool place (not the refrigerator unless you are doing this well in advance).

From your bread cut 12 circles of 3 in/7.5 cm diameter and toast these on one side only. Whisk the egg whites until stiff but not dry and fold evenly into the clam mixture. Mound this high on the untoasted side of each round of bread. Arrange on a baking tray and place in a preheated oven at 425°F/220°C/Gas 7. The soufflés should puff and brown in 5 minutes. They will then be still liquid in the middle (more so if the mixture was rather cold); if you prefer them firmer, cook for 8 minutes. Serve as soon as you can.

POLYNESIAN CRAB PLATTER

This is a pretty and interesting way to serve crab on a hot day, provided your guests have been cured of the shrimp cocktail syndrome and won't mind the combination of fruit with seafood. If it's really hot, keep everything chilled and put the crab on ice.

1 lb/450 g of crab meat should be enough for 4 people if this is to be the star dish – otherwise it might stretch to 6 or 8.

Simply arrange the crab meat on a big serving platter or tray with contrasting rows of avocado slices, fresh pineapple slices, fresh mango or papaya slices and lime or orange segments. The first three should all be dipped in lime or lemon juice to preserve their freshness and to give them a bite, but don't use any further citrus juice or you'll overwhelm the crab. You can decorate with roasted cashew nuts, which I like to do.

If mango or papaya aren't available, a good ripe tasty melon or watermelon will do nicely; the colour and crunch of the latter is the better choice.

Serve with a very light dressing; perhaps mayonnaise mixed with equal quantities of plain yoghurt (see Chapter 11).

HERRINGS

Salted and pickled herrings are a great standby of the Continental delicatessen, and a staple of the countries that border the North Sea. Rollmops, which are rolled, pickled fillets of herring are quite popular. They make a good thing to keep in the refrigerator, especially in summer, and do not always need to include onions, as the second recipe which follows will show.

There are literally hundreds of ways to prepare herrings and few of them are much better than the ones you can buy in jars or tins. But in case you'd like to play around the next time you see some fresh or salted herrings, here are just four recipes. Each is suitable as a first course, a snack or a rather daring main course. Beer, vodka, aquavit or schnapps are the accepted drinks – all ice-cold, of course.

GERMAN ROLLMOPS

Buy, say, six fresh herrings or soak six salted herrings overnight in water and then drain. Either way you remove the head, open the fish, remove the bones and then divide the flesh in half lengthwise, ending up with two boneless fillets from each herring.

Spread each fillet with a little prepared mustard. If you can't get German mustard use mild, sweet hamburger mustard. On each fillet then sprinkle a little thinly sliced onion or shallot, a slice of gherkin or pickled cucumber and, if you like them, some capers. Roll each fillet up tightly and secure firmly with half a toothpick.

Arrange the rollmops in a wide-mouthed glass jar or in a plastic container with a tight-fitting lid. Between the layers put more sliced onion, some lemon peel, black peppercorns and some mustard seeds. Also add any roes you found in the herrings. Proportions are not vital, in fact you could well get away with layering the fillets only with onion and lots of black pepper; alternatively you could scatter in some mixed pickling spices instead of the peppercorns and mustard. The important thing is now to cover the fish with white wine. or cider vinegar. Stand covered in a cool place for a few days or for 4-5 days in a refrigerator before eating.

The final texture is improved if each fillet is sprinkled with some olive oil before serving.

Rollmops are usually enjoyed with a good dollop of soured cream and slices of pickled beetroot or cucumber. A substantial potato salad topped by a few rollmops makes a sustaining and easy meal.

BAKED SPICED ROLLMOPS

This recipe will appeal more to those who cannot abide the thought of eating uncooked fish; I specially like it because it doesn't contain onion. Perhaps these aren't really rollmops at all? Never mind. They are delicious hot or cold. As in the previous recipe you can start with fresh herrings or with salted ones which have been soaked overnight in cold water. You need to end up with a nice row of neat, boneless fillets of herring, perhaps twelve, to make the effort worthwhile.

Rub a little salt, pepper and mustard powder into the flesh of each fillet. Grate onto that some fresh nutmeg, then roll up each fillet and hold each together with half a toothpick. Arrange them in a dish which will just contain them and cover with a mixture of two-thirds wine vinegar and one-third water. Sprinkle on any roe you found inside the fish plus some bay leaves, some whole garlic cloves (a big one for every three fillets) and a generous scattering of whole coriander seeds. A couple of dried chilli peppers could be crumbled in for some tang.

Cover the dish with some foil and bake in the lowest heat of your oven for 1 hour. Turn off the oven and leave to cool, without lifting the foil. Once they are quite cold they are ready to eat but will keep in a cool place for 3 or 4 days if you turn them over every day. In a refrigerator they will last well over a week, turned daily.

As with most herring dishes, soured cream makes a perfect sauce, particularly if it includes some horseradish. On cold days, heat some gently in their liquid and serve with hot or cold potato salad.

BREADCRUMBED DILL HERRINGS

I think this is my favourite way of eating herring. You can use fresh fillets, or buy salt herrings, soak them overnight in water, drain and fillet them.

You then sprinkle dried breadcrumbs on a plate and lay half your fillets skin side down onto those. Sprinkle the exposed flesh with a little salt and lots of fresh or dried dill. Make a sandwich by covering the seasoned fillets wtih the remaining ones, flesh to flesh. Press lightly, then turn over to cover the other side with crumbs, too. Fry gently in a mixture of oil and butter and serve them hot or cold as a first course or as a luncheon dish.

Option Although it is strange to our ideas, these bread-crumbed fillets can also be pickled. If you have six sandwiches of breadcrumbed dill herrings mix together 1 pint/570 ml water and at least ¼ pint/150 ml vinegar. Sweeten the mixture lightly with white sugar. Pour that over the cooked herrings then scatter in some slices of red or white onion and several teaspoons of whole allspice berries. Leave 24 hours before serving the fish cold. You may strain the pickle and use on another batch of herrings if you like.

PICKLED HERRINGS UKRAINIAN STYLE

If the herrings are fresh, a soaking in cold water will make it simpler to pull off the skins.

For 10 herrings

10 *whole herrings*	3 tbsp *soured cream*
1 tbsp *sugar*	2 *dill or salt cucumber, sliced*
2 tbsp *dried or prepared mustard*	1 *medium onion, chopped*
8 tbsp *vinegar*	½ tsp *salt*

Prepare the herrings by removing the heads and tails, splitting, cleaning, boning and skinning. Cut each into two fillets, and save the roe and milt.

Mix all the other ingredients together, then layer with the herrings in a dish. Seal and keep in a cool place at least 6 days, turning daily. They will last at least another week in the refrigerator but as they are not likely to be uneaten by that time the point is possibly academic.

MEXICAN PRAWNS

This is something I created almost twenty years ago, when I first learned of the affinity of tomatoes and oranges. It is a perfect party or buffet dish because it can be made days in advance and decorated with fresh herbs.

This is easily enough for 6-8 people as an intriguing light starter, but would probably serve more at a party buffet. Make it in a loaf tin or in a ring mould, which makes cutting and serving simpler.

2 *whole oranges*	*Salt and pepper*
1 *lemon*	2 envelopes *gelatine*
1¾ pt/1 litre *tomato juice*	*Fresh herbs*
1 dessertsp *Worcestershire sauce*	8 oz/225 g *shelled prawns*
A dash of Tabasco sauce	

Cut up the oranges and lemon roughly, leaving on the skins, and put into the tomato juice in a large saucepan. Bring to the boil very slowly and simmer gently for 5 minutes. Strain through a colander or large sieve and when the fruit is cool enough squeeze to get out the juice which remains in the flesh.

Let the liquid cool before flavouring first with Worcestershire sauce and Tabasco, and then some salt. Remember the flavour will be less sweet and the hotness of the sauces and Tabasco will thus be accentuated when it is chilled, so be careful.

Melt the gelatine over low heat with about 8 tablespoons of the mixture then pour through a fine sieve into the remaining cool liquid and stir very well.

Lightly oil a 2½-3 pint/1.4-1.7 litre mould, then strew the base with such fresh herbs as you have – especially basil, marjoram and parsley – plus the prawns which should be lightly salted and peppered. Cover with a layer of the liquid then let set in the refrigerator before adding the remainder. Let set and chill thoroughly before turning out to serve.

Options   For party buffets you may like to make this without the prawns – it is just as fascinating and unusual.

PINK SALMON SOUFFLÉ

This is one of the great store-cupboard dishes; don't be tempted to use expensive red salmon, as the difference in price is not justified by the tiny difference in flavour.

Serves 4 as a light main course; 6 as a starter

½ pt/300 ml *milk*	7-8 oz/200-225 g *canned pink*
1 *bay leaf*	*salmon*
1 *small onion, sliced*	5 *egg yolks*
1-2 tsp *dried tarragon*	2 dessertsp *grated Parmesan*
3 oz/85 g *butter*	*cheese*
1½ oz/40 g *flour*	6 *egg whites, at room temperature*

Pour the milk into a small saucepan and add the bay leaf, sliced onion and tarragon. Cover and heat gently for at least 5 minutes to extract the flavours of the onion and herbs. Melt the butter, add the flour and cook over gentle heat without browning for 2 minutes. Strain the milk then whisk whilst still hot into the butter and flour roux. Cook a further 5 minutes over a gentle heat.

Open the canned salmon and add the juices to the sauce. Discard the skin and bones from the fish then mix the flesh into the sauce. Let cool a little then whisk in the egg yolks.

Generously butter a 2½ pint/1.4 litre soufflé dish with the remaining butter, then coat that with the Parmesan cheese.

Beat the egg whites until stiff but not dry. Stir one-quarter into the salmon sauce which should be still warm, then carefully fold in the remainder; don't worry about odd lumps or streaks of egg white – it is more important to keep the mixture light.

Ladle the mixture with care into the prepared soufflé dish then run a long knife around the mixture about 1 in/2.5 cm from the rim, which encourages a better rise.

Put directly into a preheated 400°F/190°C/Gas 6 oven and turn down immediately to 375°F/190°C/Gas 5 and cook undisturbed for 25-30 minutes. The shorter time gives a soufflé still runny and moist in the middle, which is the best sort of soufflé – the proper French term for one in this state is 'baveux'.

To serve, spoon off the crusty top first and divide amongst the plates. Then spoon deeply into the soufflé giving each person both set and runny soufflé. Use a large spoon and work quickly and do not serve anything over the crisp brown crust. As a main course, I think it is best to present a salad or vegetables afterwards, to allow uninterrupted enjoyment of the soufflé while it is hot and light.

SALMON MUSHROOM SAVOURY

Serves 6-8

12-16 *opened mushrooms*
12 oz/350 g *cream or curd cheese*
2 *eggs, beaten*
2 oz/50 g *smoked salmon pieces*
Anchovy essence or pounded anchovy fillets, to taste

Crisp toast or French toast (see below)
3-4 dessertsp *olive oil*
1-2 tsp *mixed sweet and hot paprika*

Wipe the mushrooms and remove the stalks carefully. The cap of each should be about 2 in/5 cm across. Choose a rather dry cheese and fold in the eggs, keeping the mixture as firm as possible. Don't beat or you will lose the texture. Chop the smoked salmon finely and blend in well. Add anchovy flavouring to suit, without overpowering the salmon flavour.

Arrange crisp toast or rounds of bought French toast in a big, shallow baking dish and sprinkle lightly with olive oil. Use one piece for one or two mushrooms, depending on their size. Fill each mushroom generously with the cheese mixture, using a piping bag if you can. Otherwise, use a fork to build the mixture up high into a point. Arrange the mushrooms on the toast.

Bake in the oven at 350°F/180°C/Gas 4 for about 20 minutes, or until the outside of the cheese mixture is just starting to brown and crispen. The time will depend on the size of your mushrooms and the amount of filling. Sprinkle with a little mixed paprika.

Can be served as a starter or as a savoury to end the meal. You can use just salmon and a little tarragon and white wine, or you can use just anchovy, perhaps with a touch of herbs.

TONNATO SAUCE

Cold slices of braised or roasted leg of veal in a thin, tuna-flavoured mayonnaise, Vitello Tonnato, is a highlight of the Italian summer and a speciality of most good delicatessens in Italy. The idea is far more flexible than that, and although the dish is unquestionably better made classically, which includes leaving the sliced meat in the sauce for at least 24 hours before serving, you can actually make and eat it on the same day.

First the basic recipe which would make enough sauce to cover a sliced piece of veal that weighed up to 4 lb/1.8 kg before cooking, so six generous portions.

½ pt/300 ml *thick mayonnaise*	1 or 2 *anchovy fillets*
8 oz/225 g *canned tuna, drained*	Up to ½ pt/300 ml *strong stock*

Chill the mayonnaise well. Purée the tuna totally using a little of the liquid from the can if this helps. Do the same thing to the anchovies and mix both fish evenly into the mayonnaise. Then thin the mayonnaise with the chilled stock which should have the flavour of the meat over which the sauce is to be poured.

A few capers are often scattered over tonnato-sauced dishes but although unorthodox I prefer the contrasted texture of some lightly roasted flaked almonds.

Porco Tonnato

Roasted pork fillet, also sold as tenderloin, makes a delicious and elegant alternative to veal.

Buy about 6 oz/175 g per person and roast the tenderloins until just cooked on a bed of finely chopped onion, a few stalks of celery and a teaspoon of dried rosemary. Baste a couple of times with warmed dry white vermouth. Let rest before slicing into even pieces about ½ in/1.25 cm thick. Pour any juices from the meat back into the pan then add ¼ pint/150 ml white vermouth, heat and stir up all the vegetables. Simmer for 1 minute then strain and cool. Use this to thin down the tuna mayonnaise.

Arrange the pork pieces on a suitable platter, pour on the sauce and leave to chill as long as you can.

Toasted almonds are specially nice with this version.

Pollo Tonnato

Buy or prepare six large chicken supremes, that is complete but boneless chicken breasts. Arrange them on a bed of 1 chopped onion, 2 sliced stalks of celery, a couple of fresh bay leaves, a chopped carrot and pour over them a generous ¼ pint/150 ml of dry white vermouth.

Cover the baking dish with foil and seal well. Bake at 350°F/180°C/Gas 4 for 30 minutes, checking the condition of the breasts after 20 minutes to ensure they are not curling or overcooked, which will be a risk if the pieces are small. The flesh should be only just set, still very tender and moist.

Remove the breasts, boil up the cooking juices with the vegetables and simmer 1 minute to extract all possible flavour, strain and cool. (If the juices add up to more than ½ pint/300 ml, reduce them to under that amount so that nothing is wasted.)

Complete the dressing by mixing the tuna mayonnaise and the cooled stock, pour it over the supremes and let them chill as long as you can. Fresh dill or fennel fronds make an attractive and delicious garnish.

Ginger Tonnato

The clean taste of fresh ginger is exceptionally welcome on torrid days. There are two ways of gingering up your tonnato.

Just before you pour the sauce on to your veal, pork or chicken, squeeze ginger juice onto them, using your garlic press. Or make the tiniest julienne strips of ginger and sprinkle them on the assembled dish, so the flavour extends during the marinating process.

In order to establish the flavour and develop a rather softer version, include the ginger in the base of vegetables over which the meat is cooked, then simply liven up the stock with a squeeze or two of fresh juice when it is cool.

Whichever way, or whichever combination you use, you cannot fail. If your ginger is woody in the centre, don't bother with the matchsticks; use it sliced in the cooking pan or squeezed over the flesh.

Vitello Tonnato Subito

A rich and busy person's version would be to buy some escalopes of veal and cook them very quickly in a little butter. Denude them of excess butter by patting with kitchen paper, rinse out the pan with some dry white wine or vermouth and use that juice to thin down the tuna mayonnaise. There's no reason why it should not be excellent and the tang of fresh ginger would be specially appreciated here; perhaps some garlic, too?

Eggs Tonnato

Hard-boiled eggs, split lengthwise and in the thick, undiluted tuna mayonnaise are perfectly delicious when served with a bed of fresh herbs. They don't need to marinate together other than for the time between that suiting you to prepare the dish and when you wish to serve it.

Eggs cut lengthwise after hard-boiling are the perfect way to extend any of the tonnato dishes above, especially the chicken one. Cut each supreme in half and detach the long fillet from underneath, thus giving three even pieces, which when served with the eggs will confuse most guests so they will never know how many owe so much to so few.

BANGKOK TUNA AND COURGETTES

Serves 4

Butter, for frying	¼ pt/150 ml *water*
Oil, for frying	2 *garlic cloves, crushed*
1½ lb/675 g *courgettes, cut into sticks or strips, salted and drained*	1½-2 in/3.5-5 cm *green ginger, thinly peeled and chopped*
1 *chicken stock cube*	8 oz/225 g *canned tuna, drained*

Melt a little butter with some oil in a large frying pan or wok then add the courgettes, keeping heat high. Continue stirring and frying to prevent browning. When starting to soften, crumble over the chicken stock cube, add water and keep stirring.

When the liquid has reduced to about half, add the crushed garlic and chopped ginger (if your ginger is woody, use more and squeeze it through a garlic crusher and use only the juice). Mix well then add the tuna in large pieces, turn over a few times to heat the fish. Serve immediately.

This should be accompanied by rice and, as is the custom in Thailand, should be served with soya sauce and Worcestershire sauce.

Options   The ginger is not very hot. If you like hot food, slice up some small green chilli peppers or add a couple of dashes of Tabasco sauce.

Thinly sliced spring onions, French beans or whole baby corn kernels may also be added or substituted for some of the courgettes.

TUNA LOAF

What we would call water biscuits or crackers are often used in cooking. in the USA, at least they were in the old days, for they kept better than flour. This is typical of the old-fashioned technique but uses new-fangled canned tuna.

Serves 4-8, according to the occasion

Approx 12 oz/350 g *canned tuna,*	2 *eggs*
	1 dessertsp *hot horseradish sauce*
2 oz/50 g *crushed plain water biscuits*	1 dessertsp *tomato purée*
	Salt, pepper, cayenne, to taste
2 oz/50 g *butter, melted*	4 *egg whites*

Mash the first four ingredients together, including any liquid from the tuna cans, then flavour well with the horseradish, tomato purée, salt, pepper and cayenne. If you like herbs, add some chopped chives or dried or fresh marjoram.

Beat the egg whites until stiff but not dry, fold into the mixture and place in a well-buttered 1¾ pint/1 litre loaf tin. Seal with a dome of aluminium foil then stand in boiling water in a roasting tray and steam in a 350°F/180°C/Gas 4 oven for

1 hour, ensuring there is always plenty of steam and water.

Turn out onto a hot plate and serve with a suitable sauce. I was told, when I collected the recipe, to make a hollandaise with the egg yolks but I reckon that is far too fancy. Better to make a good, pouring béchamel sauce, well flavoured with onion and bay and, just before serving, to enrich it by adding those egg yolks. A light cheese flavouring would be good too. Otherwise serve the loaf sliced when cold and accompany it with a mayonnaise mixed with an equal quantity of plain yoghurt then flavoured with tomato purée, some garlic and a touch of lemon juice and Tabasco.

SALT-PICKLED FISH

Among the food fashions currently gripping the better establishments is Gravadlax – which is salmon pickled in salt, sugar and dill and served in slices with a sweet mustard sauce (unless served by me, when it is served with almost anything else). I'll give you the basic recipe, for it is easier than you can possibly imagine. The technique has always fascinated me, for it has obvious applications to all manner of other oily or delicate fish and so, following the basics, you will find variations using mackerel, fresh tuna and fresh trout.

Please be clear about the difference between marinating and salt-pickling. Salt-pickling leaves the flesh translucent whereas marinating, which uses acid of some kind, always makes the flesh look as though it has been cooked. It is silly to use alcohol, as I have seen in some versions of salt-pickled fish, for then you are falling between two stools and getting the benefit of neither.

If you use sizes of fish other than those in the recipes, remember that the weight of the combined salt and sugar should be 1-1½oz/25-40 g per 1 lb/450 g trimmed raw fish. Some Scandinavian recipes use a higher proportion of salt to sugar, but their palates are used to salt foods. Some recipes also use a much smaller total quantity of salt/sugar pickle but this runs the risk of not fully preserving the fish. If, once your pickle has liquified, you feel it is too salty for your taste, add a couple of teaspoons of sugar and let this sit an extra day, turning the fish every 6 hours.

DILL-PICKLED SALMON

The great success of salmon farming in Scotland means that fresh, whole salmon are available throughout the year, and at prices that are often 25 per cent of the wild variety. Dill-pickled farm salmon means you can serve something far more delicious and fascinating than smoked salmon at considerably less than one-third of its cost.

6 big servings, twice

4 lb/1.8 kg *fresh salmon*	20 *white peppercorns*
3 oz/85 g *sea salt*	3-4 bunches *dill fronds*
3 oz/85 g *white sugar*	

I find the best cuts to use are tail pieces, as often a fishmonger will sell these more cheaply, especially if you take a much smaller piece, say only 2 lb/900 g, then use half the above amount of sugar, salt and dill.

Have the salmon scaled and then cut the two sides free of the spine. Lay them skin side down and rub the back of a knife along the thickest part of the flesh from the head towards the tail end of both pieces. This will raise the ends of the bones, which should then be pulled out using tweezers or sharp-nosed pliers with serrated ends. Persevere and do this properly now, as it makes the serving simpler, and the ultimate enjoyment is multiplied. Wipe the pieces of fish over with a damp cloth.

Mix together the salt and the sugar, ensuring the distribution of both is even. Crush the peppercorns coarsely and mix them through, too. Take a deep flat dish in which one piece of the salmon can lie with only a little extra space around it. On the bottom of that container, strew a quarter of the pickle mix, and arrange on that a quarter of the dill. Put one of the pieces of salmon skin side down then layer two-thirds of the remaining pickle and two-thirds of the remaining dill. Now add the second piece of salmon, flesh to flesh, but head to tail. Cover with the last of the pickle and dill, then cover the fish with a couple of layers of clingfilm.

Lay on top of the fish a plate or some other flat object and weight it with at least 6 lb/2.7 kg. Leave in a refrigerator a minimum of 48 hours; in a cold larder the process only takes 24 hours but a little longer will not hurt. Either way, turn the fish over every 6 hours or so. The salt and sugar will dissolve in liquid drawn from the fish and preserve it without changing the flesh's brilliant translucency.

To serve, scrape the pepper and dill from one of the pieces of salmon and lay it skin side down on a chopping board. With a long, sharp knife slice it thinly starting somewhere about the middle, cutting towards the tail and angling slightly downwards so that after a couple of slices you end up with the knife flat against the skin, thus retrieving every scrap of the delicious stuff.

The usual Scandinavian accompaniment to Gravadlax, which is what they call this, is a perfectly disgusting sweet mustard sauce which, now you know about it, I suggest you immediately forget. Serve your dill-pickled salmon with a soupçon of the pickle poured over and some quails' eggs and add a very generous teaspoon of an excellent seed mustard for each egg. Chill that well and you will have something truly exceptional. My other favourite accompaniment is something I use a great deal – arcs of poached cucumber, glistening and jewel-like if they aren't overcooked.

Options   The choice of other herbs as a substitute for dill should be kept to those that have perfume rather than pungency. Basil is outstanding and so is a good strong peppermint.

Salt-pickling seems most successful with fish of a fatty or oily nature. Thus if you are able to buy fresh tuna (which are usually frozen, but you know what I mean) then this will be most successful. So will mackerel.

FRESH SALMON IN GREEN-GINGER PICKLE

This rather startling combination of East and West is without peer as an ice-breaker at a difficult dinner or as the first move in any kind of seduction. You could serve the crisply flavoured slices of salmon with fingers of poached cucumber, but if you can afford it the best possible accompaniment would be the finest dried Chinese mushrooms you can find, reconstituted in the usual way then sprinkled with very dry sherry and chilled. Slice thinly so you can sprinkle them around the plate.

Serves 6-8 as a starter

1½-2 lb/675-900 g *tail piece*	*trimmed weight*
fresh salmon	1-1½ oz/25-40 g *sea salt*
2 oz/50 g *green ginger,*	1-1½ oz/25-40 g *white sugar*

Prepare the salmon, then chop half the ginger finely and cut the other half into fine julienne strips. Mix the chopped ginger with the salt and sugar then proceed as in the previous recipes, strewing all the julienne strips between the pieces of salmon.

Use a fairly substantial weight – at least 7 lb/3 kg – and leave the fish in the pickle for a minimum of 24 hours in a cool place or for 48 hours in a refrigerator. Remember to turn the fish over every 6 hours or so.

This must be served very cold, on chilled plates. Please resist any temptation to serve bread and butter unless you have some really excellent, crisp and slightly sweet bread rolls. The choice of alcohol is tricky too, as anything with enough real body to complement the flavours will be fearfully expensive. A very cold Amontillado or Fino are possibly the best choices, and therefore a dry Maderia, a Sercial or Verdelho, would work, too.

MACKEREL WITH ROASTED BLACK PEPPER PICKLE

Serves 4 as a starter

2 × 8-10 oz/225-275 g *mackerel*	½ oz/15 g *black peppercorns*
½ oz/15 g *coarse sea salt*	½ oz/15 g *white sugar*

Fillet the mackerel and remove as many of the bones as possible.

Put the salt and the black peppercorns into a heavy or nonstick pan over low heat for several minutes, then turn to medium heat and agitate until the peppercorns smoulder a little and one or two pop their skins. Turn off the heat then crush the mixture slightly, so the peppercorns are little more than cracked in half. Stir in the sugar. Strew the bottom of a dish with a quarter of the mixture: this dish should ideally be only just big enough to hold two fillets lying side by side. Put two fillets in side by side, skin side down, and sprinkle with two-thirds of the remaining mixture. On that lie the other two fillets, flesh to flesh and head to tail. Scatter with the last of the salt, pepper and sugar mixture. Cover with a layer of clingfilm then place something flat over that and atop that something weighing about 2 lb/900 g.

Leave in a cool place for 12-18 hours or in a refrigerator for twice that long, turning the fillets from time to time. To serve, cut into long slices, in the same way as you would smoked salmon. Moisten with a very small amount of the strained pickle – you really will not want too much of the peppercorn about.

Soured cream with horseradish or with a mixture of beetroot and horseradish would go well with this.

TROUT IN FRESH PARSLEY PICKLE

Serves 4-6 as a starter

2 × 12-14 oz/350-400 g *fresh trout*	1 oz/25 g *coarse sea salt*
	1 oz/25 g *white sugar*
2 oz/50 g *fresh parsley*	

Prepare four fillets of the trout, removing as many bones as is possible or practical for you. Chop the parsley coarsely and include every bit of the stalk, which is where most flavour lies. Mix the parsley with salt and sugar.

Layer as in the previous recipe and, in this case, if you have extra parsley lay whole sprigs on the bottom of the dish and in between the fish. Leave in a cool place for 12-18 hours or for double that time in a refrigerator, turning from time to time.

To serve rub the parsley from the pickled fillets, then cut each into long slices as though cutting smoked salmon. Strain any extra pickle and remoisten each slice.

Arrange on individual plates accompanied by cold scrambled eggs and very thinly sliced baby turnips which have been quickly cooked, drained and topped with a little whipped cream flavoured with mustard. Equally good would be new potatoes cooked in their skins, sliced thickly and topped with horseradish-flavoured whipped cream and served warm.

5 Pasta

The trouble with making and serving your own pasta is that it is so simple, it doesn't seem like real cooking. Relax, listen only to the appreciation of your guests, and pretend you've been at if for hours! Frankly, I get pleasure merely from the thought that with flour, a couple of eggs and a tap that works I have the basis of food at any time.

You do not need to include egg in pasta dough but it helps both appearance and flavour. You do not even need special flour but results are unquestionably better and so is the flavour when you use strong white bread-making flour. The reason is simple: strong white flour has a higher quantity of gluten – the protein that stretches to form bubbles in bread dough – which allows you to roll pasta dough thinly without it breaking.

HOME-MADE PASTA

This recipe makes two generous servings of noodles, but rather more if you are going to stuff the pasta.

8 oz/225 g *strong white (bread) flour*	2 tsp *olive oil*
	Water, as required
1 *egg*	

Mound the flour in a warm bowl, make a well in the centre and add the egg and oil. Use your fingertips to work them into the flour then slowly add water until you have a soft dough which kneads easily without sticking to your flesh. Many Jewish women would add a pinch of nutmeg and I think this is worth doing. Knead for at least 5 minutes and if you are good at it, knead another 5 minutes, too. Cover the dough with a slightly damp cloth and leave quietly to develop its gluten elasticity (about 1 hour) while you relax in some other way.

Pasta dough must be rolled very thinly indeed and a multitude of pasta rollers and cutters have now appeared on the market. The exact thinness is very much a matter of preference but if you do not have one of these machines, and want thin pasta, you will have to employ the method of rolling the dough around the pin itself as you roll. Ensure both sides of the pasta are well floured when you do this. To avoid early death through apoplexy caused by coping with huge amounts of pasta, divide the amount of dough into four or even eight pieces before you start rolling by hand. As with making phyllo pastry, nothing is better than a straight broomstick, perhaps amputated of one-third its length, for rolling pasta and pastry thinly.

SHAPING PASTA

Noodles
Long thin strips of pasta are the simplest to make even if not the simplest to eat. Once you have some sheets of rolled-out pasta, leave them to dry for 20 minutes. Ideally the sheets should be 4-6 in/10-15 cm wide and as long as you like or reckon you can manage to manipulate from plate to mouth. Lay the sheets atop one another and cut across or lengthwise into strips. A light tossing with your fingers will separate them. Alternatively, flour the sheets well and roll up quite tightly and cut through as for a jam roll. Each snail of pasta will unfold during cooking.

Ravioli
Suddenly, equipment for making ravioli is in the shops, too. When using them ensure you put no more filling into the hollows of the ravioli trays than will lie flat or it squishes everywhere. Without ravioli trays, simply roll out two equal sheets, dot a filling evenly over one, cover with the other, press firmly together the space between the rows of filling, then cut with the special serrated wheel, to give the classic finish, or with any sharp instrument.

Cappelletti and Tortellini

The former is supposed to look lie a woman's head in a scarf and the latter like an especially attractive feminine navel, but either looks like the other a lot of the time. Cappelletti should probably be made from circles of pasta but this is time-consuming and wasteful and not necessarily authentic either. So use 2 in/5 cm squares for both.

Once you have prepared your squares, dot the centre of each with the filling you have chose. Fold one corner over so it just covers the filling, but not so far that it folds the dough in half. Fold over once again, still leaving a small triangular tail visible. Flatten the two arms by pressing them lightly. Now join the two arms by turning the pasta around your fore finger, with the flat, triangular 'headscarf' uppermost. Press the ends together. That's your first cappelletti.

To make a belly-button, proceed as above, but do not worry so much about leaving a tail. When you turn the pasta around your finger, twist both arms before pressing them together; good trick, isn't it?

PASTA STUFFINGS AND SAUCES

The classic stuffings for pasta are often very bland, based on pork or veal with a few herbs or spices, and whatever delicacy there is seems lost when they are boiled. Be a little bolder, so that when you bite into your belly-buttons or ravioli, they bite back a little.

Few stuffings are better than the simple Italian idea of flavouring Ricotta cheese with herbs, and spices. You can substitute any of the soft cheeses, even sieved cottage cheese; the common combination is to add some chopped spinach and lots of nutmeg plus a hint of garlic. Masses of parsley together with some grated lemon peel is simpler and perfectly delicious, especially when served with a simple dressing of warmed olive oil and lemon. If you want to use a meat stuffing, use the time you have to wait for pasta to rest to make a really good and simple Bolognese Ragù, which can go into or over pasta. It also keeps very well, so make plenty.

BOLOGNESE RAGÙ

Although there are many versions of this mince and tomato sauce, the simplest are the most satisfying, so don't be bullied into buying sirloin steak or other expensive ingredients. The real secret to such sauces is long slow cooking – you simply cannot get good results by frying mince, throwing in some tomato and letting it heat through.

When you buy your mince ask for the leanest possible; at the utmost you could ask for some chuck steak to be minced for you.

The celery is vital to this recipe and the quantity will serve from two to four people depending on whether you like lots of sauce or make it go a long way as the Italians do.

---

1 lb/450 g *beef mince*	Approx 2 lb/900 g *canned plum*
2-3 tbsp *olive oil*	*tomatoes*
1 *very small onion, chopped*	1-2 *bay leaves*
1 *carrot, finely chopped*	*Salt, to taste*
½ *celery stalk, chopped*	

Brown the mince in the olive oil then add the onion, carrot and celery; the man who taught me this recipe was from Bologna and swore this sauce should never contain garlic or wine. Keep cooking until the vegetables too have a little colour. Add the tomatoes, juice and all, and the bay; don't salt at this stage as the sauce must reduce radically and mistakes could be made.

Turn the heat to low and simmer at least an hour, turning over from time to time. By now most of the liquid from the tomatoes should have gone and thus you can add a little salt so it will penetrate each morsel of meat. Continue cooking gently until the pieces of meat can be crushed to a pulp on the roof of the mouth by the tongue.

If allowed to reduce until really quite dry this ragù makes an excellent stuffing for ravioli, cappelletti and tortellini, but flavour further with some freshly ground nutmeg and lots of chopped parsley.

RED-WINE RAGÙ

This sauce of my own creation is richer and thinner than the previous, more authentic sauce. It makes the simplest dish seem more filling and satisfying and is excellent for the Macaroni Party Pie in Chapter 9.

Serves 2-4

1 lb/450 g *beef mince*	2-4 *garlic cloves (optional)*
2-3 tbsp *olive oil*	¼ pt/150 ml *red wine*
1 *small onion, chopped*	2-3 dessertsp *tomato purée*
14-16 oz/400-450 g *canned*	2 *dried bay leaves*
plum tomatoes	*Salt and pepper, to taste*

Brown the beef in the oil, then add the onion and let it brown a little, too. Add the tomatoes and all the juice from the can plus the whole garlic, the red wine, tomato purée and bay. Cover and cook over a gentle heat for 45 minutes by which time the meat should be very tender – the extra acid content from the wine means it will cook faster than the previous ragù. Flavour with salt and pepper and use on any plain or filled pasta.

Note   Before adding tomato purée to anything, it should be fried in a little oil as this somehow intensifies the colour and stops it turning the sauce brown. Simply fry a dessertspoon or so in oil until you see it thicken somewhat and look a little fluorescent; then add some of the ragù (or other sauce) to it before mixing it back into the main mixture.

TOMATO SAUCES

If you are an assiduous shopper and bully enough to convince your greengrocer to stock decent, knobbly sun-ripened tomatoes such as the Beefsteak or Marmande, then making a delicious tomato sauce is a matter simply of denuding them of skin (and seeds if you are picky) and letting the flesh cook with a little olive oil, butter, a tiny amount of onion and/or garlic and nothing else. Once reduced, more colour or flavour can be added with tomato purée if you like (see above). Then just before serving stir in masses of almost any fresh green herb.

Basil is the classic addition, but there's nothing wrong with good old parsley, as long as it isn't chopped finely; and fresh mint makes a wonderfully simple dressing when added to this basic sauce. If you think any of them need a touch of sharpening, add vinegar drip by drip and the change will be remarkable.

The combination of tomato with green pepper is something of a cliché in such sauces, and badly overworked too. The best way to use the flavour is not to cook the pepper long and hard in the sauce but to chop it finely and add at the last minute so that it erupts into a vivid greenness and is served immediately. Incidentally, pizzaiola sauce should never include peppers, but invariably does; it should be tomato with lots of olive oil and garlic plus oregano, fresh or dried, a herb more associated with Greek than Neapolitan food. And speaking of Greece, the tang of their salty cheese, Fetta, is an excellent ingredient in pasta sauces.

Chop up some tomatoes and cook them in a good amount of olive oil, which will combine with them to make a sort of mush. Add plenty of garlic then crumble in Fetta cheese – at least half the volume of the sauce. Let it heat through then add an equally large amount of coarsely chopped parsley and a sprinkle of dried oregano. Serve on cooked pasta immediately.

Another simple sauce is bacon and tomato, made by frying small pieces of fatty bacon until the fat is running freely and then cooking the tomato down to a mush in that fat with a lot of garlic and a little onion. Finish with a handful of coarsely chopped parsley and plenty of black pepper.

And if you cannot find decent tomatoes, by all means use canned plum tomatoes in their own juices. Chop them slightly to release the juice inside the fruit, then once reduced, strain well. To ensure that the sauce is reduced enough, put a spoonful onto a plate and if a watery edge soon appears you still have some reducing to do.

Tomato purée by itself should never be used as a sauce, but a spoonful or two can be employed to brighten up other sauces.

BUTTER AND OIL SAUCES

Some of the pasta dishes I have most enjoyed on the edge of a Mediterranean beach relied simply on olive oil and fresh shell-fish. Those experiences are somewhat difficult to emulate exactly in either bedsitters or mansions. But those ever-wondrous cans of shellfish from Spain, Italy or Japan can do you very well.

Thin spaghetti, sometimes sold as spaghettini, seems best for such simple dishes, provided you also choose small seafood, such as baby clams. If you can only buy something bigger, like mussels, or smoked clams or squid pieces, then choose conchiglie (shells) or something else with holes and interstices.

Melt equal quantities of butter and oil together and pour into that the juice from the can or cans of seafood, unless you are using something smoked, in which case not only discard the liquid from the can but rinse the fish in lemon juice.

Cook down until most of the can's liquid has disappeared then add finely chopped garlic and masses of parsley. Add salt, then the seafood and keep warm with the absolutely minimal heat or they will toughen. Once the pasta is cooked, serve it directly onto warm plates, let it steam itself dry and then spoon on the hot sauce. By varying the proportions of butter and oil you can make this sort of pasta dressing as Mediterranean as you like.

CREAM SAUCES

The serving quantities for all the following cream sauces are tricky, but would generally be enough for two main courses, or four starters.

ARTICHOKE CREAM SAUCE

½ pt/300 ml *double cream*	½ *garlic clove*
6-8 *canned artichoke bottoms*	Salt and pepper
½ *small can sweet peppers*	

Reduce the double cream by half by simmering, then add the sliced canned artichoke bottoms. If you have bought artichoke hearts, cut off the top three-quarters which are leaves, to discover the bottoms. Finally, add half the contents of the can of sweet red peppers, sliced finely, with garlic, salt and pepper.

BROCCOLI BLUE-CHEESE SAUCE

½ pt/300 ml *double cream*   *Black pepper*
1-2 dessertsp *Danish blue cheese*   *Parmesan cheese*
3 oz/85 g *small broccoli florets*

Reduce the double cream by boiling for 10 minutes or so, until a good coating consistency, then flavour with crumbled Danish blue. When that has melted and been amalgamated, add a couple of dessertspoons of florets from the top of the fresh green broccoli and a little black pepper. By the time they have heated through they will be cooked enough. If you have to use frozen broccoli, because everything had to be bought from the deli, use only 2 oz/50 g and cook it even less. Provided you haven't overdone the blue cheese content, sprinkle some grated Parmesan over each serving.

PROSCIUTTO AND DRIED MUSHROOM SAUCE

Two of the most expensive things in a delicatessen will be Italian dried mushrooms and real Parma or other air-dried ham. But ask. Often the knuckle end of a prosciutto can be bought more cheaply and this very dry meat is excellent in all pasta sauces when diced.

3-4 oz/85-115 g *dried mushrooms*   2 oz/50 g *prosciutto*
½ pt/300 ml *double cream*   *Lemon juice and black pepper*

Put the dried mushrooms into the double cream and reconstitute them slowly by simmering gently for 10-15 minutes, during which time the cream will also reduce to a proper sauce consistency. Meanwhile, prepare the ham by cutting into fine dice and add to the sauce. Little extra flavouring should be required except a squeeze of lemon juice and some black pepper.

FRESH MUSHROOM SAUCE

If you can only get fresh mushrooms, then they must be added to pasta sauces at the last moment otherwise they will release their juices and you will have to wait ages for the sauce to reduce again before you can eat; never be tempted to use canned mushrooms unless they are of the oriental persuasion or they are the wilder French types – even then it's better to reconstitute dried morels or cornes d'abondance in cream than to use those that have been preserved in some other way.

If you are able to afford or find wild mushrooms, the best have an excellent flavour which is enhanced by the blandness of pasta. Reduce double cream very vigorously until starting to brown somewhat. Cook the wild mushrooms very quickly in lots of butter with some garlic, splash with white wine or brandy, smother with coarsely chopped parsley, pour in the very thick cream and serve over pasta at once. Only the ignorant or pretentious would put cheese on such a heavenly dish.

SEAFOOD CREAM SAUCE

½ pt/300 ml *double cream*	½ *garlic clove*
8 oz/225 g *canned baby clams or*	2 tbsp *white wine*
Danish mussels	1-2 tsp *tomato purée*

Add to the double cream the juice from the can of clams or mussels, plus a squeeze of garlic, the white wine, and tomato purée – just enough to make a blush. Reduce this to half the original amount by boiling for 15 minutes, then just as the pasta itself is ready to serve add the clams and let them barely heat through. A pinch of the pungent oregano is a nice surprise with this, and because the sauce is lumpy it is appropriate to serve this over pasta shells which will entrap the unctuous sauce and the shellfish, thus making each mouthful rather more rewarding.

LASAGNE

It has escaped the attention of most caterers, but the sauce used between layers of lasagne should be rich and creamy, a combination of béchamel and of a Bolognese ragù. Lasagne made with mince, masses of onion and chopped tomato has every right to weep copious amounts of water, as indeed it usually does. (But you cannot simply blame the caterers; instructions in many languages on the packet of lasagne I buy include béchamel as an ingredient in every language but English!)

To make a successful lasagne dish make equal quantities of a thick white sauce (use milk flavoured with onion and carrot and bay leaf) and of thick, well-reduced ragù. When you are constructing the dish, start by scooping some of each sauce into the bottom of the dish (perhaps using more béchamel than ragù) then use the scoop to swirl the two together, paying particular attention to working it well into the corners. Cover that with a layer of cooked and drained lasagne sheets then repeat the process of swirling the two sauces together; don't try to mix them evenly but leave them marbled, which is one of the pleasures of the dish. Strew the sauces with grated Parmesan or Pecorino cheese, then add more pasta etc., finishing with a beautifully marbled top layer of the two sauces. For maximum enjoyment of lasagne always err on the side of using too much béchamel sauce for at least this will give a moist, creamy dish; too much meat gives something dry and unsatisfying. It's easy when you know how, isn't it?

For four people, cook 8-12 oz/225-350 g of lasagne and use my recipe for Ragù Bolognese at the beginning of this chapter, plus at least 1 pint/575 ml of béchamel sauce and lots of Parmesan. Layer in a dish about 10 in/25 cm square and bake a full 30 minutes at 350°F/180°C/Gas 4.

SEAFOOD PASTA SALAD MARSEILLAISE

Serves 6-8

8 oz/225 g *pasta shells or shapes*	3 *garlic cloves, chopped*
Olive oil	*A generous handful of parsley,*
½ pt/300 ml plus *mayonnaise*	*chopped*
Lemon or lime juice	8-12 oz/225-350 g *mixed*
1-2 sachets *saffron*	*seafood (see method)*

Cook the pasta in plenty of boiling salted water until just tender, drain then dry well by rolling gently in a towel. While still warm, toss in just enough olive oil to coat each piece lightly.

If you are using a commercial mayonnaise, sharpen it somewhat with a tablespoon or more of fresh lemon or lime juice. Warm the saffron gently and add together with the very finely chopped garlic and parsley; you can use less saffron, but if you use large cloves of garlic or more than 3 cloves you will certainly need 2 sachets. Mix the pasta into the mayonnaise.

The seafoods you use can all come from cans if that is easier. They should be drained and are better if they have been in brine, stock or oil rather than in vinegar; mussels, cockles, prawns, baby clams, smoked clams or oysters, crab flesh – all or any would be good. Mix these in too, using a light hand. Chill for several hours during which time the saffron flavour will develop further.

If you keep this longer than a couple of hours you may find the pasta absorbs a great deal of the mayonnaise; so be prepared with more, or reserve a little of the juices from the cans of seafood and moisten the mixture with that.

This recipe doubles easily for buffets and parties. If you can't find saffon, turmeric, curry powder or a mixture of coriander and cumin would all be worthwhile.

FETTUCINE FLING

Katie Stapleton from Denver, Colorado, is a renowned food broadcaster and entertainer. She called this Fettucine Fling because as soon as you taste it you fling your hands up in amazement at its simplicity and goodness.

Serves 6-8

12 oz/350 g *green fettucine*	2 *garlic cloves, chopped*
Salt	1½ tsp *dried oregano*
1 bunch *parsley*	½ pt/150 ml *olive oil*

Tomato sauce

2 lb/900 g *canned plum tomatoes in their own juice*	2 *garlic cloves, crushed*
	Herbs (see method)

Cook the the fettucine in masses of boiling water with 1 teaspoon salt – you can also use tagliatelli, and although green pasta is better, plain or mixed noodles will taste the same.

Meanwhile chop the parsley and add it with the garlic and oregano to the olive oil, and stir in some more salt. Drain the cooked fettucine, put onto a platter, allow to dry then pour over the herb/oil mixture, toss very gently and let cool.

You need 1 pint/575 ml of tomato sauce which is why you start with twice that amount of plum tomatoes in their own juice. Cook the tomatoes down until really thick together with the garlic; it may take as much as an hour. When it is thick, flavour the sauce by adding a favourite herb for just 5 minutes. Katie suggests a little sage, which is excellent and unexpected. If you feel safer with what you know, basil or mint are very good. Use fresh or dried, but only cook gently for 5 minutes to keep the freshness of flavour. Strain out the herbs and pips. Chill thoroughly, adding some more fresh basil or mint if that is what you have used when the sauce was cooking.

Make a well in the cold pasta, pour the sauce into the middle and put on the table like that. Mix together and serve. Although the pasta should not be chilled, the sauce should be as cold as possible.

Options Add one or two cans of baby clams or mussels to the oil and herb dressing for the pasta, then incorporate the liquid from the cans into the tomato sauce. To simplify the flavours, use only parsley and garlic, but spike the tomato sauce with a touch of celery salt towards the end of its cooking time.

The classic thing to do when you have masses of basil is to make pesto pasta; but what if you have unexpected guests, or can't be bothered or just don't have pine nuts or the money to buy them? Flavour the olive oil for the pasta with a great deal of chopped basil and only a little parsley and enliven the mixture with a few dessertspoons of grated Parmesan or Pecorino cheese. Cook the tomato sauce with garlic and add masses of basil a few minutes before it is due to be ready. Once the savour has been extracted, strain the herbs out by pouring through a sieve.

Or, when the oil and herb mixture is poured onto the fettucine, also add 3-5 oz/85-105 g prosciutto in small dice (you can only afford this when you have bought a knuckle end – if not use ordinary ham or tongue).

To enjoy a real Greek flavour, add crumbled Fetta cheese to the fettucine and flavour the tomato sauce with extra oregano. Yes, you are right, this is either Fettacine Fling or Fetta Fettucine Fling, both of which are terrible names.

CONCHIGLIE COSTANZA

The only pasta dish I've dared invent for an Italian – she loved it so it is named after her. It will feed four quite well.

1½ oz/40 g *butter*	Approx 6 oz/175 g *canned*
3 tbsp *flour*	*Danish mussels,*
1 tbsp *tomato purée*	*drained weight*
1 *bay leaf*	At least ½ pt/300 ml *milk*
1 *small clove garlic, chopped*	1 lb/450 g *conchiglie (shell pasta)*
Approx 9 oz/250 g *canned baby*	At least ¼ pt/150 ml *white wine*
clams, drained weight	

Melt the butter, stir in the flour and cook gently for a couple of minutes. Stir in the tomato purée, bay leaf and chopped garlic and leave over a very low heat.

Open the cans of seafood, reserving the liquid. Make the liquid up to 1 pint/575 ml with milk and bring to the boil. Add all at once to the flour and butter roux and whisk until thickened. Leave to simmer very slowly, covered.

Cook the conchiglie according to packet instructions, drain, toss in butter and keep warm as you quickly finish the sauce. Remove the bay leaf and reduce the sauce to a thin coating consistency by adding white wine (use more or less according to preference). Stir in the seafood and heat just enough to warm through. Put the pasta shapes into an attractive dish pour over the sauce and serve at once.

A very little Parmesan is all right, but the usual lavish dose would swamp the delicate, rosy-pink sauce. A spinach and bacon salad is good with this; otherwise introduce green by strewing the pasta heavily with coarsely chopped parsley.

6 Pulses and Grains

I know it is silly, but I inevitably feel inhibited when trying to write or talk about pulses and grains – I suppose I'm trying hard not to appear faddish, for these important and delicious foods are inextricably associated with the long skirts and sandals of health food stores. If we ate more of them we would save money and, more important, drastically reduce our intake of cholesterol, for they are all marvellous substitutes for meat . . . there I go again!

In an attempt to avoid the fad problem, this chapter is planned to be entertaining rather than plain educational, a collection of ancient and newly-created recipes from as far apart as Russia, China, Venice and Notting Hill Gate, London, where I live. I've concentrated on some of the lesser-known varieties and techniques, such as making a genuine risotto.

Frankly, canned beans are one of the best products you'll find in any deli, and each shop should sell a wide range. It takes only a little effort to make most types taste just as though you have made them all yourself, and usually any differences may be ignored. My sole suggestion as you explore the delights of red kidney beans, borlotti, pinto and butter beans, Arborio and Basmatti rice, millet hash and buckwheat cakes is to get boring 'three-bean' salads out of your repertoire and off your list as soon as you can. There is a fabulous world of pulse and grain dishes beyond that limiting horizon.

As with so many basic foods, some of the simplest ideas are by far the best. Follow my suggestions in *The Delicatessen Food Handbook* to use toasted barley as the base for winter stews and casseroles. And I specially recommend you try buckwheat or burghul wheat as an alternative to rice – both are fail-safe and, I think, more delicious.

BARLEY WATER

So extraordinarily good and so astonishingly refreshing, this simple, old-fashioned treat is almost permanently in my refrigerator during summer. It goes to prove that many of the best things in life are amazingly cheap if not free.

Makes 2 pt/1.2 litres

2 oz/50 g *pearl barley*   4 pt/2.3 litre *boiling water*
1 pt/575 ml *cold water*

Put the barley into the cold water and bring slowly to the boil. Let it simmer for 15 minutes then pour off the water and discard it. Put the cooked barley into a large saucepan and pour onto it the freshly-boiled water. Let this simmer uncovered until the volume has been reduced by half. Strain off – this time you keep the liquid and discard the barley.

Once cooled and chilled the barley water may be enjoyed a number of ways, the most common of which is to sweeten it with sugar then to give it tang with lemon, orange or lime juice. Whatever you do it may be further diluted, as its exceptionally smooth texture will be thought too unusual to be enjoyed by some. The addition of soda or of a sparkling mineral water to a mixture of barley water and fresh lime juice is the best of all, to my mind.

BOSTON BAKED BEANS

Serves 4-6

1 lb/450 g *dried haricot, navy or*   3 tbsp *molasses*
   cannellini beans   1 *large onion (optional)*
2 tsp *salt*   6-8 oz/175-225 g *salt pork or*
½ tsp *mustard powder*   *unsliced bacon*
3 tbsp *dark brown sugar*

Soak the beans overnight, drain, then cook in 2 pints/a good litre of cold water *without salt*. Drain again and put into a heavy casserole with 1 pint/575 ml of water plus the salt, mustard, sugar and molasses. A large sliced onion can also be added but is not very usual. The salt pork or piece of bacon should be pushed down into the middle of the beans – I always think smoked bacon is best.

Cook first at 400°F/200°C/Gas 6 for 1 hour, well covered. Then reduce the heat to 250°F/130°C/Gas ½ for 4 hours. Remove the lid and bake a further hour. Stir only very occasionally, adding water if the beans are drying too much.

Serve with bacon or ham, sausages and hot bread. Note that tomato has no place in this recipe; for that you need the following recipe.

MY BAKED BEANS

Like so many dishes based on beans, this version of baked beans is fail-safe (provided you don't salt the beans too soon) and allows enormous scope for you to make your own version.

To serve 6-8

1 lb/450 g *haricot or cannellini beans*	3 *dried bay leaves*
28-32 oz/800-900 g *canned plum tomatoes in their own juice*	8-12 oz/225-350 g *smoked bacon, cubed*
1 or 2 *onions, sliced*	8-12 oz/225-350 g *garlic sausage, sliced*
4-6 *garlic cloves*	¼ pt/150 ml *red wine (optional)*

Soak the beans overnight, drain, then cook until tender in fresh unsalted water. Drain once more then put into a casserole with all the other ingredients except the wine. Although the beans can be baked in the oven I prefer to cook them over a very low heat on top of the stove, as it makes supervision of their state that much easier.

It will take at least 2 hours of very slow cooking for the fat to melt and be absorbed, and some of the beans should have melted, too, to form a thick sauce with what is left of the tomatoes. Adjust the texture of the sauce by adding extra water if it is too dry, cooking without the lid if it is too wet.

Ten minutes or so before serving, dribble in the red wine, which gives an astonishing lift of flavour. A spoonful or two of mustard is another excellent addition to baked beans.

Options   Neither the bacon nor garlic sausage is necessary, particularly if you are trying to cut down on cholesterol, nor need they be in the proportions outlined; you simply need 1-1½ lb/450-675 g of bacon, sausages or smoked poultry and any mixture will work well if that is what you like.

LAMB AND BEAN CASSEROLE

Hearty and filling, this dish is the perfect winter lunch or informal dinner for friends. Make it a day or two in advance if you can, for the flavour improves dramatically if left to its own devices. You can change the proportion of beans or meat as you like and by adding more or less tomato, make a sloppy or a dry casserole.

I prefer to use the big flat butter beans or dried broad beans for this, mainly to make a change, but white haricot beans are perfectly marvellous, too.

Serves 4-6

1 lb/450 g *dried beans*	4 *fresh bay leaves (or* 2 *dried)*
1 or 2 *neck of lamb chops,*	*Fresh or dried thyme*
per person	½ pt/300 ml *robust red wine*
Oil (optional)	1 *large can Italian plum tomatoes*
1 *large onion, sliced*	*Prepared mustard (see method)*
3 or 4 *garlic cloves, in their skins*	*Parsley, coarsley chopped*

Soak your chosen dried beans overnight in cold water, drain, and then cook in plenty of unsalted water until tender. Drain again.

Then take the neck chops and brown slightly in a nonstick pan or in a little oil. Add to the beans together with the onion, whole garlic cloves, bay leaves, and a good sprinkling of fresh or dried thyme.

Stir in the red wine and the tomatoes in their own juice. Cook covered on a low heat or in the oven so that the mixture only just bubbles. It will take several hours for the lamb to tenderize, by which time some of the beans should have mushed up to help make a nice sauce.

If it is too wet for your liking (give it a good stir to be sure first), continue cooking without the lid; if it is too dry, add more wine or some water. Just before serving, stir in several teaspoons of prepared mustard. Take the whole pot to the table liberally covered with very coarsely chopped parsley and a little more fresh thyme, if you have it.

HOPPING JOHN

I've not yet found an explanation for the name of this, which is yet another variation on the mixture of beans and rice endemic to the southern states of the USA and the Caribbean. This one uses black-eyed beans, which are confusingly known also as black-eyed peas and which have a delicious slightly spicy-peppery flavour. It is served instead of potatoes.

Serves 6, generously

1 lb/450 g *black-eyed beans*	1 *onion, finely chopped*
Approx 8 oz/225 g *salt pork or*	1 or 2 *bay leaves*
fatty bacon	*Cayenne pepper*
1 pt/575 ml *water*	*Salt and pepper*
8 oz/225 g *white rice*	

Start by soaking the black-eyed beans overnight. Drain them well and cook in unsalted water until tender. Meanwhile gently cook the salt pork (perhaps from your own brine bath) or, if you can't get that, a piece of fatty bacon in the water in a large saucepan with a lid. Then add the beans plus the white rice, onion, a bay leaf or two and a pinch of cayenne pepper (also sold as chilli pepper).

Simmer covered until the rice is cooked and the liquid has been absorbed. Season to taste. The pork should be tender enough to be pulled apart, so that everyone gets a share. Don't hesitate to add a little more water during the cooking if the liquid has been absorbed before the rice is tender.

ROASTED BUCKWHEAT PILAFF

A buckwheat pilaff is what is generally called kasha, but in fact any grain that is prepared like this is a kasha.

For 4-6 generous portions

1 oz/25 g *butter*	¾ pt/425 ml *water or stock,*
8 oz/225 g *whole roasted*	*boiling*
buckwheat	½ tsp *salt*

Melt the butter in a saucepan, add the buckwheat and stir until it has darkened in colour. Add the boiling water or stock and the salt, stir quickly then put over medium heat until the liquid has been absorbed, usually a matter of minutes only. I like to eat it almost immediately but it is traditional now to leave the buckwheat covered on the lowest heat, possibly for hours, which certainly fluffs it up, but any texture or bite it has disappears and I think that a loss. Up to you.

Options   The most popular variation is to use bacon rather than butter. Cut 4-6 oz/115-175 g into small pieces and let the fat run before adding the buckwheat to brown. Some finely chopped onion would also be good with that, and so would garlic. My favourite version starts by reconstituting up to ½ oz/15 g of dried mushrooms (depends on your budget) in ¾ pint/425 ml of water. Then I fry up 4 oz/115 g of bacon pieces, brown the buckwheat in that and add the mushrooms and mushroom flavoured stock. It is good enough to eat just by itself, but wicked spoonfuls of soured cream make it quite ambrosial.

If the frying is done in butter and the liquid used is hot milk, you get a sweet dish to serve with soured cream, sugar and melted butter.

BUCKWHEAT GALUSHKI WITH BACON

Galushki are Russian gnocchi, basically lumps of pasta served as a main course or as an accompaniment. These ones are cut into squares, but you (and the children) might enjoy making them different shapes through rolling, folding or stamping out. It is good to make small balls of the dough and to flatten these against the floured tines of a fork, giving a flattened shape with ridges which is then folded lightly in half so it will collect the maximum amount of sauce, oil or butter.

Serves 4-6

6 oz/175 g *bacon, cubed*
2 *medium onions, chopped*
1 *large egg*
½ tsp *salt*

4-5 fl oz/115-150 ml *water*
8 oz/225 g *buckwheat flour*
Butter, oil or soured cream,
    to taste

Gently fry the bacon pieces until the fat is running freely then add the chopped onions and sauté until softened and well cooked. They can be browned or not according to your preference.

Mix together the egg, salt and water, add the flour, mix and then knead until smooth but not sticky. (Add extra buckwheat or wholemeal flour if stickiness is a problem.) Roll out the dough to about ¼ in/6 mm and cut into squares – bite-size is best.

Boil a large saucepan of well-salted water and dribble in the galushki. They are cooked when they rise to the surface, which takes only minutes. Drain well then serve with the bacon and onion, including all the fat, and top with extra butter, some oil or, best of all, soured cream.

Options You might like to cut down on the onion and/or add some garlic. A little horseradish is excellent in the soured cream, and indeed the galushki could be served with neither bacon nor onion but mounds of well-flavoured soured cream.

BUCKWHEAT PAMPUSHKAS WITH GARLIC

Pampushkas are a type of yeasted dumpling and go excellently with roasted meats and poultry or with juicy stews.

Serves 6-8 as accompaniment

½ oz/15 g *fresh yeast*
¼ pt/150 ml *warm water*
12 oz/350 g *buckwheat flour*

4 tbsp *oil*
1 oz/25 g *fresh garlic cloves*
1 tsp *salt*

Dissolve the yeast in the warm water; if you can only get dried yeast, use 2 teaspoons plus a pinch of sugar. Stir in a quarter of the flour and leave to stand in a warm place until foamy and well risen. Knead in the remaining flour plus the oil and leave to double in bulk once more. The mixture should be rather soft – if not add a few extra spoons of water.

Lightly form the dough into small dumplings (use two dessertspoons to get an even shape, or simply roll lightly between oiled palms), cook in masses of gently boiling water for at least 20 minutes, drain and keep hot.

Peel the garlic and mash it well with the salt. If the flavour really is too robust, cook the garlic purée in a little oil or butter until it has softened and weakened. Then serve the two together. Like so much Russian food, dollops of soured cream would make these even more enjoyable.

TOASTED BURGHUL SALAD WITH GREEN GINGER AND ALMONDS

The most famous burghul salad is the Lebanese tabbouleh, which is increasingly found in restaurants and houses. It relies on masses of parsley and lemon plus raw onion for its special flavour but, as I don't like raw onion much and certainly do not approve of it being served in any serious meal, I invented this version.

Serves 6-12 depending on accompaniments

8 oz/225 g *fine burghul*	½ oz/15 g *mint, finely chopped*
4-5 tbsp *nut oil or olive oil*	1 *large cucumber*
4-5 tbsp *fresh lemon juice*	*Salt and pepper, to taste*
2 in/5 cm *green ginger root*	1 oz/25 g *flaked almonds*
3 oz/85 g *parsley, finely chopped*	

Lightly brown the burghul by stirring or tossing in a nonstick pan with no added fat. Remove and let cool, then cover with cold water and leave for 30 minutes. Drain and gently squeeze out excess water. Mix together the oil and lemon juice, peel and slice the green ginger, then squeeze out the juice with a garlic crusher directly into the vinaigrette. It should be rather sharp, and you will find you need to squeeze each slice of ginger several times to get all the juice from it.

Mix the liquid through the burghul very well then add in the parsley and mint and put to one side for at least 30 minutes to allow the flavours to mingle. Meanwhile slice the cucumber in half lengthwise, scoop out the seeds then cut the cucumber halves into ½ in/1 cm pieces. Toss these into boiling water until only just beginning to soften then drain and cool under running water until they turn translucent and bright green. Drain well and mix into the salad.

This can be finished and served immediately but I find it is better when left several hours in the refrigerator. Before serving, season with salt and pepper and consider whether or not you need to add more ginger juice – I like to be aware of the slight sting of the ginger without knowing exactly what the flavour is.

Toss the almonds in a nonstick pan with care until golden brown. Arrange the salad in a neat mound surrounded by lettuce leaves, and sprinkle with the nuts.

Serve as an accompaniment to cold or hot meats or as part of a mixed hors d'oeuvre, in which case the salad can be scooped up in the lettuce leaves or with pieces of hot or cold pitta bread.

Options Opinions varied when I made this as to whether the use of the more expensive nut oil made sufficient difference to justify its cost. I thought it did, but as it is marginal you may wish to use olive oil instead. Be careful not to overdo the mint.

The fact that this has no onion in it means it is super with salmon or smoked salmon, cold game and fine hams.

BURGHUL PILAFF

Burghul, incorrectly known as cracked wheat, is also sold as bulghur and as pourghourri. It is a fail-safe alternative to rice, and tastes far better too. To my mind the onion usually added is unnecessarily intrusive, for a pilaff should be merely a background to a more important dish unless it is to be the star dish, in which case it can be packed with whatever you like.

So here is my way and, if you like, a finely chopped onion may be cooked in the oil or butter before adding the burghul.

Serves 4-6

1 oz/25 g *butter*	8 oz/225 g *burghul*
2 tbsp *olive oil*	½ pt/300 ml *hot stock or water*

Melt the butter with the oil in a saucepan, add the burghul and keep stirring until it has turned a delicious golden brown. Then add the hot stock or water, stir once and put over a low heat until the liquid is all absorbed, which doesn't take long at all. Now turn the heat down even lower, put the lid on the pan and leave it as long as it suits you. If you eat the burghul fairly soon it will have a little crunch in the centre, which I prefer – the longer you leave it over the heat to cook in its own steam the softer and fluffier it becomes, but I find that can become amazingly boring, unless it is to accompany really highly flavoured food.

Traditionally, you would add extra melted butter to the burghul before steaming it or before serving it but in these cholesterol-conscious days I think that can be forgotten . . . it is quite delicious enough without.

Options   As the food to accompany the pilaff becomes simpler, the pilaff can be proportionately more complicated. Armenians would sauté a handful of almonds, seedless raisins and dried apricots in butter and pour those over the top with a scattering of cinnamon. A great treat. Good melting cheeses can be cubed and stirred in just prior to serving, and any of the Middle Eastern spices like coriander, cumin, nutmeg, clove or cardamom may be incorporated with discretion.

TOMATO BURGHUL WITH EGGS

Here is an original, fresh-tasting dish for a hot or a cold buffet; or you can serve this well chilled to start a sit-down luncheon or dinner on a sizzling day. Served hot or warm it is a delightful lunch dish.

Serves 2 as a main course; 4-6 as a starter

8 oz/225 g *canned plum tomatoes*	*Salt and pepper, lemon juice,*
4 dessertsp *parsley, coarsely*	*to taste*
chopped	1-2 oz/25-50 g *butter*
1 *garlic clove, chopped*	4 *eggs, lightly beaten*
2 oz/50 g *burghul, coarse or*	2 dessertsp *cream or milk*
medium	

Coarsely chop the canned tomatoes and put together with the juice from the can into a saucepan. Once simmering, add the parsley and garlic and cook for just 1 minute until the parsley is very bright green. Take from the heat and stir in the burghul. Cover and leave away from heat for 15 minutes, by which time all the moisture from the tomatoes will have been absorbed. Stir gently then flavour with salt, pepper and a little lemon juice. Keep warm in the oven if you plan to serve warm, otherwise let cool then cover and chill.

To complete the warm dish, melt the butter in a saucepan, add the eggs and cream or milk and scramble over a low heat stirring constantly. Once clotted but while still soft and creamy, remove from the heat. Quickly shape the warm burghul into a ring and pile the eggs in the centre. Serve immediately, perhaps sprinkled with chopped chives, soured cream or both.

To serve cold, let the scrambled eggs also chill then arrange in the centre of a ring of burghul as above. Top with chives, soured cream or both. As a special alternative, leave the chives for another time and dust with cinnamon – a spice equally at home with burghul, tomato, parsley, garlic or lemon.

SWEETCORN SOUFFLÉ

This simplest of all soufflés is delightful at any time of the year, as a satisfying starter in summer or as a light, sweet summery main dish.

To serve 4 generously

Approx 10 oz/275 g *can of creamed sweetcorn*	5 *egg yolks*
1 tbsp *plain flour*	*Salt and pepper, to taste*
1 oz/25 g *butter*	6 *egg whites*

Butter and flour a straight-sided soufflé dish of about 3 pint/ 1.7 litre capacity, and preheat the oven to 400°F/200°C/Gas 6.

Turn the contents of the can of creamed sweetcorn into a small saucepan and mix the flour in well. Heat slowly, adding the butter, and stirring until the mixture has thickened. Let it cool a little then whisk in the egg yolks and salt and pepper to taste, remembering to allow for the egg whites which are still to be added.

Whisk up the egg whites until firm but not dry. Fold the two together, ladle into the prepared soufflé dish and put directly into the oven for 25 minutes, which gives a high soufflé that is runny in the middle.

To serve nicely, cut just the crust into the number of portions required and carefully lift it off onto hot plates. Then serve the rest of the soufflé beside the crisp crust by cutting a large spoon deep into the centre and lifting back towards you. (Starting from the outside tends to flatten the soufflé.)

A little salad or some grilled bacon are the best things to have on the side.

Options   Green peppers or green chilli peppers are a common flavouring for sweetcorn dishes, but both tend to be rather overpowering, so go easy. Chunks of precrisped bacon would also be nice in the soufflé itself. My favourite flavouring for sweetcorn is garlic and parsley – add garlic to the soufflé and cover each serving with parsley, or make a garlic and parsley butter as a sauce.

CHILLI-GREEN SWEETCORN IN LETTUCE

Hot spicy food served in crisp cold lettuce leaves is very much a Chinese idea. But this is all mine, and the contrast of texture and flavour makes a worthwhile talking point.

Serves 4 as a main meal; more as a starter

1 lb/450 g *boneless belly of pork,* *trimmed weight*	2 *fresh chilli peppers* *Oil for frying (optional)*
2 *garlic cloves, chopped*	Approx 12 oz/350 g *whole*
1 tsp *ground allspice*	*kernel corn*
1 tsp *ground cumin*	1 *large lettuce*
1 *small green pepper*	

The belly of pork should be cut into slices and then into smaller pieces about 1 inch/2.5 cm long. Sprinkle the pieces with garlic and the spices and leave for an hour or so in a cool place. Meanwhile, cut the green pepper into strips and slice the chilli peppers thinly into circles – take out the seeds first to reduce excessive heat, but be careful to wash your hands afterwards.

Stir-fry the pork pieces in a nonstick pan with very little oil – or none at all – until cooked through and still juicy. Add the drained corn and keep stirring until it is well heated through then add the peppers. When they have turned bright green, quickly put the mixture into a hot bowl and serve at once with lots of washed, very well dried and then thoroughly chilled lettuce leaves.

Each person takes a lettuce leaf, then adds a spoonful of the pork and corn mixture and rolls the former about the latter. This is also delicious when cold.

CREOLE CORNFLOUR CAKE

This incredibly simple pudding continuously surprises me. There seems to be almost nothing that does not go with it or on it or in it. Its pale colour and strangely rich flavour is often welcome after complicated food, and once a slight tint is added to it, such as with Crème de Menthe, it almost becomes a decorative feature in itself.

Make it in something ovenproof and transparent if you can, so that the full effect can be appreciated.

4 oz/115 g *cornflour*	3 oz/85 g *butter, just melted*
2 pt/generous litre *boiling milk*	*Caster sugar, to taste*
2 *large eggs*	*Flavouring, to taste*

Dissolve the cornflour in some of the milk in a saucepan, then pour in the remaining milk. Keep stirring over medium heat until the mixture is quite dry and not floury to the taste. Let it cool then beat in the eggs, butter, sugar and flavouring, according to your peculiar preference. Put into a greased dish and bake in a 350°F/180°C/Gas 4 oven until the top is lightly browned. Serve hot or cold – the latter being better, I think.

Options   The old recipe I found used vanilla as the flavouring but a combination of vanilla and rum is quite fabulous. Indeed you could use just black rum, when the cake would be perfect as a base for fresh cherries.

Crème de Menthe gives a frosty green colour and a refreshing flavour that is surprisingly good to accompany strawberries, and all the orange liqueurs would also be good. I think toasted nuts would be nice in or on this, as would almost any spice. Jane Stapleton, who experimented with this for me, sliced peaches, sprinkled them with liqueur and brown sugar and having layered them atop the cake, put it under a grill until the sugar was melted and the peaches were heated through but not too soft. This could be done to the pudding when freshly baked or chilled.

Bananas with rum, orange or lime juice, plums with brandy, apple slices with Calvados or pears with Maraschino or Tia Maria would also be more than worth your while to try.

RICE, ITALIAN STYLE

A genuine risotto of short-grain Arborio rice, one of the staples of northern Italy, is nothing like the piles of dry rice and vegetables we call risotto. It is actually rather like a rice porridge and made by a method that breaks every rice-cooking technique you have ever been told about, for you must stir and whisk it constantly as it cooks. What this does is break up the starch that is released, which is then polished and smoothed to make a deliciously unctuous sauce around each separate cooked grain. Risotto is rich in butter and cheese, and because of the special and continuous care required it is almost always served as a first course, for it cannot be kept warm once it is ready.

The basic recipe is given first then one of my favourite variations.

Serves 2

1 pt/575 ml *hot chicken stock*	*Extra butter and grated*
2 oz/50 g *butter*	*Parmesan cheese*
4 oz/115 g *Arborio rice*	

If you have no home-made chicken stock, boil 1 pint/575 ml water and dissolve in that a single stock cube which, although not as concentrated as recommended by the manufacturer, is less aggressive and more chicken-like in flavour.

Melt the butter in a small saucepan then cook the rice gently in that until glistening and golden but not brown. Pour in all of the hot stock and start whisking while keeping the mixture just simmering. It will take 12-15 minutes to cook the rice so that every grain is separate and the sauce is thick and smooth. If the rice is not cooked by the time the sauce is thickened, add a little more stock or water. It is up to you whether you serve your risotto thick or rather sloppy – it doesn't matter as long as the rice itself is neither undercooked nor overcooked.

Once the risotto is ready, take it from the heat and stir in butter and grated Parmesan cheese to taste – about 2 teaspoons of each per serving. Don't be tempted to use a Cheddar or other cheese as this will give precisely the nasty stickiness you have laboured to avoid. Serve at once. Well worth the trouble for you and a friend, but I would think twice about doing it for more unless you are an experienced cook with a strong whisking action!

RISOTTO WITH FRESH-HERB GREMOLATA

Serves 2

2 oz/50 g *butter*	1 pt/575 ml *hot chicken stock*
4 oz/115 g *Arborio rice*	

Gremolata

1 or 2 *garlic cloves*	*chopped*
2-3 tbsp *mixed fresh herbs,*	1-2 dessertsp *grated lemon peel*

If you have no home-made chicken stock, use a chicken stock cube as described in the previous recipe. Then you must prepare your gremolata, the deliciously silly name given to a mixture usually made from parsley, garlic and lemon. You can make it with those ingredients for this dish, but if you use other sweet herbs, like basil, thyme, marjoram or, minimally, mint, you will have something wonderful. The garlic and herbs should be chopped together then mixed with the lemon peel until the flavour is just right. Do not overchop the herbs or they will develop a rather grassy flavour.

Make up the risotto as explained in the previous recipe and once it is ready, mix in the prepared gremolata, stirring gently until the herbs have turned a very bright green. Serve on fairly large plates, as a good risotto should spread.

AN INDIAN TRIFLE

Trifles were once a great variety of puddings and cakes, having in common only that they were layered with a fascinating range of flavours, textures and fillings. Thus it means there is no such thing as a classic trifle.

The first of the two recipes which use rice flour for trifled confections is a nineteenth-century one, and for those of you with time to spare it presents an ideal opportunity for artistic licence. It can also use up lots of leftover pieces of fruit, scrapings of jams and the last of some nuts, raisins or dried fruits you have in the cupboard. It is based on an Indian recipe and hence its name.

Serves 6-8

Base

7 oz/200 g *rice flour*	1 *cinnamon stick*
2 oz/50 g *white sugar*	*Flavourings (see method)*
2 pt/generous litre *milk*	

Fillings

As many or as few as you want, have, can afford or would like, including fruit purées, jams, creams, nuts and fruit

Mix the rice flour and sugar together then slowly stir in all the milk. Put into a saucepan together with the cinnamon stick and stir while heating gently until thickened. Cook for a few extra minutes to ensure no starchy flavour remains.

Remove from the heat, extract the cinammon, then flavour exotically. I used 8 teaspoons of rose-water and a dash of orange flower water. Try any combination of the two, or some good essence of vanilla or of almond. Freshly grated lime and lime juice is marvellous; so is toasted grated coconut.

The custard is then left to set into a slab – or slabs – at least 1 in/2.5 cm thick, thus you pour the flavoured custard into one or two flat-bottomed dishes that are that deep. Let the custard set and chill thoroughly. Now comes the good bit.

To proceed, you cut the set custard into shapes which you will eventually pile upon one another to make a sort of castle. By sandwiching each layer of shapes and dribbling things over or scattering and chopping you can make a truly fabulous effect. One attractive way to start is to choose a round plate in which to set the custard. Cut a star shape into the custard, then carefully remove the extra pieces of custard leaving the star on the plate.

Start decorating by filling in those excavated spaces. Fill them all with a delicious fruit purée, say of mango or some passion fruit pulp, or some raspberry jam with brandy in it. Or make each space different by putting a little fruit in one, some cream in another and so on. Once the spaces have been filled, you start again. Make a layer of something else over the star then arrange some or all of the remaining pieces of custard – you can cut them into smaller more interesting pieces if you like.

Make the shape as fantastic as you can, even if you only use a couple of extra flavouring ingredients. Just before serving, scatter over some toasted nuts.

If you like, the custard can be prettily coloured and one of the nicest finishing touches is to serve the sliced Indian Trifle with a cold sugar and water syrup flavoured with a liqueur.

A TRIFLE RICE CAKE

This is an adaptation of one of Mrs Beeton's recipes and is a good way to use up any otherwise useless rice flour you own. Rice flour gives a rather dry texture to baked goods unless used with a high proportion of butter.

Perfectly nice eaten quite plain, rice cakes lend themselves admirably to being cut decoratively and then being piled together with extra flavourings, sauces and creams.

8 oz/225 g *rice flour*	6 oz/175 g *caster sugar*
8 oz/225 g *white flour*	2 tsp *grated lemon or orange rind*
8 oz/225 g *butter*	4 *eggs*

Sieve the flours together. Cream the butter and sugar particularly well then stir in the citrus rind. Beat in the eggs one a time then fold in the flour. The final consistency will be the classic dropping one of a cake batter. If it is stiffer, loosen with a little milk.

Pour the batter very gently into a greased mould or tin and bake at 350°F/180°C/Gas 4. It may take 1½ hours before the centre is cooked. Leave to cool in the mould or tin for 15 minutes then turn out to cool thoroughly on a wire rack.

To trifle the cake, use a sharp pointed knife to make a diagonal cut from the top outside edge of the cake down to a central point an inch/2.5 cm above the bottom of the cake. Slowly turn the cake cutting with the knife until you can remove the inverted cone you have cut. Reserve.

Spread the exposed surface of both pieces of cake with raspberry, strawberry or blackcurrant jam. Then spread with thick cold custard, flavoured or plain, or with flavoured whipped cream. Carefully replace the cone and smooth off any filling.

Properly this cake should now be covered with something called a High Whip, which is really a syllabub so perhaps make the Blackberry Syllabub in Chapter 14. Otherwise simply sprinkle with a sherry, port or a liqueur and then cover with more whipped cream.

DUTCH SPICED RICE TART

This is a late eighteenth-century recipe I have adapted. It's delicious eaten with apple sauce or a crisp apple.

For a 10 in/25 cm pie dish

1 *prebaked shortcrust base*
4 oz/115 g *short-grain pudding rice*
1/2 pt/300 ml *milk, cream or mixture*
1/2 *cinnamon stick*
4 *eggs, lightly beaten*

2 oz/50 g *butter, melted*
1/4 pt/150 ml *single or double cream*
3 oz/85 g *sugar, white or brown*
2 tsp *orange-flower water*
Grated nutmeg, be generous

Soak, the rice in warm water for half an hour then drain. Cook covered with the milk, cream, or a mixture of both, plus the cinnamon stick, until soft. Allow to cool a little then remove the cinnamon stick.

Stir in the eggs and remaining ingredients, except the nutmeg. My preference is for brown sugar as it suits the spicy taste better.

Put the mixture evenly in the baked pastry case and sprinkle quite freely with nutmeg – freshly grated or scraped is noticeably better.

Bake in a preheated 350°F/180°C/Gas 4 oven for 30 minutes, by which time the rice mixture should be nicely set and lightly browned on top – if not, a few extra minutes won't hurt. Serve warm or cold.

7 Cheese and Cheese-making at Home

With very few exceptions, cheese is made from solidified casein, the major protein component of milk. When full milk direct from the cow is allowed to stand, it will slowly sour, the result of an increase in acid manufactured as a by-product of an enzymic action which consumes lactose, the milk sugar. At a certain acid level the casein will begin to solidify. This solid mass is curd, and as it separates out it leaves behind a liquid known as whey.

This acidic curd can only make an acidic-tasting cheese and for countless centuries most cheeses were so based. But the discovery of rennet, which is made from the stomachs of young suckling mammals such as calves and kids, meant that sweet milk could also be formed into curds and a whole new range of flavours was available to the cheese-maker, who was, as often as not, a housewife. Until the turn of this century it was common for a woman to turn her own cows' milk into curds if she wanted a soft curd cheese to make cheesecakes. Vegetarian and country-lore lovers will know that certain flowers and plants can also be used to curdle milk, including the artichoke, dandelions, the grass known as Ladies' Bedstraw – even the Venus Flytrap.

Exactly when you form milk into curds, the temperature of the milk, and whether or not you assist the whey to separate out, will all affect the flavour, texture and style of your cheese; and it is these variations of technique which are responsible for the world's huge variety of cheeses. When you then start tampering with the curd itself – heating it or pressing it, salting it or dipping it into a brine bath – further variations present themselves. Considering there is but one basic ingredient, the curd, and an extremely limited variety of cheese-making techniques, it is astonishing that there are quite so many cheeses to tempt us.

At one time the range was even greater, for before pasteurization became standard, cheeses would vary in flavour from day to day, for they would reflect exactly the food eaten by the animals; just as wine differs from yard to yard, the mixed grasses of each field would result in different tasting milks and thus a variety of cheese. Pasteurization kills *all* the bacteria in milk, including the ones responsible for those nuances of flavour. Pasteurized milk won't even form unrenneted curds naturally; when such milk in your carton or bottle solidifies it is almost certainly due to some contaminating bacteria that is dangerous to you (you should never drink or eat thickened pasteurized milk and it must never *ever* be used for cheese-making).

To restore to pasteurized milk its ability to curdle naturally and safely, and to develop the characteristic textures and perfumes of the cheeses we know, milk destined for cheese-making is inoculated with a 'starter'. This is a carefully controlled and nurtured collection of bacteria which will give back to the milk a chosen range of characteristics otherwise destroyed by the pasteurization process. After inoculation with the starter, the milk is left to 'ripen', allowing the introduced colonies of bacteria to increase and raising the acid level and flavour of the milk to a carefully defined and consistent level.

Although once so commonplace as barely to merit mention in cookbooks, the home manufacture of soft cheeses – known commercially as curd cheese or cream cheese – has all but disappeared. The ingredients necessary to make good cheese from pasteurized milk are difficult to obtain; and the cost of the milk itself means that in most instances it is more expensive to make these cheeses at home than to go out and buy them. Yet it is a pleasurable thing to do, and such techniques should not be forgotten.

Unless you own milking animals (and sheep or goats are simpler and safer than a cow) the manufacture of hard, pressed cheeses, like Cheddar, cannot be entertained, for even the smallest and simplest such cheese requires large quantities of milk. If you do have access to supplies, there are some good recipes in my small book *Cheese and Cheese-making* (Macdonald Guidelines). Even if you do not see yourself making cheese from scratch, there is enormous pleasure to be found in flavouring and maturing soft cheeses bought from a shop.

I hope this whole section inspires you to be creative and, even if not, I hope it will give you more respect for those who do make cheese for you; and that you will resist the admonishments of those who insist it is toasted upon every dish that has a sauce, or who make soup from Stilton or who serve it sweaty or crusted from beneath a cheese bell. Whatever cheese you have, you will only get a maximum flavour from it if it is wrapped tightly, for air is the worst enemy of cheese – it is totally wrong and unproductive to let cheese 'air' before you eat it. The best wrapping is clingfilm and the best storage place is somewhere very cool or a refrigerator, especially for such delicate ones as Brie or Camembert. You must bring cheese to room temperature before serving, but do so in its wrapping and only expose the cheese to the air as you serve it.

CHEESE-MAKING AT HOME

INGREDIENTS

Milk   Autumn milk gives the heaviest yields of cheese even when pasteurized, but nowadays flavour varies imperceptibly all year round, for you must always add a starter or buttermilk to pasteurized milk to restore flavour-giving bacteria.

If you are able to use raw cow's milk be absolutely certain the animal is accredited tuberculosis- and brucellosis-free. Also try to discover if the donating cows have been given antibiotics during the previous 3 or 4 days; if so these will kill the cheese-making bacteria in the milk.

Sheep's and goats' milk do not normally need to be pasteurized, although current thinking on the subject is best checked out with such authoritative bodies as the British Goat Society.

High-fat milk, such as Jersey or Guernsey, makes richer cheese, but is more difficult for the learner to use, as it requires more rennet and higher temperatures; better start with silver-topped milk. It is very important to understand that pasteurization kills all the harmless lactic acid-producing bacteria. When pasteurized milk turns sour and curdles at home, it could be the result of harmful, contaminating bacteria. *Pasteurized milk that has 'turned' must never be used for cheese-making.*

Starter   'Starter' is sterile milk injected with a culture of specially selected and isolated bacteria to replace those destroyed by pasteurization. Some of the bacteria will govern flavour, some the formation of holes or aroma, others will manufacture lactic acid and thus help form curds.

Starters for domestic cheese-making are available from the supplier give below.

There is also an easier starter for use at home – buttermilk. This is widely available, cheap, and gives excellent results. Cultured buttermilk is produced by adding a starter culture to the liquid by-product of butter-making. The bacteria mix is almost identical to that used as the basis for most cheese starters.

Rennet   Proper cheese rennet, which is stronger than junket rennet, is mandatory for most cheeses. With some experience, you can increase the proportion of junket rennet and successfully use this, but it is unreliable.

Rennet has two main functions: to curdle fresh, unripened milk without souring it, thus providing a sweet curd; and, in cheese made with ripened or sour milk, to hasten the solidification process without further altering the acidity. The use of small quantities of rennet results in a soft, moist curd; more rennet means a hard, dry curd. Both affect the speed at which the whey drains, which in turn affects the texture and flavour of the cheese.

Annatto   This is the most common cheese colouring and is a natural product made from a West Indian tree. Marigold petals and saffron can also be used.

Salt   This brings out the flavour of cheese and acts as a preservative. Ordinary household salt can be used, but iodized salt is not recommended; the complicated flavour of good sea salt is a considerable plus in cheese-making.

Lard   Pure lard is used to coat pressed cheeses, sealing them while they cure.

Deceit   You cannot hide many cheese-making mistakes but you can get away with most. As long as your hygiene is reasonable your cheese will be edible. Don't let on what you expected the cheese to be like and they will never know.

EQUIPMENT

Thermometers   A floating dairy thermometer is important.

So is a room thermometer, for the ambient temperature has a marked effect on results.

Measuring Jugs   These should be of glass or stainless steel: plastic can retain odours, and if scratched will be difficult to sterilize.

Mixing Bowls   Large stainless steel bowls are best and a good investment, but a bucket or two might be more in order for you. Never use any uncoated metal other than stainless steel. Unchipped enamel is good and there are cheaper, light dairy buckets of special plastic.

Water Bath   The temperature at which you add rennet to milk for cheese is critical but often low enough to be reached simply by standing a bowl or bucket of room-temperature milk in hot water in a sink or bath and stirring. For higher temperatures, milk heated slowly in a bowl or bucket directly on your cooker, but protected by a couple of asbestos mats, is perfectly suitable. But stir constantly.

Utensils   Apart from teaspoons and tablespoons for measuring rennet and annatto, you will need something with a long handle to stir the milk, a perforated spoon or slice, a ladle for transferring curd and a long-bladed knife for cutting curd. Stainless steel is best.

Colander   A large colander, even of plastic, is essential.

Moulds   A large range is available from the supplier below. Otherwise improvise with tins of various shapes and sizes, details of which are given with the relevant recipes. Watch for signs of rusting and remember always to punch the necessary drainage holes *from the inside* or you will never get your cheese out again. Round coffee tins and square tea tins (both 8 oz/225 g size) are useful.

Drainage Mats   While whey drains from the curds, your cheese needs to stand on something like table mats made of wooden strips or straw, cannibalized bamboo curtains, or plastic-strip table mates. Cheesecloth, folded a couple of times can be used.

Drainage Boards   Many cheeses drain on wooden boards and a basic small wooden chopping board will do as long as it is not pitted or scored. Make sure it is big enough to hold the number of moulds that you will use at any one time. In many cases – and always when using the Coulommiers hoops – you will need two.

 If you are lucky enough to get hold of some stout, stiff straw mats from your local cheese shop, you may be able to make do with these balanced over your whey collector.

Whey Collector   The drainage of cheeses results in a lot of free whey. You will need to stand your mould on its drainage board and/or mat in something such as a large roasting pan.

Cheesecloths   Use cheesecloth or butter muslin, both easily available. You nearly always use it folded double. If it is *not* easily available, get some from your butcher, boil it well, then rinse very thoroughly.

A Cheese-making Book   These are used to record every step in making cheese – from the age of the milk to the room temperature, the time that elapses between each operation, the acidity, and so on. You will then have a record of your mistakes, your corrections, and your triumphs. It pays big dividends.

Cheese-making Supplies   Contact the address below.
Self-sufficiency and Smallholding Supplies Limited
The Old Palace
Priory Road
Wells
Somerset BA5 1SY
Tel: Wells (0749) 72127

This company specializes in domestic cheese-making supplies and equipment by mail order, and can offer a full range of products for the home cheese-maker. The range includes 40 different designs of cheese mould, as well as starters, rennet and colouring, and a full catalogue is available on request.

METHODS

Temperature   The room temperature for cheese-making is all-important. The best range is 65-70°F/18-21°C. Otherwise, decrease the milk renneting temperature by the number of degrees by which your room exceeds 65°F/18°C.

Stirring   'Deep stir' means stir right to the bottom of the container in wide circles.

'Top stir' means agitate only the top ½ in/1.25 cm of the milk. This stops the cream rising, protecting flavour and texture.

Recognizing Coagulation   The easiest way to recognize coagulation is to float a piece of straw or a toothpick on the top of the milk. Stop stirring the moment it stops moving or you will break up the curd and release the whey much too early.

Curd Cutting   To test the state of readiness of the curd, insert an index finger into the coagulum and move it forward an inch/ 2.5 cm or so. The curd should split cleanly and should not adhere to your finger. The whey released should be clear and greenish.

The time-honoured formula for checking when curd should be ready to cut is: *Time taken to coagulate plus 2½ times that time.*

If your cheese took 15 minutes to coagulate, it should be ready to cut in another 15 minutes plus 37½ minutes, or 52½ minutes after cutting the rennet. If ready to cut earlier your curd is higher in acidity than you thought; if later, lower.

Sterilization and Washing   Everything you use, including working surfaces, must be sterile, which may be achieved by boiling for at least 20 minutes or using a sterlizing solution – 1 fl oz/ 5 ml ordinary household bleach (hypochlorite) to 1 gallon/4.5 litres water. Rinse very thoroughly indeed, and then some more. Infinitesimal amounts of residual bleach will kill the bacteria in the milk and your cheese will not ripen.

All equipment that has been in contact with milk must be rinsed thoroughly with cold water before washing with hot, otherwise an undesirable film forms.

Never wear anything woolly, for fine hairy strands always find their way into the cheese. Remove rings, make sure that nails are clean and tie back and cover your hair. Beards are a problem – they really should be covered too.

TESTS AND TECHNIQUES

Milk Acidity   The acidity of milk affects the speed and texture of the curds formed. Normally, milk for pressed and matured cheeses should have an acidity of 0·21-0·23 per cent. Soft cheeses use unripened milk, with an acidity of only 0·18-0·20 per cent.

Test 1   Measure 56 drops fresh rennet into a warm cup, add a straw or a toothpick and then 4 fl oz/115 ml milk at 84°F/28°C, noting the time exactly on a watch with a second hand.

Stir for a few seconds, then note the exact time the straw stops moving.

The shorter the time to coagulation, the higher the milk's acidity:

24 seconds   = 0·20 per cent
21-22 seconds = 0·21 per cent
20 seconds   = 0·22 per cent
18 seconds   = 0·24 per cent
. . . and so on.

If milk varies more than 1 degree from 84°F/28°C it will affect the result by 2 seconds for every degree. Milk at 83°F will take 26 seconds to indicate 0·20 per cent, milk at 85°F will take only 22 seconds, and so on.

This test does not convert easily into Centigrade, but for use as a very rough guide, the milk should be at 28°C and fluctuations of 0.5° will affect your result by 2 seconds; milk at 27.5°C, for instance, will take 26 rather than 24 seconds.

Test 2   This is much more accurate without being much more difficult. Add 2 drops phenolphthalein to 10 cc of the milk or whey to be tested. Fill a well-calibrated plunger (acidometer) with N9 caustic soda solution: both chemical liquids are available at most chemists. Slowly drip the caustic soda solution into the whey or milk until it turns and *remains* pink. Each cc of caustic soda used shows the presence of 0·1 per cent acidity. Thus 2.5 cc = 0·25 per cent and so on.

If you have too high or too low an acid count, you can compensate. If development of acidity is lower than required, for soft unscalded cheeses you simply let the milk sit longer until the right level is reached; for pressed cheeses heat the curd more slowly and to a lower temperature than usual to give slower drainage.

When making soft cheese, a high-acid milk gives a fast-working curd which must therefore be cut small or sliced thin to hasten drainage; for making pressed cheese, both scald at a higher temperature and take up to that temperature as fast as possible.

POSSIBLE PROBLEMS

Mould can be wiped off with a damp cloth; dry cheese can be mixed with cream or butter; and wet cheese should be eaten fast, before it sours.

Failure to Coagulate   Often caused by residue of sterilization solution, wrong or weak rennet; in unpasteurized milk it may mean antibiotics are present.

Tainted Flavour   Invariably this is from unsatisfactory personal or kitchen hygiene.

Cheese which will not Ripen   You have probably killed the bacteria in the curd by contact with sterilization solution (usually in the cheesecloth which is better boiled than soaked in such a solution).

SOFT CHEESE RECIPES

Before you start, please always remember that, as with bread, there is no definitive cheese-making recipe. Each time you make a cheese, something will be different – the milk, the temperature, the humidity, even you and your concentration. Just as you must always work towards making a bread dough of the same consistency rather than work with exactly the same proportion of ingredients, each time you make a cheese you will have to fine-tune your technique if you wish consistent results. If this is not so important, there is just as much pleasure from anticipating and enjoying the variations. Although hygiene is of the greatest importance, the majority of soft cheeses are eaten relatively fresh and not so prone to spoilage and contamination as those which are kept longer. Soft cheeses that are to be ripened longer than a week demand very high standards of hygiene.

This small selection of recipes starts with those that do not use rennet and goes on to show what you can do with bought soft cheeses.

LACTIC-CURD CHEESE

This is unrenneted cheese, relying on the natural formation of lactic acid to solidify the casein. A gallon/4.5 litres of good creamy milk will make about 2-2¼ lb/1 kg cheese, depending on the time of the year and how much you drain it; you can halve or quarter the recipe.

| 1 gallon/4.5 litres *pasteurized milk* | 1 fl oz/25 ml *cultured buttermilk* Salt, to taste |

Slowly heat the pasteurized milk to 76°F/24°C then add the cultured buttermilk. Stir deeply and well for a full minute, cover the milk and leave for 2 hours or more in a room with a temperature of 65-70°F/18-21°C. When the curd is firm enough to split cleanly in front of you when you move a finger gently through it, line a bucket or large bowl with a large dry sterilized and rinsed cheesecloth, pour in the curd, breaking it as little as possible.

Pull up the corners of the cloth, tie them tightly, and suspend the lot to drain for 36-48 hours at approximately the same temperature as before.

Every 3 to 4 hours (or as convenient) you should gently mix the dry, drained outer curd with the soft inner curd in the cloth.

When you judge it is ready, salt it to your taste and then proceed to flavour it as in some of the ideas later in this section. If you whip it with an electric beater it will be smoother. You can also fold lightly whipped double cream into the curd to make it richer.

As explained before, the addition of cultured buttermilk restores to pasteurized milk some bacteria similar to those required to safely make cheeses. If you can't get hold of buttermilk, then try one of the next two recipes.

ACID-CURD CHEESE

This simple, fast method specially suits those who can't get or don't like to use rennet. By artificially raising the acidic content of the milk it will quickly curdle. Goats' milk is very suitable.

| 3 pt/1.7 litres *milk* 1 fl oz/25 ml *lemon, orange or* | *lime juice (or vinegar)* |

Heat the milk just to boiling point then stir in the lemon, orange or lime juice, or the same quantity of vinegar (which could be tarragon, garlic, cider, chilli or whatever you have).

The curd forms very quickly and should be put into a sterilized and rinsed cheesecloth to drain. As the milk has not ripened and you have added nothing to help it do so this curd has little flavour and needs spiking. The simple addition of herbs, a little softened butter, pepper and salt make it into a delightful spread or dip which can also be moulded into little shapes. If put into a larger mould it could be pressed under about 4 lb/1.8 kg weight, and, when well dried and solid, cut into cubes as an unusual addition to curries – it is called panir in India.

Otherwise, you add 1 egg, 1 oz/25 g of butter, nutmeg and sugar to taste, and a few currants and peel to each 8 oz/225 g of curd, bake that in little pastry cases and you have home-made cheesecakes.

RENNET-CURD CHEESE

This is a basic, milk cheese using ordinary junket rennet, which does not give as firm a set as cheese rennet. You will get better results if you add the cultured buttermilk some hours before you start and leave the combination in a warm place to ripen further and increase in flavour.

2 pt/a good litre *pasteurized milk*	1 tbsp *cultured buttermilk* Rennet

Mix the pasteurized milk and buttermilk together. Slowly raise the temperature to 100°F/38°C, stirring all the time. Then make a junket according to the instructions for the type of rennet you have bought. Stir very well for 1 minute, cover and leave in a moderately warm place for at least 2 hours.

When you can cut a clean sharp line through the curd with your index or little finger it is time to drain the curd. Line a colander with sterilized and rinsed cheesecloth and ladle thin slices of the junket into this (I use a flattish slotted spoon or a flat egg slice). Lift the four corners of the cloth, tie them together and suspend to let the whey drip into a bowl until the drainage is complete. Remove it from the cloth and wrap it in waxed paper – that from your breakfast cereal is ideal. This is good to eat almost immediately, but better if left a couple of days for the flavour will continue to develop. It can be added to, making it sweet or savoury, eaten just with cream or sugar, or cured in dock leaves or chestnut leaves.

SINGLE-CREAM CHEESE

1 pt/575 ml *single cream*	14 drops *rennet*
¼ fl.oz/7 ml *buttermilk*	*Cold boiled water (see method)*

Gently heat the single cream to 75°F/24°C, add the buttermilk and mix well. Remove from heat cover the mixture and leave to ripen for 2-3 hours. Then add the rennet, diluting with six times its volume of cold boiled water; stir it in very well. Cover and leave at a temperature of 70-80°F/21-27°C for 8-12 hours, or until the cream coagulates. Ladle this curd into folded cheese-cloth and hang it to drain in a cool, airy room.

At 4 to 8 hourly intervals, scrape the harder curd from the cloth and mix it with the softer central curd.

When the curd is thick and grainy, add salt and any flavour that suits you, sweet or savoury. Mix well and shape by hand or pack into a yoghurt container or teacup. Even when kept in a refrigerator it will continue to develop in flavour.

Double-cream Cheese   Uses the same proportions of cream and buttermilk as the previous recipe for single-cream cheese but it is neither ripened nor renneted. And you obviously use double cream instead of single.

Heat the cream to 75°F/24°C, add the buttermilk and at least ¼ oz/7 g salt, stirring in well. Cover and leave in a warm place to coagulate.

Mould and flavour in exactly the same way as single-cream cheese, but take even more care, in view of its cost.

FRENCH CREAM CHEESE

1 gallon/4.5 litres *milk*	15 drops *rennet*
2 pt/1.2 litres *double cream*	*Cold boiled water (see method)*
½ fl oz/15 ml *buttermilk*	

Mix the milk with cream and buttermilk. Heat slowly to 60-65°F/16-18°C. Add rennet diluted with six times its volume of cold boiled water. Stir in 4 minutes, then top-stir for a minute.

Put the container, covered, in a safe, cool place and top-stir for 2 minutes twice during the next hour. It will be at least 12 hours before you can break the curd cleanly.

Ladle the curd into the cheesecloth, tie up the cloth by its corners, and hang it in a draught-free place until the whey is only dripping slowly. Every hour, scrape the dry cheese from the cloth and mix it back. Once the cheese is good and firm – after about 12 hours – salt to taste and pack into small moulds of about 2½ in/6 cm diameter on drainage mats.

As soon as the cheeses have taken the shape of the moulds they may be removed. They are ready for immediate consumption or may be stored in waxed paper or aluminium foil for up to a week.

Alternatively use half as much rennet and leave to coagulate for 24 hours. Let the cheese drain on a board rather than hanging it and mould it in much larger moulds.

FLAVOURED FRESH CHEESES

The following ideas can be used for any of the preceding cheeses or for playing about with cream or curd cheese you have bought commercially. Once you have confidence there is almost no limit to the possibilities.

Fine herbs
Finely chop fresh parsley, chives and tarragon. Add a little garlic and a touch of grated lemon peel. Let the cheeses reach a stage of almost-readiness and then roll them in this mixture and wait for another full day.

Green peppercorns
Crush some green peppercorns in a little of the brine in which they are canned and roll the cheeses in this. You could also add a very few to the curd itself. Try adding vodka, too.

Herbes de Provence
This coating can be bought dried and expensive, or made in high summer with fresh savoury, thyme, rosemary and a few lavender flowers. It is recommended that you leave the cheese in this for a full week to draw out the smoky flavour of the herbs.

Paprika
Roll the cheeses in sweet paprika, perhaps with a little of the hot variety as well; it takes about 5-6 days to reach its peak.

Bacon
Either crumble some crisp, smoked, streaky bacon into the cheese, or wrap the cheese in strands of raw smoked bacon; you can eat the former fairly soon but leave the latter till later. In neither case should you add salt as the bacon will do this for you.

Geranium
Add a little rose-water to the milk before turning it and cure the cheese wrapped in leaves of rose geranium. Wonderful served chilled in slices with cream and raspberries or strawberries. You can use the other scented geraniums too, such as lemon, peppermint, orange, pineapple and cologne varieties.

Elderflower
Either sprinkle with elderflower wine or add a few fresh or dried elderflowers to the curd before draining. Excellent served with gooseberry fool or for use in baking cheesecakes.

Other fragrant flowers can be used but not all are as nice to taste as they are to smell. Jasmine is excellent but you should simply soak a quantity of them in your milk overnight and remove them before making the cheese. If using bought cheese, pressing some blossoms into the made cheese and storing them wrapped in the refrigerator for some days should work as well. Try nasturtium flowers and leaves.

Dried fruit
Any soaked dried fruit makes a nice coating for fresh cheeses, but the best plan is to soak raisins in a little dark rum and to press these swollen raisins into the surface and leave for a little while. Served in small amounts, chilled, on a pretty dish with an extra puddle of rum at the bottom and a slice or two of fresh orange, this really combines cheese and pudding in one – always a good idea if you can get away with it. A sprinkling of cinnamon, nutmeg or allspice is also nice.

Fresh fruit

One of the simplest ways to flavour cheese, especially when very fresh, is with a purée of fruit, perhaps with a little complementary liqueur of some kind. A small tin of drained, crushed pineapple; a little crushed fresh mint and some gin (yes, gin!) is excellent; raspberry with rose-water or strawberry with Cointreau; banana with Tia Maria; pear with Poire William or melon with port or ginger wine; mango with lime juice; passionfruit with orange juice; lychees with orange flower water . . . as you can see its simply a matter of what's in the cupboard. And don't forget nuts, preferably slightly toasted first.

The prettiest presentation of such combinations is the simplest. Instead of mixing the fruit or liqueur into the cheese, sit the plain cheese on a bed of the fruit and pour the liqueur over the top. Truly a stunning end to a meal.

CURED SOFT CHEESES

Soft cheeses, including those made from bought cheese may be eaten fresh or allowed to cure for a week or two in many different ways.

The most traditional assistants to curing cheese in Britain were dock or nettle leaves, chestnut leaves and pewter plates; the tannin and other ingredients in each of these affects the texture and flavour of the cheese in different ways. Dock and nettle are used as they are, but chestnut leaves are first soaked in boiling water for a few minutes (see Banon cheese).

The whole cheeses can also be dipped into, or painted with, a sharp spirit, such as marc or grappa and cured without wrapping.

But, the simplest method of interfering with the natural chemistry of the cheese is to interfere with the surface, especially once mould appears. By wiping this off daily with a dry cloth or by wiping it off then rubbing salt into the cheese, or by washing it off with a brine, different results can be obtained. The introduction of salt or brine inhibits the growth of mould but allows the development of bacterial growths, which are usually reddish and smelly but make creamy and sweet cheeses.

Experimentation is the key, and as long as the cheese is kept in a fairly cool place and you have been careful with your initial hygiene you will always make something edible. But do keep track of what you have done in a cheese-making book so you may avoid repeating mistakes and you can repeat a success.

To encourage you, here are some of the best successes I have had, and there seemed to be no marked difference whether a low-fat curd or a high-fat cream cheese was used.

SPICED CHEESE

1 lb/450 g *soft cheese*
Salt
2 oz/50 g *butter, softened*
Brandy

2 dessertsp *mixed whole pickling spices*
2 *mace blades*
Vine leaves

Salt the soft cheese then work in the softened butter. Wrap in sterilized muslin and shape into a disc about 1 in/2.5 cm thick. Turn daily for a week until the surface is dry. You can unwrap it for the last few days.

Brush the surface with brandy and grind the mixed pickling spices together with the mace. Press all over the cheese, wrap in vine leaves and tie securely. Then wrap in waxed paper. Leave in a cool, airy place for 2 weeks, turning daily. Once softening, it may be transferred to the refrigerator. If you leave off the waxed paper you will get a much drier cheese.

OIL-MARINATED CHEESE

6-8 oz/175-225 g *curd or cream cheese, unsalted*
Salt
Oil
2-3 *garlic cloves, crushed*
2 *bay leaves*

6 each *juniper berries and black peppercorns*
2 *dried chillies*
1-2 tsp *mixed pickling spice, ground*
½ *lemon, grated peel of*

Line a straight-sided cup with sterilized muslin then press into that the unsalted curd or cream cheese. Lift out, wrap then dry as in previous recipe. When the surface is quite dry, rub it all over with salt, then put into a small bowl, cover with olive oil or a mixture of olive and another decent oil. Into that put the slightly crushed cloves of garlic, bay leaves, juniper berries, black peppercorns, dried chillies and mixed pickling spice. Finely grate in the peel of half a small lemon. Let this sit for a couple of weeks, giving the cheese an occasional turn.

The marinade can be used again and again and you might like to make this cheese smaller so you can dip in and out of the treasure trove as it suits you. Serve with a little of the marinade.

Oil-marinated cheese is especially good if made with goats' milk cheese; you could do this more easily if you were able to buy fresh small cheeses from a farm.

VINE-LEAF CURED CHEESES

These are really a variation on the Banon (see later).

Once your small cheeses have dried enough, rub salt into the surface then brush over with a sharp spirit. I used ouzo, which seemed specially appropriate as an accompaniment to vine leaves. Make sure the leaves have been soaked long enough in warm water to rid them of most of their brine, then pat them dry.

Wrap up the cheese well then tie and leave a couple of weeks in a cool place. Once ripening and softening, you could transfer to a refrigerator. If drying too fast, wrap in wax paper.

LIPTAUER CHEESE

This Hungarian treat is highly spiced and is eaten fresh. Original recipes use low-fat quark, but a good full cream cheese can be substituted. Into it stir and knead softened butter, a good dollop of anchovy paste, caraway seeds, prepared mustard, a dash of hot or sweet paprika, capers according to taste, salt and pepper and finally, a hint of chopped onions.

No proportions have been given since, traditionally, every cook finds her/his preferred taste. It should be very spreadable, and have almost a whipped consistency.

In Austria and Hungary it is served with rye bread and the light new white wines or lager. There is no more delightful summer snack, but beware, the combination of tangy cheese and sunshine will make your wine, beer and senses disappear as if by magic!

COULOMMIERS-MOULD CHEESE

Moulded soft cheeses will vary from sweet to pungent, depending how you treat the curd – be sure your hygiene is as perfect as possible. Tall, round Coulommier moulds, open at both ends and punctured with holes are the easiest cheese moulds to buy. For this recipe you will need three of them. If you can't buy them, take the top and bottom out of 8 oz/225 g tea or coffee tins and use these – taller tins would be even better.

For 3 cheeses

1 gallon/4.5 litres *milk*	56 drops *cheese rennet*
2 fl oz/50-60 ml *cultured buttermilk*	*Cold boiled water (see method)*

Heat the milk: cows' to 95°F/32°C. goats' or sheep's milk to only 85°F/29°C. Remove from the heat, add buttermilk and stir well.

Dilute cheese rennet with six times its volume of cold boiled water. Deep-stir for a couple of minutes, then top-stir into coagulation. It takes at least an hour before the 'clean finger' test works.

Always prepare 'tops' for moulded soft cheeses, by gently pressing the mould, about 1 in/2.5 cm, into the curd, scooping out the shape, and slipping it onto a clean plate; make one top for each of the three cheeses.

Stand the moulds on mats on drainage boards and ladle slices of curd into each mould in turn, so each is filled to the same height.

If your milk was rather acid, cut thin slices, so you hasten drainage; thick slices impede it. Let the curds settle, then put on the three tops.

Drainage in a warm place will take about 24 hours. Then turn the mould over so the cheese gently slides to the other end. Put onto a clean mat and board. Repeat this process everyday until the curd has shrunk from the side of the mould – usually 3 days. Rub about ½ oz/15 g salt into the surface of each cheese. Leave the cheeses a few days longer. Wipe off any mould which grows or leave it on just one cheese to see what change in flavour results.

You might actually eat one cheese fresh, leave another for a couple more days and the third a bit longer, wrapped in wax paper in the refrigerator. Then you will know which flavour you prefer.

When you are adept, try putting layers of fresh herbs or pepper between the layers of the curd in the mould.

A Coulommiers mould is in sections so that as the curd drains and shrinks you can remove the top hoop, thus making it simpler to turn the curing cheese.

COLWICK CHEESE

This traditional moulded English soft cheese does not need turning as it cures, and it develops a characteristic curl to the edges. A gallon/4.5 litres of milk makes two cheeses and you could use round or square moulds. The recipe is exactly the same as the Coulommiers-mould cheese. But your moulds must be lined with enough cheesecloth to allow you to fold the ends over the top of the cheese.

Slice off a top for each mould you are using (see previous recipe), then ladle in the curd in thin slices. When it has drained a little, slide on the tops.

After an hour or so – the time is not critical – pull the muslin up and inwards to curl the outside edges of the curd, a characteristic of this cheese. Do this another three or four times during the next 4 hours.

After draining for up to 36 hours – certainly a minimum of 24 hours – the cheese will be firm enough to handle. Remove the mould and peel off the muslin carefully.

The cheese is eaten straight away, usually as a sweet. The hollow on the top lends itself admirably to being filled with fruit and whipped cream. It is not traditional to salt it, but there is no reason why you should not make it into something savoury.

CAMBRIDGE OR YORK CHEESE

This famous cheese is still sometimes sold. The proper mould is about 8 in/20 cm long, 5 in/12.5 cm wide and 6 in/15 cm deep, but it's almost impossible to buy. Alternatives include square or rectangular cake tins of the same capacity, with the bottom cut out.

This recipe makes one cheese in such a container. The cheese should have an orange stripe through the middle, but it is better to forget this than to use anything other than annatto for the colour.

1½ gallons/6.75 litres *milk*	*Cold boiled water (see method)*
½ fl oz/15 ml *buttermilk*	56 drops *annatto*
56 drops *rennet*	

Start by heating cows' milk to 90°F/32°C, or 85°F/29°C for goats' milk. Add the buttermilk, and then the rennet, diluted with six times its volume of cold boiled water. Stir for 2 minutes then remove 4 pints/2.3 litres and colour it with annatto.

Do not top-stir the remaining milk as this time you want the cream to rise. Cover both containers and leave for 1-1½ hours or until the finger test is successful.

Now press your mould onto the creamy, uncoloured curd and slice off one top. Put the mould on a straw mat or cheesecloth on a drainage board and carefully fill with slices of curd – first put in two-thirds of the uncoloured curd, then all the orange curd, then the rest of the plain. This should get the stripe in the middle of the drained cheese. Finish with the creamy top.

The curd should drain for up to 3 days without turning or salting. Eat as it is.

YOGHURT CHEESE

The thicker yoghurts called for in a lot of Indian and Middle East recipes are often obtained by draining basic unflavoured yoghurt to a greater or lesser degree. There is no secret to it, although yoghurt made from full cream milk does give a nicer cheese than that made with skim milk. You simply wrap the yoghurt in sterilized cheesecloth, tie the corners and suspend it to drain overnight or until it is firm enough to spread. This is what is known as labna in the Near and Middle East. You use it the way you would any other such cheese, making it sweet or savoury, with fruit, herbs, flower waters or honey.

You lose about 20 per cent of the original weight.

GOAT AND SHEEP CHEESES

If you have goats or sheep that you are certain are free from diseases, they offer the chance to make a lot of traditional cheeses, with or without the use of rennet. The simplest white cheese is made by letting the unpasteurized full milk sour and curdle naturally, putting the curd gently into sterilized cheesecloth and letting it drain for 48 hours in a cool place. When you judge it is ready (or suits your taste) simply add salt or sugar. Of course you can be very inventive and complicated with this cheese and some flavouring ideas are given under the Banon recipe (see below). In France goat cheeses are known as 'chèvres', sheep cheeses as 'brebis'.

FROMAGE PAYSAN

Many people who raise goats or sheep are Vegans, that is they don't include anything in their diet that comes from a dead animal and thus cannot use rennet to curdle their milk if they wish a sweet curd; there are a few vegetarian rennet substitutes on the market but at the right time of the year you can make your own by boiling some artichoke flowers in a little water; dried artichoke flowers apparently work as well, but I don't know anyone who has tried this.

For a Chèvre or Brebis Paysan, mix the milk from two milkings; the extra acidity that will have developed in the first yield will help coagulation. Stir some of the artichoke flower water quickly into the tepid milk and the curd should form immediately. Put the curd into a sterilized cheesecloth, tie the ends and suspend to drain. Each day, gently turn the curd on itself so it drains evenly. Traditionally the ball of curd is put in fresh cheesecloth each day, but this is not strictly necessary.

Depending on the weather, and you, it will be ready in 1-4 days and only needs to be salted. Of course, if you are not a Vegan, you could use some cheese rennet.

You may also drain this cheese in small moulds or shapes made of reeds, pottery, porcelain, metal or plastic – anything as long as it has holes through which the whey can drain at the bottom. Put these moulds on a draining board that is slightly tilted or on something like a cake rack.

When they are drained, remove the cheeses from their moulds, shape them by hand and then let them mature further in a cool dark and dry room, covered with netting or under one of those metal garde-manger things that the French have but we don't.
Note You can also make these cheeses with fresh unpasteurized cows' milk or with pasteurized milk if you have some cheese rennet. Junket rennet can be used but doesn't give such good results; don't forget the addition of buttermilk to pasteurized milk will give speedier and more flavoured results if you let the milk rest and ripen in flavour before it is curdled.

BANON

This cheese can be made with goats', sheep's or cows' milk, or any mixture, depending on the assets of your village, commune or smallholding. Start with any of the preceding recipes and drain the curd in small round moulds, which should stand on straw mats. They will need up to 5 days to become really dry. Unmould them, plunge them into an eau-de-vie or brandy and wrap in chestnut leaves, which have been soaked in hot water for just 2 minutes, drained and dried. Wrap securely with sterilized string or raffia and store in a cool place for some weeks. The curing will continue, the cheese paste turning creamier and being perfumed by the tannin in the leaves. You can eat this cheese relatively fresh or quite ripe but I always prefer it slightly chilled. You could use nettle or dock leaves instead of chestnut but then it wouldn't be your actual Banon.

8 Yeast Baking and Breads

Perhaps the most important requisite of a delicatessen or speciality food shop is a variety of excellent breads, made by different methods, containing differing grains and representing, as far as is practicable, several countries and their style of food.

Even the most earnest of shopkeepers can be defeated in this apparently simple task. For much of what is shaped or presented to look like speciality bread is simply modern, fast-risen, additive-filled dough. I don't suggest you always bake your own bread, but it is interesting to have done so, to have a real yardstick by which to judge what you buy. And, being able to run up a loaf or two of your own, particularly of the sour-dough variety from a starter in your refrigerator, is the sort of casual ability I reckon we all owe to ourselves.

Recipes for some of the other most maligned or disguised delicatessen foods are here to give (a) the customer some idea of what is often missing and the ability to praise and recognize real effort and (b) some guidance to the independent shopkeeper who is defeated by suppliers.

Believe me, I know that a great deal of adjustment needs to be made to domestic recipes so they are suitable for delicatessens. If the adjustments are major, my feeling is that you don't attempt it or you call it something else; if the differences are minor, you are all the better for having a secure platform from which to launch your experimentation.

FRENCH BREAD – C'EST IMPOSSIBLE . . .

Elizabeth David and other much revered food pundits have often said the reason we cannot get authentic French bread outside of France is that we cannot get French flour. French flour is certainly different from other flour, having a very high proportion of soft wheat, which absorbs little water, thus accelerating the staling of bread made from it.

Having accepted this as gospel, shoppers have contented themselves with bread that is long and thin and, regardless of its composition, texture or crustiness, it has been known as French bread or French sticks. Only in France, we have been told, is it possible to have thin bread with a chewy but crisp crust and a light interior with an uneven scattering of holes. I accepted this story, too, blaming it on the flour. But much more research showed me that this is not the case at all.

The flavour and appearance of the long French loaves is actually a matter of the technique used in making the bread. The flavour is largely due to the high proportion of crust to crumb. The texture of the crust is the result of injections of steam into the oven, which must be critically controlled during baking. But the most important factor of all in making an authentic French stick loaf is a long final proving of the dough, and it is this which gives the vital open, uneven interior.

Some of the larger supermarkets are now selling excellent French loaves and, here and there, there are small French bakers who turn out excellent breads, often using fairly standard flours but specialist techniques.

So, shy can't the home bread-maker make bread like the French, if it is that simple? First, it is far from simple. And second it is easy to forget that bread of this type is rarely made in French homes. Other white loaves, the pain de mie or pain de ménage may be made out of necessity or out of interest occasionally, but the making of stick loaves is as foreign to the French housewife as kilts are to Scandinavians. The manufacture of baguettes and ficelles belongs firmly in the realms of the professional baker, and it is time the amateur bread-maker stopped attempting the impossible.

By all means shape your white dough into sticks, especially if it is sour-dough leavened, for the high crust-to-crumb proportion does give a wonderful flavour. Give your shaped loaves a long second rising in cool conditions, to help develop that open texture which is so important; and spray the dough with water just before going into the oven. But whatever you do, you will only make an authentic looking and tasting French stick by accident unless you have professional ovens.

NO-KNEAD WHOLEMEAL BREAD

This is the simplest of all breads to make and especially suitable for the elderly, who might not have the strength, vitality or interest to knead a white-flour dough.

You really should not knead this dough, for kneading wholemeal flour has an adverse effect on the important Vitamin E content. However there are many who do knead a little and swear they get a lighter loaf. The truth is they have found the dough mixture they like best, for the balance of liquid to flour is the real art of this recipe and can only be learned by experience. As with all bread recipes you must try to achieve a consistent texture of dough each time you bake rather than slavishly following a set balance of ingredients.

For 1 large or 2 small loaves

2 lb/900 g *100% wholemeal flour*	Approx 1 pt/575 ml *lukewarm*
½ oz/15 g *salt*	*water*
1 oz/25 g *fresh yeast*	½ oz/15 g *muscovado or*
(or half as much dried yeast)	*Barbados sugar*

Mix the flour and salt together well then warm in the oven. Activate the yeast in some of the warm water, adding a pinch of sugar only if using dried yeast. When the yeast is working well – after 10 minutes or so – dissolve the brown sugar in that, too.

Make a well in the middle of the warmed flour and pour in the yeast and sugar liquid and most of the warm water. Mix gently but firmly with a wooden spoon until you have a soft, somewhat wet mixture. It must not be sloppy so you must adjust water and flour until you get something which a regular baker would recognize as something rather firmer than the dropping consistency of a cake batter.

Put the dough directly into the oiled tin or tins. Cover and let rise by a third to a half. It is important that the dough is not overproved or underproved so until you are expert actually measure the tin accordingly. Don't forget, the slower bread rises, the better the flavour.

Bake the bread at 400°F/200°C/Gas 6 for 30-35 minutes for small loaves and 45 minutes or so for a large one.

Stored properly this bread improves in flavour over several days.

Options When you wish to make larger amounts, double the above recipe but only use 1½ oz/40 g fresh yeast. If you like a softer crumb, a little fat may be added to the dough. A maximum of 2 oz/50 g butter or oil is enough, and so is a few tablespoons of milk. It is a temptation to use half milk and half water but your bread will be rather too cake-like for most tastes.

A BASIC WHITE BREAD

Makes 1 large or 2 small loaves

1½ lb/675 g *strong white flour*	½ oz/15 g *fresh yeast*
¾ pt/425 ml *warm water*	2 level tsp *salt*

Warm the flour thoroughly in the oven; it should not be so hot you cannot put your hand into it and keep it there. Take about a third of the warm water and crumble the yeast into it. Cover and keep warm until it has dissolved and is clearly frothing – about 10 minutes or so. Dissolve the salt in the remaining liquid.

When the flour is warmed and the yeast is working well, make a hollow in the flour, pour in the yeast mixture (it is as well to strain it) then start adding the rest of the liquid, stirring as you do. Mix well then turn out onto a floured surface – not marble or you will quickly lose the heat of the dough. Because no flour is exactly the same from day to day you may find the dough is too slack and sticky, in which case work in more flour; if it is too dry and will not blend together, add more liquid. Knead for about 10 minutes as previously explained then put into a lightly oiled bowl and cover loosely with clingfilm. Cover the bowl with a damp cloth and leave in a warm place to double in bulk. Do not put in or on a hot place or the dough will rise too quickly and this always gives terribly coarse results.

Punch down the dough, knead for just a minute or two and shape as you wish. Leave to rise again until doubled. Bake at

450°F/230°C/Gas 8 for 45-50 minutes for one large loaf, 30-40 minutes for two small ones. Elizabeth David recommends you reduce the heat by about a quarter, down to 400°F/200°C/Gas 6, after 15 minutes and that after a further 15 minutes, the large loaf is carefully turned out of its tin to crispen up. For a smaller loaf, the timings should be 15 and 10 minutes.

Options   This recipe can also be used for a mixture of white and wholemeal flour, or more easily for one of the 81% or 85% extraction flours.

You could replace up to a quarter of the water with milk and add up to 2 oz/50 g of butter or lard.

SHORT-TIME WHITE BREAD

The only new technique involved in making bread worth knowing about is this one, which cuts down on the rising time for dough without major changes of taste or texture. The addition of vitamin C, which is broken down and disappears during the baking, means you need just one rising. Fresh yeast works better than dried – or at least it works faster. But neither will eventually give the same flavour as bread using less yeast and much longer risings.

1 large or 2 small loaves

1½ lb/675 g *strong white flour*	½ oz/15 g *butter*
1 oz/25 g *fresh yeast*	½ oz/15 g *salt*
25 mg *ascorbic acid/vitamin C*	1 level tsp *sugar*
14 fl oz/400 ml *warm water*	

Put the flour to warm in the oven. Crumble the yeast and the ascorbic acid/vitamin C tablet into the water, then add the butter in small pieces, so that it melts. Once the yeast is working well, add the salt and sugar to the warmed flour then add the strained yeast liquid and after mixing turn out onto a floured board and knead very well.

Leave the dough to rest, covered with a damp cloth for 10 minutes, then knead thoroughly again and shape the dough into a loaf or loaves or into rolls. Cover with a damp cloth and leave to double in bulk, brush with beaten egg or dust with flour for a more rugged effect. Bake at 450°F/230°C/Gas 8 for 30-35 minutes for small loaves, about 50 minutes for a big one, lowering the heat after 15 minutes, as explained in the previous recipe.

OPEN PLAIT LOAVES

This attractive idea can be used for sweet or savoury fillings. You can make one or two little loaves or use the full quantities of a dough recipe to make several larger ones for slicing. Roll or stretch the dough to about ¼ in/6 mm thick, in as square a shape as possible.

For a sweet pudding version, spread sliced fruit down the middle third (use apples, peaches, bananas and raisins, apricots, soft fruits such a blackberries, currants or raspberries, pears with a little ginger, and so on). Slice the remaining thirds at angles, from the middle third to the edges, several times, to make flaps to plait. Sprinkle brown sugar and spices over the whole, together with a little rum or liqueur, if desired. Plait. Fold in the end flaps to form a tight loaf.

Leave to rise just 20-30 minutes, then bake at 350°F/180°C/Gas 4 for about 1 hour.

Soaked dried fruit can be used and, whether dried or fresh, the fruit will be especially good if placed on a bed of thick custard.

For a savoury loaf, either add flavourings to the flour, or spread them on the dough and roll it up like a sponge roll. The following ideas are for a dough made with about 3 lb/1.3 kg flour.

A minced onion and ½ oz/15 g dill weed; a minced onion, clove of garlic, minced parsley (for less bite but more flavour, use some grated lemon peel instead of the onion); 8 oz/225 g grated cheese (more if mild); cheese mixed with chopped chives, chives and garlic, or curry powder; 1 oz/25 g mixed or Italian dried herbs; or 8-12 oz/225-350 g grated carrots, mixed with nutmeg and orange juice and/or grated orange peel.

Liquid additives to the dough itself include stock made with a chicken stock cube and herbs or tomato juice (or thinned tomato purée), possibly spiked with Worcestershire sauce.

MONKEY BREAD

Unlike the eponymous tree, the derivation of whose name is obvious, the reason for this bread's name is a real puzzle. It is another recipe developed from an idea given me by Katie Stapleton from Denver, Colorado.

This is better eaten all at once while warm, but the high fat content means it reheats very well.

For 6-8 people

1 lb/450 g *strong white or*	(*or* 2 tsp *dried yeast*)
85% flour	1 tsp *salt*
¼ pt/142 ml *soured cream*	1 dessertsp *sugar*
¼ pt/142 ml *warm water*	3-4 oz *butter, melted*
½ oz/15 g *fresh yeast*	*Herbs, spices or cheese (optional)*

Put the flour to warm in the oven. Then mix a small carton of soured cream with the same volume of warm water, using the carton as a measure. Pour about a quarter of this into a warmed bowl and crumble the yeast into that (adding a pinch of sugar only if using dried yeast).

Stir the salt and sugar into the rest of the diluted soured cream and keep warm. When the flour is well warmed and the yeast is working, add the yeast to the other liquid then mix into the flour. Add a little extra water or flour to get a dough that comes cleanly away from the bowl and your hands. Knead thoroughly until the texture changes into a satisfying satiny feel, then cover and let rise in a warm, not hot, place.

Once the dough has doubled in bulk, punch it down and roll or stretch it out to somewhere between ¼-½ in/1-2 cm thick and then cut that into pieces about 2 in/5 cm square (alternatively you can make circles or even little rolls).

Take a large, circular tube pan or deep gugelhopf mould and butter it well, with a little of the melted butter, and also brush the tops of the pieces of dough with the butter.

Make a ring of the buttered pieces then keep building, buttering each layer generously. Pour any leftover butter over the top.

Let the dough rise once more then bake about 30 minutes in a preheated 400°F/200°C/Gas 6 oven. Be most careful when turning out the baked loaf as it falls into as many pieces as you made.

Put a plate over the loaf pan and hold firmly while inverting and remove the mould with care. Everyone takes the pieces they want, as they want them.

Options Although pretty good like it is, this bread lends itself admirably to flights of flavouring fancy. I first made Monkey Bread with butter that was loaded with garlic and that went down very well; but try using Italian seasoning to go with ratatouille, cumin and coriander to go with something Indian, dill to go with fish, saffron to go with anything expensive and any fresh herb or combination to go with almost everything. Butter sweetened with sugar and rich with spice would be excellent, I'm sure, and you might even consider making the bread itself spicy – simply sprinkle the spices (or herbs or nuts) as you go. The important thing is to be generous with buttering the pieces of dough so they don't stick to one another. It may look as though it is swimming in fat when it goes into the oven, but all will be absorbed.

BAGELS

These rolls with a hole are especially associated with Jewish food, particularly in the USA. Indeed, New York has adopted the bagel as its own, and lox and bagel – smoked salmon and cream cheese on a hot bagel – is a classic breakfast there during the weekends. The crust is fairly tough, an effect obtained by poaching the rolls before baking.

½ oz/15 g *fresh yeast* (*or half as much dried*)	1 oz/25 g *white sugar*
	1 tsp *salt*
½ pt/300 ml *warmed milk*	2 oz/50 g *butter*
1¼-1½ lb/575-675 g *strong white flour*	1 *egg*

Crumble the yeast into a little of the milk; if using dried yeast add some of the sugar. Put the flour to warm in the oven. Add the sugar, salt and butter to the milk and warm gently. Once the yeast is working well, add it to the milk, then beat in the egg.

Make a well in the warm flour, add the liquid then knead until smooth and shiny. Use more flavour if necessary. Cover the dough with a damp cloth and leave in a warm place to double its bulk. Knock down, knead lightly then divide into six to twelve pieces depending on how big you like your bagels.

Roll out each until the thickness of a thick finger and form into a ring, pinching the join together. Leave the rings to recover, no more than 10-15 minutes – they should look and feel lighter but should not have begun noticeably to rise much.

Boil up a large saucepan full of water and drop in the bagels one or two at a time. Classically, like pasta, they should drop to the bottom and float to the surface when cooked. But if you have let the dough rise too much, they will float. Never mind, turn them over after a minute and cook the other side for another minute, then remove with a slotted spoon to an oiled baking tray. Bake at 400°F/200°C/Gas 6 for about 15 minutes.

Bagels are better served warm and reheat wonderfully. Variations are almost limitless and all achieved by the addition of something atop the rolls before baking. Poppy seeds, sesame seeds, chopped onion or such herbs as oregano are the most popular. But nothing beats a plain bagel with cream cheese and smoked salmon.

CHOLLAH

Traditionally associated with Jewish festivals, this is a semi-sweet plaited loaf, sometimes made with milk, sometimes eggs, sometimes both. Make a dough with about 3 lb/1.3 kg strong white flour and 1 oz/25 g fresh yeast. Use 8 oz/225 g sugar. Mix with 4 eggs plus milk or water, probably about 1¼ pints/ 750 ml. The dough needs good kneading and two risings.

Proportions of egg, milk and sugar are infinitely variable; but do not add too much sugar at the start.

VIENNA BREAD

This indiscriminately applied name is properly used for a highly special type of enriched white loaf rarely found. For domestic purposes a good Vienna-style loaf can be simply made by making the basic bread with all milk, and sprinkling it with poppy seeds. It is usually shaped and slashed as a bloomer.

NUT-OIL BREAD

This fascinating bread has a texture and appearance somewhere between brioche and croissants. It is light and flaky inside, crisp and golden on the outside. I like it just as it is, but if you add nuts and raisins, the haunting aftertaste of the nutty oil is even more dramatic. It lasts extremely well, improving in flavour each day and is quite wonderful toasted. Use walnut, hazelnut or almond oil.

To make 2 small loaves or 12 rolls

1 lb/450 g *strong white flour*	1 oz/25 g *demerara sugar*
8 fl oz/225 ml *milk*	*(optional)*
¼ pt/150 ml *nut oil*	2 level tsp *dried yeast*
	2 level tsp *sea salt (be generous)*

Warm the flour through in the oven. Warm the milk, adding the nut oil, and the sugar if you are using it (it gives the bread only slight sweetness which makes it more suitable for both sweet and savoury toppings, but it is nice either way).

Dissolve the yeast in just half the milk, adding a pinch or two of sugar if you've not put some into the liquid. Leave to froth and dissolve the salt in the remaining half of the milk and oil liquid.

Once the yeast is working well and the flour is warm, make a well in the flour, pour in the two liquids and work to a dough. Add extra flour if necessary but expect a light oily dough that although soft will not stick to your hands. Knead well until slightly bubbly and very smooth on the surface.

Turn into a warmed bowl, cover the surface with clingfilm or the bowl with a damp cloth, then leave in a warm place until doubled in size. Knock down, then shape according to your preference, and put into oiled moulds or on a baking sheet.

Let the dough double in bulk again under a damp cloth in a warm place then bake at 400°F/200°C/Gas 6 – the loaves for 30-35 minutes, the rolls for 15-20 minutes. Leave them in the tins for a soft crust, take them out for a crisp one.

Option You really do need quite a lot of salt unless you plan to serve with very sharp cheese. This recipe will easily support

8 oz/225 g of added nuts and raisins or more if you insist. After the first rising of the dough, roll or stretch it flat into a rectangle about ½-1 in/1.25-2.5 cm thick then scatter that with half of your mixed seedless raisins and broken walnuts or of just one of those. Roll up the dough tightly, then flatten again and scatter with the remaining ingredients. Roll up again then cut and shape as before. The technique of rolling in the nuts and raisins at this stage means there is no likelihood of breaking up soft fruits like raisins through having to knead them.

Thin slices of nut bread make a delicious difference to canapés or pre-dinner drinks. Use them as the basis for anything – avocado purée and shrimps, slices of tomato and Mozzarella, blue cheese creamed with butter.

BRIOCHES

I have never understood why croissants are so much easier to buy than brioches, for brioches are far easier to make and this is usually what one would expect to attract manufacturers. Still, it means you will appreciate even more the heady, yeasty aroma of hot brioche baking in your oven.

Bought brioches, if you are lucky enough to be able to buy them, and they are not too sweet, are excellent ways to put on a bit of a show at lunctime or to start a dinner party with a gasp. As an accompaniment to a soup or as a piquant opener, scoop out a brioche slightly and stuff with well cooked, roughly chopped mushrooms, enhanced with Tabasco, lemon juice and garlic. A saffron-flavoured seafood sauce tastes even better in brioches.

If you are adept at making brioches you can be even more breathtaking. Buy a can or two of quenelles de saumon or quenelles au brochet, plus several cans of those excellent *French* seafood sauces, Nantua or Américaine. Wrap one or two quenelles, according to size, in brioche dough, first putting a generous spoonful of one of the sauces over the fish dumpling. Glaze with egg. When baked, serve with more of the sauce or another one. These are specially good if a lump of chilled saffron butter is slipped into a cut made into the top of each hot brioche. Quenelles de saumon with saffron butter are equally good cold and make an uncommon and uncommonly good picnic ingredient.

Among the many variations of recipes for brioche dough it is the quantities of milk, water, eggs and butter that vary, but the major liquid content should always be egg. My recipe is quite typical but not oversweet – you can add more sugar if you like.

To make 12 small brioches

½ oz/15 g *fresh yeast*	1 tbsp *white sugar*
2 tbsp *lukewarm milk*	4 oz/115 g *unsalted French butter*
8 oz/225 g *strong white flour*	3 *large eggs, beaten*
A *pinch of salt*	

Activate the yeast in the warm milk (use 2 teaspoons of dried yeast and a pinch of sugar as an alternative).

Sift the flour, salt and sugar together and warm them slightly in the oven. Melt the butter and cool so it is just at room temperature but still liquid (I think French unsalted butter has the best flavour for this type of baking but others are quite satisfactory).

Mix flour, yeast, butter and eggs together and beat with a wooden spoon for 5 whole minutes, or until smooth and supple. Although very sticky, the mixture should look at least as though it is making an effort to cling together and leave the sides of the bowl; if not, mix in a handful or so more of flour, but don't make a firm, dry dough. Leave to rise, covered with a damp cloth, until doubled in size then knead lightly for 1 minute. If you grease your hands slightly with butter this will be infinitely less frustrating.

If the brioches are to be baked and eaten for breakfast, leave the dough in a cool place overnight, then knock down. You can put it in the refrigerator but will have to wait an extra half hour in the morning for it to come back to room temperature. If you wish to get on with baking immediately, it would be some advantage to let the dough rise once again before shaping it, but this is not strictly necessary.

To make small brioches, roll the dough lightly out into a sausage shape and cut with a very sharp knife into pieces. Oil or butter small moulds, which can be of almost anything – you don't need special brioche moulds, but you *do* need moulds. Pop in the pieces of dough.

To make brioches with top-knots, use three-quarters of each

piece of dough in the base of each mould, then poke a floured finger deeply in to each. Roll the remaining quarters of dough and plug them firmly into the holes.

To make just one large brioche loaf, put all the dough into a large mould. Traditionally this is round and with fluted sides but even a loaf tin will do – the shape doesn't alter the flavour.

Leave to rise until the dough is very light and puffy – an hour or so depending on how cool your dough was. Note that if you leave the dough in too cool a place at this stage the butter content will be quite hard and the dough will not be able to rise easily. A temperature of 70-75°F/21-24°C is about right, for if it is very much hotter the butter will actually melt!

Preheat your oven to 450°F/230°C/Gas 8 and bake the small brioches for about 10 minutes and the large loaf for 20-25 minutes. They burn easily so watch carefully and perhaps reduce the temperature to 375°F/190°C/Gas 5 if this seems imminent.

The larger brioches look more attractive if they either have a large top-knot or if you run a sharp knife blade around the centre just before baking. This allows the dough to rise through the middle and gives a soufflé-like cap. Brioches may be glazed with egg just before baking or with a sugar glaze when they emerge – a few tablespoons of milk, and of sugar, boiled together for a couple of minutes is enough.

Options   A small amount of lemon juice makes brioches more suitable for tea-time consumption. Adding a little mixed peel with raisins and currants will produce something closer to Italian pannetone, usually made at Christmas.

For an eighteenth-century style of treat, make a large sweet brioche and have it ready and hot after dinner. Make a deep diagonal cut and almost lift off the lid. Into the centre pour a rich sweet sauce of cream or butter heated with sherry or Madeira, sugar and a touch of brandy or liqueur. Or serve plain hot slices with flavoured whipped cream and a glacé fruit or two.

SAUSAGE IN BRIOCHE

This classic recipe is excellent hot or cold and as both a starter or a main course. The type of sausage used is often called a boiling sausage and should be free, or as free as possible, from bread or cereal binding. The texture should be coarse and quite fatty and those with a garlic or smoke flavour have a distinct advantage.

The Polish mazurska or a portion of a Polish boiling ring are both suitable. German bratwurst is wonderful if of high quality and the pure Italian or French sausages are more expensive but perhaps more rewarding. Of course, if you have made your own sausages, especially the Camargue sausage (in Chapter 3), this combination would be unsurpassable. (As they probably have no skin, a proportion of binding would be acceptable.) Or you could quite simply use frankfurters.

Normally you would use a sausage weighing somewhere around 1 lb/450 g but several smaller ones of a particularly interesting type would be just as good, baked in a line or separately.

Although you won't believe it when you make it, the dough should not be strengthened with additional flour; use the previous recipe and reduce the sugar to about 1 teaspoon.

The sausage should be cooked and at room temperature by the time the dough has been proved once (or twice if that is your preference). Roll out the dough until quite thin and wrap up the sausages, tucking in the ends. Ensure the seals are nice and tight. Leave the package on a baking tray for just long enough for the top layer of dough to rise nicely – 30 minutes or so – then bake at 425°F/220°C/Gas 7 for 20-25 minutes. Slide onto a folded white napkin on a dish and slice at the table.

BRIOCHE WITH PESTO

If you want to experiment with stuffing other goodies into brioche dough, take my long and hard-learned advice – it only works if that stuffing is very fatty or very rich and unctuous and oozes out when bitten or cut.

The small jars of pesto sauce – a Northern Italian piece of magic based on fresh basil, pounded pine-nuts, Parmesan and olive oil – are ideal. Into 12 oz/350 g of cream or curd cheese mix a generous 4 oz/115 g of pesto from which any surplus olive oil has been spooned off but reserved. Beat together an egg plus an extra yolk then mix them well into the cheese and pesto.

Wrap the mixture in brioche to make a roll, or divide the

dough between two large moulds, lining each with half the dough, adding the flavoured cheese, and top up with remaining dough. Cook as for main recipe after the dough has risen, and serve warm rather than hot; smaller ones would be perfectly stunning served with a chilled tomato soup or with ratatouille, hot or cold. The large loaf could be sliced and served with a small salad as a stunner of a first course or as a light luncheon on a hot day.

CINNAMON BRIOCHE RING

Yeasted cakes rich with butter and spices are popular for breakfast or with coffee throughout Europe and in America. This recipe of mine is suitable for either occasion.

Start by making a double quantity of the brioche recipe but *do not* double the amount of yeast. After the dough has risen once, you do not leave it overnight but continue by knocking it down and letting it rest whilst you make the cinnamon filling.

Filling

4 oz/115 g *unsalted butter*	2 tsp *ground cinnamon*
4 oz/115 g *muscovado sugar*	1 tsp *vanilla essence*

Soften the butter a little then cream together with the other ingredients, being generous with the cinnamon.

Roll out the dough into two oblongs, approximately 15 × 5 in/ 37.5 × 12.5 cm. If the dough is too sticky to roll easily, grease the rolling pin rather than using flour. Spread the filling evenly over both pieces, leaving a narrow border all round each one. Form both into long rolls by rolling from the long side. Seal well all round, twist the two together (having first greased your hands if necessary) then form into a circle. Transfer to a greased springform or cake tin that is at least 10 in/25 cm in diameter.

Cover with a damp cloth and leave until at least doubled in size. Paint the top with a little beaten egg then put into a preheated oven at 425°F/220°C/Gas 7 for 30-35 minutes.

CROISSANTS

1 oz/25 g *fresh yeast*	1 oz/25 g *butter or lard*
(or half as much dried)	12 oz/350 g *strong white flour*
1 tbsp *sugar*	4 oz/115 g *French unsalted butter,*
1 tsp *salt*	*well chilled*
¼ pt/150 ml *lukewarm, scalded*	*Egg and milk for glaze*
milk	

Activate the yeast in a little warm water, adding a pinch of sugar if using dried yeast. Meanwhile, dissolve the sugar and salt in the milk. Melt the first quantity of butter or lard, and stir that in too. Add the yeast. Work in the flour, then knead thoroughly until the dough is really smooth and supple. Leave to rise, covered, until doubled in size. Knock the dough down, then chill.

Roll out the dough on a floured board to make a strip three times longer than it is wide. Flake the unsalted butter and arrange it evenly down the centre of the dough (if following the simple method), or flake one-third of the butter over two-thirds of the dough (alternative method).

Simple method Continue by folding one-third of the dough into the centre and folding the other third over that.

Give it a half turn, roll out to the original size, then chill for 10-15 minutes. Fold, turn, roll and chill at least twice more. Chill thoroughly before proceeding.

Alternative method Fold the dough into thirds, folding in the unbuttered third first. Give it a half turn and roll out to the previous size.

Chill for 10-15 minutes. Then butter, fold, turn and roll again. Chill, then repeat.

After this third chilling, fold, turn and roll the dough at least three more times, but without adding more butter and without chilling between times. At the end of this process, chill the dough once more.

Finishing The croissant dough can be treated in various ways. It can be wrapped and frozen, or the croissants can be made up then left in the refrigerator overnight.

When shaping the croissants, work as fast as you can and in reasonably cool surroundings: a warm kitchen will melt the butter and make the desired flakiness impossible. Divide the dough in half, roll each half into an even strip or a circle and cut out triangle shapes with a base of about 6 in/15 cm. It is important that the triangles of dough are not equiliateral. So, as you start to shape each croissant, hold the base firm and roll the point away from you, extending it by several inches. The dough's tip can be much thinner than the base, for this gives a more elegant finished shape to the croissant by not leaving too much dough in the central mass.

Now, take each corner of the base in thumb and forefinger and pull apart a little to stretch the dough, then roll up, tucking the tip of the triangle underneath. Form into a crescent shape and space out on a greased baking tray. Either put the croissants into the refrigerator overnight to rise slowly, letting them return to room temperature before baking, or let them prove in a warm place for 20-30 minutes, then chill them for just 10 minutes to ensure butter is set.

Brush the croissant with lightly beaten egg and bake at 425°F/220°C/Gas 7 for 15-20 minutes.

JANE STAPLETON'S PEACH CROISSANTS

This recipe, using a full quantity of croissant dough is enough to cover 10-12 peach halves, depending on their size and your dexterity, of course.

1 recipe *croissant dough*	1 tsp *sugar*
5-6 *fresh peaches*	*Cinnamon*
2-3 tsp *almond extract*	

Filling

6 oz/175 g *cream cheese*	2-4 tbsp *sugar*
4 tbsp *ground almonds*	2-3 tbsp *Cointreau*

Peel and stone the peaches and into the pit of each half dribble a few drops of almond extract, a teaspoon of sugar and a dusting of cinnamon. Let them soak that up for 10 minutes or so, while you make the filling.

Mix all the filling ingredients together, adjusting the sugar according to the sweetness of the peaches (the riper they are, the less they need sugar). Incidentally, if you toast the ground almonds first the flavour will be markedly improved.

Divide your prepared croissant dough into the same number of pieces as you have peach halves. Roll each piece out to three times the size of a peach half. Spread the cheese mixture evenly over each dough piece, put a peach on, upside down, then fold the pastry over to make a neat parcel, or whatever shape you like.

If you want to make your peach croissants in the traditional croissant shape, then spread the filling along the side of the triangle closest to you. Slice each peach half into thirds or quarters, line them up and roll the dough around them.

Then you let the pastry recover and bake them as usual. Better warm than hot, and toasted ground hazelnuts would be just as good as the almonds.

SAVOURY CROISSANTS

These make sophisticated and filling breakfast fare for leisurely weekend mornings.

To start, make croissant dough with only 1 teaspoon of sugar and, if you like, about 1-2 oz/25-50 g more butter.

When you are ready to roll up the croissants you can go to town. To my mind the best ingredients to incorporate are smoked ham or smoked salmon. In either case trim a good slice to the size of the dough and roll the croissant up around this.

Grated cheese flavoured with herbs and garlic might also be used, with a little egg to bind.

It is not strictly necessary to form the combination into croissant shapes. A nice lump of flavoured cheese or pieces of fresh salmon, or some flavoured cheese atop smoked salmon or ham, could be placed on a square of dough which is then folded to make a triangle; or you might use a circle and either fold it in half or crimp it across the top like a pasty. Either would make a scrumptious addition to breakfast or picnics.

When serving, don't feel obliged to serve butter, at least not plain butter. Think about dill butter to go with your smoked salmon croissant or saffron butter. For something more substantial, serve some cream cheese instead of butter, a mustard flavoured one with smoked ham croissants for instance, or a mixture of cheese and chives which is easily bought in tubs.

PIZZA

Often misunderstood and misrepresented the pizza is now irreplaceable. Most home-made ones are merely repositories for leftovers; many commercial pizzas have become savoury tarts on a biscuit-like base.

True pizza has a light, milk-dough base, cooked to a slight crispness round the edge and only a few restaurants aim for this. Pizza toppings should be simple but rich, always blending into the dough rather than curling and crisping on top. To be fair, some of the modern inventions and versions are truly delicious. But none is more so than the original.

For pizza base to serve 3-4

8 oz/225 g *flour*	*Warm milk*
1 oz/25 g *fresh yeast*	1 *egg*
(or half as much dried)	

Topping

2 *large onions, chopped*	*Oregano*
Garlic, to taste	*Anchovy fillets*
Olive oil, as necessary	*Black olives*
1 lb/450 g *tomatoes*	

For the base, you could use just water instead of the milk and egg, but the dough won't reheat so well. Make this basic bread dough – makes about 1 lb/450 g – as described at the beginning of the chapter. You could take some from a batch you are already making. Knead well and leave to rise in a warm place until doubled in size.

To prepare the topping, gently fry the onions and as much or as little garlic as you like in good olive oil until soft and mushy. Add fresh tomatoes, or the equivalent of canned tomatoes, drained. Sprinkle in oregano, cook for a minute or so, then leave to cool.

Using a rolling pin and your fingertips, roll and stretch the dough into a circle or square on a baking tray well coated with olive oil. The dough should be about ½ in/1.25 cm thick. Spread the mixture of tomato evenly, almost to the edge. Then decorate with anchovy fillets and small black olives. Leave for

10 minutes or until the dough just starts to rise. Sprinkle generously with olive oil, then cook at 425°F/220°C/Gas 7 for 15-20 minutes. Eat straight away.

Options   Leave out the onion and garlic altogether. Drained, canned plum tomatoes, gently squeezed between the fingers make an excellent base; sprinkle generously with oregano. If you are making a very big pizza, which will have to cook a long time, just crush the tomatoes lightly and use both them and the juice.

Cheese has become a popular pizza ingredient: almost any hard variety can be used. Strong Cheddar is good if you cannot find something Italian. The anchovy fillets and olives should be put on top of the sliced or grated cheese.

Slices of salami and Mozzarella, green or hot peppers, gherkins, baby clams, prawn, chorizo or chopped ham can all be used for pizza toppings.

SAVARIN

Savarin is a simple but exotic end to a meal.

Batter

½ oz/15 g *fresh yeast*	*A pinch of salt*
(*or half as much dried*)	2 tbsp *sugar*
2 fl oz/50 ml *warm, scalded milk*	2 oz/50 g *butter, just melted*
2 *eggs*	8 oz/225 g *strong white flour*

Syrup

6 oz/175 g *sugar*	*Liqueur*
¾ pt/425 ml *water*	

Activate the yeast in the warm milk, adding a pinch of sugar if using dried yeast. When it is working well, beat in the eggs, salt and sugar, then the butter which must be only just melted. Pour gradually onto the flour, beating with a wooden spoon all the time: aim for a thick batter rather than a dough.

Butter a 7-9 in/17.5-22.5 cm ring mould, fill with dough, sprinkle with flour, cover with damp cloth and leave to double in size. Bake at 400°F/200°C/Gas 6 for 20-25 minutes. Meanwhile, prepare the syrup by boiling together the sugar and water for just 1 minute. Flavour the liquid with liqueur: for a fruit-filled savarin, Kirsch or Cointreau; for one to be served simply with its syrup and cream, rum or a strong sharp liqueur, such as Poire William.

As soon as the Savarin is a rich golden brown, remove from the oven and from the mould, put it on a wire tray resting on a dish and gently prick it with a fine fork or skewer. Pour over the lukewarm syrup, spooning it back again and again so that the excess is soaked up. Savarin may be decorated with almonds and cherries but it is usually served plain.

Rum Babas

Use the recipe for Savarin, but bake for 15 minutes in twelve small ring moulds, include a handful of currants, and use rum, of course, to flavour the syrup.

POPPY-SEED LOAF

¼ oz/7 g *fresh yeast* (*or half as much dried*)	1 *lemon, grated rind of*
3 fl oz/85 ml *lukewarm milk, previously scalded*	2 oz/50 g *unsalted butter*
	1 fl oz/25 ml *clear honey*
2 oz/50 g *butter*	*A little double cream*
4 oz/115 g *sugar*	6 oz/175 g *poppy seeds, roasted*
1 tsp *salt*	2 oz/50 g *grated orange rind or chopped crystallized orange peel*
8 oz/225 g *strong white flour, warmed*	4 oz/115 g *almonds, crushed or chopped*
3 *egg yolks, beaten*	2 *egg whites*

Activate the yeast with some of the warm milk, adding a pinch of sugar if using dried yeast. Melt the 2 oz/50 g butter in the remaining milk. Dissolve the sugar and salt in this and keep warm. Make a well in the middle of the warmed flour, pour in the yeast and milk mixture, plus the beaten egg yolks and lemon rind. Gradually mix the flour into the liquid, using your hands.

Knead the mixture until it is elastic and satin-like. Leave the dough to double in size.

Cream together the unsalted butter and honey and add just a trickle of thick cream. Mix in the poppy seeds, orange rind or peel and the almonds. (If you have not been able to buy poppy seeds ready-roasted, simply put them into a medium-hot oven and keep turning them over until they are ready.) Beat one of the egg whites until stiff, then fold this into the seed mixture.

Punch down and knead the dough, then roll it out to a rectangle about 14 × 8 in/35 × 20 cm, which should be about ½ in/1.25 cm thick. Spread the seed and nut mixture evenly on the dough, allowing a border all round. Moisten this border with milk. Roll up the dough (from one of the narrow sides). Seal the ends and then join with a little pressure. Put the roll, seam down, on a baking sheet. Tuck the ends under if they are a little untidy, but avoid doing so if possible.

Cover with a damp cloth and leave until doubled in size again – about 45 minutes – in a reasonably warm, but not hot, place. Brush with the remaining egg white, lightly beaten. Bake for 40 minutes at 350°F/180°C/Gas 4. The loaf should be a very deep golden brown. Glaze again if need be, just before you take it out. The loaf should be cooled completely just before being served.

Option Ground hazelnuts and chopped almonds or any other mixture of chopped or ground nuts are delicious with the poppy seeds, or instead of them.

ORANGE GUGELHOPF

There are dozens of names for these turreted yeast cakes, which can vary from pale and uninteresting to golden and rich and wonderful, but Kugelhopf is perhaps the most common other name.

The cake in question seems to be Alsatian in origin and usually contains raisins. Because it is a breakfast or tea cake it is often eaten with butter and jam hence the somewhat blander or drier versions. When very fresh it is wonderful just as it is, but even the richest needs a little help after an hour or so – I like liqueur flavoured cream or clotted cream and jam.

This orange flavoured version was created when I began to make one but discovered I had no raisins. I knew the inclusion of candied orange peel was an acceptable alternative but having none of that either took the orange idea and made this.

1 large or 2 small moulds

½ oz/15 g *fresh yeast*
  (or half as much dried)
7 fl oz/200 ml *warm milk*
4 oz/115 g *unsalted French
  butter*
5 *egg yolks*
4 oz/115 g *white sugar*

Orange flower water
A pinch of salt
12 oz/350 g *strong white flour*
1 *orange, grated rind of*
*Extra butter and almonds,
  for lining mould*

Crumble the yeast into the milk. If you are using dried yeast add a pinch of sugar. Soften the butter, then beat it well with the egg yolks and sugar until light and fluffy. Add 3 teaspoons of orange flower water and the salt.

Beat in the flour alternatively with the warmed and foaming yeast and milk mixture. Beat well then stir in the orange rind. (If you add the rind while using an electric beater you will find most of it remains on the beaters.)

Cover the rather sticky dough and leave in a warm place until doubled in size. You could put it directly into your mould or moulds but two risings give an infinitely more refined cake.

Rub orange flower water over your palms, knock down the dough and give it a very light kneading. Use extra orange flower water to stop the dough sticking to your fingers. While the dough relaxes, butter your mould or moulds (which should be deep and decorated, with a tube through the centre) very generously, then stud with whole or flaked almonds.

Put the dough into these, piece by piece, not worrying if it is somewhat uneven, cover and leave in a warm place until risen to 1 in/2.5 cm below the rim. Bake at 350°F/180°C/Gas 4 for 40-50 minutes for one large mould or for 25 minutes if using small moulds. Remove from tins while hot, and cool on wire racks. A scattering of icing sugar or thin water icing will add what I think is a necessary touch of sweetness. Chocolate icing would be even better.

Options   If you wonder what to do with 5 leftover egg whites, I suggest you stuff the centre of your cooled cakes with some chocolate ice cream, use the whites to make a meringue mixture and mound this up into a mountainous shape over all. Bake quickly in a fierce oven then cap it with a flaming spirit or liqueur which should drizzle down the sides. Call it a Vesuvius and it will leave the somewhat passé Baked Alaska in the shade. Of course if Mount St Helens or the volcanoes of Hawaii are in eruption you might wish to be more topical with the name.

CHEMICALLY RAISED BREADS

WHOLEMEAL SODA BREAD

This is a specially easy way to enjoy wholemeal flavour, but the soda kills the flour's vitamin E.

18 oz/500 g *wholemeal flour*	10 fl oz/285 ml *buttermilk or*
2 level tsp *salt*	*soured milk*
1½ tsp *bicarbonate of soda*	

Sift the flour, salt and bicarbonate of soda twice to ensure a thorough mix. Work in the buttermilk or soured milk (it must be sharp and clean, without any offensive smell), working in as quickly as possible. Lukewarm water can be added if the dough is too stiff; hot water will overactivate the soda and lead to disaster.

Soda breads are usually shaped into a flattish round and marked with a deep cross.

Put the shaped dough on a floured baking sheet and straight into a hot oven at 450°F/230°C/Gas 8 for about half an hour.

Soda breads may be cooked under an inverted cake tin, which should be large enough for the dough not to be in contact with it and removed about two-thirds of the way through cooking, so that the crust can brown.

IRISH OATEN BREAD

I have adapted this bread from a recipe that came to me from Co. Dublin. The technique of cooking the bread under cover for the first 10 minutes gives a lighter bread with a crisper crust, but is not necessary. Note the rather modern addition of white flour, which should be plain and *not* bread flour, as plain flour gives better results in chemically raised doughs.

To make 1 loaf

12 oz/350 g *wholemeal flour*	2 heaped tsp *baking powder*
4 oz/115 g *plain white flour*	½ pt/300 ml *milk,*
3 oz/85 g *oat flakes*	*at room temperature*
2 tsp *salt*	¼ pt/150 ml *water*
2 tsp *sugar*	

Mix together the flours and oat flakes (which can be directly from your packet of porridge), salt, sugar and baking powder. Add the milk and mix to a firm but moist dough that will hold its shape with as much of the water as is needed. Quickly tumble a couple of times in wholemeal flour then shape into a round about 6 in/15 cm diameter on a floured baking tray. Cut a cross atop the dough, then cover the dough with a metal or ovenproof bowl which gives plenty of space to the loaf. Put this into a preheated 450°F/230°C/Gas 8 oven. After 10 minutes carefully remove bowl and leave another 15 minutes or until the underside of the loaf sounds hollow when tapped with your knuckles.

Options   If you have, or can make, buttermilk or something similar (see previous recipe), replace the baking powder with 2 teaspoons of baking soda and 2 of cream of tartar. If you have no baking powder and have sweet milk use 2 teaspoons of baking soda and 4 teaspoons of cream of tartar.

BOSTON BROWN BREAD

Soda breads often used to be steamed in tightly closed containers. This is the most famous one.

4 oz/115 g each *wholemeal flour,*	1 level tsp *salt*
corn meal and rye flour	6 fl oz/175 ml *molasses*
2 level tsp *baking soda*	¾ pt/425 ml *soured milk*

Mix the dry ingredients very well. Stir the molasses into the milk. Combine the two mixtures, then pour the combination into well-greased tin moulds. This mix makes two loaves steamed in tins of 1¾-2 lb/800-900 g capacity (I use coffee tins). Seal the moulds well (cooking foil and string will do) and stand them in a large saucepan on a trivet or upturned saucer in cold water that reaches about two-thirds of the way up the containers' sides. Once the water has boiled, cook the bread gently for 2-3 hours; dough in tall, thin containers cooks faster than dough in something squat. Add more boiling water as necessary.

Remove each container from the water, take off the seal, and put the tins into a medium-hot oven. After about 10 minutes, remove the bread from the tins, then put back into the oven to crisp (about 30 minutes).

Old American cookbooks recommend that this bread is eaten with plates of hearty Boston baked beans, as a pudding with sweetened soured cream and nutmeg, or as a hot tea-bread. If using it as a tea-bread, add a handful of raisins when mixing and, possibly, substitute fine oatmeal for the rye flour.

If you wish to try steaming soda bread made only with wholemeal flour, you can put your container straight into boiling water, but starting in cold water is more traditional. The well greased top of a double-boiler could also be used. Whatever container you use, do not fill it more than two-thirds full.

CORN BREAD

Cornmeal is also known as polenta and this is sometimes easier to buy. The bread can be steamed or baked, though most people will find baking more convenient. Always include buttermilk or soured milk and some quantity of egg, and you must put the batter into a very hot, greased shallow pan in order to obtain a crisp undercrust.

Spoon bread, also known as pone, is another name for corn bread. It is always eaten from the pan, straight from the oven, the diners helping themselves with a spoon.

1 level tsp *white flour*	4 oz/115 g *cornmeal*
½ tsp *baking soda*	1 *egg*
1 level tsp *baking powder*	8 fl oz/225 ml *soured milk or*
½ tsp *salt*	*buttermilk*
1 level tbsp *sugar*	1 level tbsp *melted butter*

Mix flour, soda, baking powder, salt and sugar together. Sift into the cornmeal and mix lightly. Beat egg and add to milk, mix into dry ingredients, then add melted butter. Turn into a heated, greased 9 in/22.5 cm pie dish. Place immediately in an oven at 425°F/220°C/Gas 7 for about 30 minutes.

Serve straight from the oven. If you use sweet milk, use 3 teaspoons baking powder and omit the soda.

CORNMEAL HUSHPUPPIES

These small rolls from the southern US states are firmer in texture than cornmeal bread, but also need to be enjoyed hot because they are fried, not baked.

2 oz/50 g *strong white flour*	*(or polenta)*
½ oz/15 g *baking powder*	1 *egg*
½ oz/15 g *sugar*	6 fl oz/175 ml *milk*
A pinch of salt	1 *small onion, chopped (optional)*
6 oz/175 g *yellow cornmeal*	*Oil, for frying*

Combine dry ingredients, add egg and milk and stir lightly. Add onion, if using.

Fry a few rolls at a time, dropping the dough from a teaspoon. Use either a frying pan or a deep-fryer; the oil should be heated until just smoking. Drain on absorbent paper and keep hot.

PEAR AND RUM BREAD

Chemically-raised breads filled with fruit are more like a cake because of their sweetness and they may be treated as such, especially at picnics, when their shape is easier to pack and slice. Once you have made one, you might like to experiment by reducing the sugar or by putting some spice into the main mixture. I think they are better served cold or only just warm; when they are hot they can be a little bland.

Makes a 9-10 in (approximately 25 cm) loaf

8 oz/225 g *pears, peeled and diced*
4 tbsp *black rum*
1-2 tsp *grated lime peel*
4 oz/115 g *butter*
6 oz/175 g *demerara sugar*
2 *eggs, beaten*

8 oz/225 g *plain flour*
2 heaped tsp *baking powder*
½ tsp *salt*
2 tbsp *milk*
½ tsp *vanilla essence*

Topping
1 oz/25 g *butter*
1 oz/25 g *demerara sugar*
2 oz/50 g *plain flour*

1-2 tbsp *black rum*
1 tsp *ground allspice*

Prepare the pears, which should be ripe and fragrant but quite firm, and pour over them the rum and grated lime peel. Butter and flour a deep 9 × 5 in/22.5 × 12.5 cm loaf tin and preheat the oven to 325°F/160°C/Gas 3.

Cream the 4 oz/115 g butter and sugar very well, beat in the eggs then add the dry ingredients and mix well. Stir in the milk and essence then fold in the pears, incorporating all the rum and liquid that may have accumulated. Spoon evenly into the prepared tin then quickly make the topping.

Rub the butter and sugar into the flour and mix in the rum to form a mixture like large breadcrumbs. Sprinkle in the allspice then spread the mixture evenly over the batter in the pan. Bake without disturbing for at least 1 hour – depending on the wetness of the pears you may need a further 10-15 minutes to complete the baking, which is tested in the usual way. Turn out onto a wire rack to cool.

Options This is a basic recipe that can be adapted to another firm fruit. Simplest is to exchange the pears for sharp cooking apples and to use orange juice instead of rum (perhaps some grated orange peel, too) and to use cinnamon instead of allspice in the crunchy topping.

PINEAPPLE BREAD

The walnuts suggested in this recipe are expensive, I know, but the original recipe from Nashville actually specified pecans, which are even more so. Actually either can be left out, or you can halve the amount and just use them in the mixture instead of coating the baking tin as well. Whatever your version, it will be very good with Cheddar-style cheeses, provided they are full of bite and flavour due to being aged properly.

Makes a 10 in/25 cm loaf

4 oz/115 g *chopped walnuts*	2 heaped tsp *baking powder*
4 oz/125 g *butter*	1 tsp *salt*
6 oz/175 g *sugar*	Approx 8 oz/225 g *crushed*
½ tsp *grated lemon rind*	*pineapple*
1 *egg, beaten*	2 fl oz/50 ml *milk*
10 oz/275 g *plain flour*	

Butter a 10 in/25 cm loaf tin (or 2 × 7 in/17.5 cm tins) then shake in walnuts to cover completely. Turn out the ones that do not stick and reserve for the bread. Then also sprinkle the pan lightly with sugar.

Cream the butter and sugar very well, add the lemon rind and the beaten egg. Mix together the flour, baking powder and salt and mix thoroughly into the basic batter. Drain the pineapple well then stir into the mixture alternatively with the milk. Lastly fold in the remaining walnuts evenly. Spoon the batter into the tin trying not to disturb the walnut coating, then bake in a preheated oven at 350°F/180°C/Gas 4 for 60-75 minutes. Let stand in tin for 10 minutes then turn out and complete cooling on a wire rack.

NUT TEA-BREAD

Nut breads, particularly those containing walnuts, or walnuts and raisins are fashionably appearing as an accompaniment to cheese, and they are quite good. But one mustn't be too impressed at the novelty for it is an old combination, as old as the simple idea of including nuts in bread. Here is a basic tea-bread recipe which I have seen published as an authentic recipe from the Limousin district of France and in New Zealand's seminal Edmonds' *Sure to Rise* cookery book; as baking powder, the foundation of the Edmonds fortune, was only perfected last century I suspect the recipes are as old as one another – not very! The inclusion of walnut oil is optional in this recipe but does make more of the nut's flavour, which can be somewhat elusive, I find.

8 oz/225 g *plain flour*	5-6 oz/150-175 g *chopped*
2 heaped tsp *baking powder*	*walnuts*
½ tsp *salt*	8 fl oz/225 ml *milk*
1 *egg*	1½ tbsp *walnut oil*
4 oz/115 g *demerara sugar*	

Butter a 10 in/25 cm loaf tin well. Stir together the dry ingredients. Cream the egg and sugar very well, then mix in the dry ingredients and the nuts. Gradually add the milk to form a pliant batter. Fold in the walnut oil and turn the batter into the prepared pan. Bake in a preheated 325°F/160°C/Gas 3 oven for an hour, or perhaps up to 1 hour and 15 minutes. Turn out onto a wire rack and serve cold. It is better left for a day.

Options   You can economically replace half the walnuts with raisins, use a mixture of nuts, or choose other nuts from the humble peanut to the cashew, hazelnut or pecan. Cashews and hazelnuts are better slightly toasted before use. If you have no nut oil, use another oil, or, rather better, use a tablespoon of melted butter. Don't use margarine in cooking. A mixture of half white and half wholemeal flour is specially good.

See also Nut-Oil Bread.

SOUR-DOUGH BREADS

Sour-dough bread is leavened with a proportion of previously-made dough, and usually relies on the action of naturally occurring ambient yeasts for fermentation.

This sour-dough starter will originally have been left in a warm place to turn sour and create gas. Once such a starter has been made it will last indefinitely, as each time you bake, only part of it is used and the remainder is replenished with some of the new dough.

It is said that many of the immigrants who went to the United States last century carried their favourite sour-dough starters with them and there is no reason to doubt this. Certainly the nickname for California gold-prospectors – sour-doughs – was based on their habit of carrying a sour-dough starter on their persons, which habit may well have been detected many yards away. Some starters pong horribly, and yet the more sour and horrid the starter, the more delicious might the bread be. You don't need yeast to start a sour-dough starter, but you get more assured results if you do. If you did happen to find yourself stuck in the bush without dried or fresh yeast you could simply mix some flour with milk or water and leave that uncovered and warm for a few days. The addition of a few teaspoons of sugar would help. The whole process is fairly arbitrary but if you use equal quantities of your chosen flour (white, wholemeal, rye or barley are best) and of your liquid to form a brimming cupful of thick batter, you'll be well on the way. If water were short and milk unobtainable, beer makes an interesing substitute for milk or water.

Once your starter has been started, keep it in a cooler place, such as a refrigerator. But as this will slow down the regrowth each time you use it, don't expect to be able to bake more than every 4 or 5 days. Obviously, you can always take the stored starter out and leave it somewhere warm if you wish to hasten it. Overnight would do.

You'll always get better results if you use potato water, even if mixed simply with a flour and sugar.

POTATO SOUR-DOUGH STARTER

1 lb/450 g *large potatoes, scrubbed, unpeeled*	1 lb/450 g *flour*
	2 oz/50 g *white sugar*
Water	2 tsp *salt*

Cut the potatoes up and just cover with cold water. Bring to the boil and cook until soft. Remove the peel from the potatoes then mash back into the water. Mix in the flour which can be any type of mixture you choose. Both rye and barley flours make excellent starters, but plain white flour is fine, too. Mix in the sugar and salt. The texture should resemble a newly made scone dough, light and almost sloppy. If it is rather heavy, beat in some more water or, even better, some milk.

Put the starter into an earthenware bowl and cover. After 3-4 days in a warm place the mixture will become bubbly and smell strongly. It is then ready for use. Be assured, the smell disappears during cooking.

I find this starter irritatingly inconsistent and difficult to control – sometimes it bubbles, sometimes it sinks. You could add a little yeast or, more simply, make half the quantity and use it all when it is ready.

YEASTED STARTER

1 oz/25 g *fresh yeast*
(*or half as much dried*)
1 pt/575 ml *warm water or*

potato water
2 level tsp *honey or sugar*
12 oz/350 g *flour*

Dissolve the yeast in some of the water with the honey or sugar. Mix in the flour and make a thick paste of it. Leave to ferment for at least 4 days, stirring back any liquid that rises.

SOUR-DOUGH WHOLEMEAL BREAD

Evening session: the sponge
8 oz/225 g *starter*
1 lb 2 oz/500 g *wholemeal flour*

1¾ pt/1 litre *warm water*

Morning session
4 fl oz/115 ml *cooking oil*
1 oz/25 g *salt*

1½ lb/675 g *flour, strong white or rye*

Add the starter to the flour, then add the water until a thick porridgy batter is formed. Beat well with a wooden spoon. Cover and leave overnight in a moderately warm place.

In the morning, remove about 8 oz/225 g of the risen sponge and incorporate it into the original starter. Cover and place in the refrigerator.

Fold the oil, then the finely ground salt, into the remaining sponge. Work in the flour to give a dough that is rather slacker than a yeasted dough. Knead for 5 minutes, adding more flour if it is too sticky.

Form into two loaves and prove for about 2 hours in well-oiled tins. If using rye flour, shape into flattish rounds instead. Bake for 20 minutes at 425°F/220°C/Gas 7, then turn down the heat to 375°F/190°C/Gas 5 and bake for at least 30 minutes longer.

SOUR-DOUGH RYE BREAD

Sour-dough is unquestionably the best way of making a rye loaf, and this is one of the simplest recipes for sour-dough rye bread.

8 oz/225 g *starter*	1 oz/25 g *salt*
4 pt/2.3 litres *potato water*	4 fl oz/115 ml *molasses or honey*
Approx 3 lb 5 oz/1.5 kg *rye*	1 oz/25 g *caraway seeds*
flour	*(optional)*

Add the starter to the liquid and half the flour. Mix, cover and stand for 3 hours in a warm place. Leave to sour longer if desired.

Stir well, then remove 8 oz/225 g of the mixture to replenish the starter. Add the rest of the ingredients to the remaining sponge to make a rather stiff dough.

Knead on a floured board until no longer sticky. Shape into two loaves and leave to prove, covered with a damp cloth, on a greased baking sheet. This may take 4 hours, but your patience will be rewarded.

Bake at 350°F/180°C/Gas 4 for 1 hour and then test.

Options   Leave out the caraway. Substitute scalded milk for the potato water (scalded milk can be used in any case if you think the dough is too stiff).

If the bread is a bit heavy for your taste, one of the most popular rye breads substitutes strong white or 85% flour for 50 per cent or more of the rye flour and does not use molasses. This will obviously also alter your starter's flavour and composition. It is very common to have a rye flour starter and continue with only white flour or a mix of rye and white.

SOUR-DOUGH WHITE BREAD

With a white flour, rye or barley flour based starter, truly delicious white breads can be made.

8 oz/225 g *starter*	1 pt/575 ml *warm milk or water*
3 lb/1.3 kg *white flour*	Approx 1 oz/25 g *salt*

The starter is mixed with half the flour and the warm milk or water and left to stand for several hours. 8 oz/225 g of that mixture is mixed back into the original starter then you continue by adding the remaining flour, liquid and salt to your dough.

I reckon that this dough makes excellent French-style bread, as it more or less forces you to let the dough develop long and slow.

CHEAT'S SOUR-DOUGH BREAD

The use of vinegar in a yeasted dough to help approximate the sour-dough flavour without the initial uncertainty of success is specially popular in San Francisco; it is the basic technique for many fanciful West Coast breads, which are as numerous as its religious groups.

½ oz/15 g *fresh yeast*	1 *large egg*
(*or half as much dried*)	1 fl oz/25 ml *cider vinegar*
2 fl oz/50 ml *warm water*	12 oz/350 g *strong white flour*
1 level tsp *salt*	*Oil*

Add the yeast to the warm water and after 10 minutes add the salt, egg and vinegar and half the flour. Pile the rest of the flour on a board, then work in the first mixture to make a soft dough. Knead lightly (working in and kneading should take about 5 minutes).

Shape into a round and place in an oiled 9 in/22.5 cm cake tin. Allow to double in size, then bake for 1 hour at 350°F/180°C/Gas 4.

Options　Add more egg or cider vinegar, or about 1 teaspoon molasses or raw sugar.

9 Pastry, Pies and Flans

Frozen pastry is probably the only product I always keep in the freezing compartment of my refrigerator, for nothing enhances simple food better than a crisp case, base or top of well-cooked pastry. My favourite types are puff pastry and phyllo pastry. With those on hand you know you can make stunning starters, main courses or puddings at will. Simply to bake little squares of pastry and scatter them on a top of a relatively plain fish in white sauce is a masterly and much appreciated touch. And you just cannot go wrong serving a first or last course in a light sandwich of puff pastry, usually known as a feuilleté or a millefeuille.

Because so little frozen pastry is now made with butter, I found a way of putting butter's flavour back – a great success, and at the same time began to experiment by flavouring pastry with fruit, herbs and spices. All these ideas are in this section and amongst the recipes are some of the best in the book. A Tortellini, Artichoke and Wild Mushroom Pie, for instance, and, to compete with the horrors of misnamed and weeping quiches, five savoury flans based on such combinations as carrot and green ginger, or onion, olive and anchovy.

I've also including the pastry recipes I find most useful and most impressive, Rough Puff Pastry and Choux Pastry. You can't buy anything like the latter, but you can fill it with almost anything fruity, creamy or cheesy. Both pastries are infinitely easier to make than most people imagine and almost impossible to muck up, provided you do what you are told, of course.

CHOUX PASTRY

If you are going to eat cream you may as well gorge and eat it sandwiched by a crisp cloud of choux pastry shaped like a bun or a long cigar. I think most people will be amazed to learn that choux pastry is actually the simplest pastry of all to make, and also that it may be used for savouries as well as for sweets.

The major problem that arises with making choux pastry is that it sometimes goes very soft very quickly. I was given the answer by Lady Harlech, who knows lots of good things about food. The hotter and steamier the day, or the more humid your kitchen, the fewer eggs your should use. Therefore, if you are to make this recipe a day in advance, use small eggs or reduce the total number by one or even two. It really works.

**Makes 48 mini profiteroles, 25 medium ones,
12 pretty huge ones and so on**

½ pt/300 ml *boiling water*	5 oz/150 g *strong white flour*
4 oz/115 g *butter, soft*	4 *eggs*
1 tsp *sugar (optional)*	

Boil some water in a kettle, then measure the ½ pint/300 ml into a saucepan. Add the butter in small pieces and leave until the butter is all melted – it will float on the surface. Add sugar now if you are making sweet pastries.

Put the saucepan over high heat until the liquid boils. Pour in all the flour at once, remove from the heat and stir vigorously until it forms a soft ball that comes away from the side of the pan. Put back over a low heat to cook through a little. Keep turning the ball of paste but do not beat it as this can make the final pastry tough.

Let the pastry cool until it is warm rather than hot then beat in the eggs one by one. This can be rather boring to do, as it takes a while to begin the incorporation of each and you must be certain the one egg is fully dissolved into the mixture before adding another. Use an electric beater if you can; a food processor is even better and gives lovely light results. The final texture of the paste should be like a thickish batter and have a dropping consistency.

For small profiteroles use a piping bag or a teaspoon to divide the paste into small piles on a dampened baking sheet. A dessertspoon does for shaping medium ones, a tablespoon for the biggies, which can be a couple of dabs of paste. I reckon the lumpier and more mishapen the paste is, the nicer these things look. Remember to leave room for them to expand.

Bake at 400°F/200°C/Gas 6 for 15 minutes for little ones, 20-25 minutes for bigger ones. But bake even longer if they are not well risen and crisp and golden brown. Then remove from the oven, make a small incision towards the base of each, then return to the oven at a very low temperature for 10 minutes to dry out the centre. Let cool.

No matter how assiduous you are in the cooking and drying there is often still a lump of nasty soft paste left inside each shape. Remove this when you cut each open and before you fill them. The most interesting way to cut choux buns open is not straight across but diagonally from one edge of the upper surface down almost to the base at the other side.

SPICED VEGETABLE ECLAIRS

This is a cheat's recipe, using leftover or frozen vegetables. It is a delicious lunch, yet could be adapted, by making smaller pastry shapes, into a most elegant and original starter.

Serves 4 as a lunch; 8 as a starter

1 recipe *choux pastry*	*(see method)*
Approx 2 lb/900 g *cooked vegetables*	*Salt and pepper*
	1-2 tsp *ground cumin*
1 pt/575 ml *white sauce*	

Make the choux pastry and either divide it into four long eclairs or make a large circle out of it on a damp baking tray. Bake for about 45 minutes, perhaps painting it with an egg-yolk glaze from time to time. Then cut into the pastry and return to dry and crispen further.

Meanwhile collect your vegetables, which can be nice left-overs, specially cooked, or a mixture. For best effect you need at least three types and frozen ones work quite nicely, especially broccoli. If you want to use mushrooms, do not precook them but simply cut into large pieces and add at the last moment. Vegetables like broccoli and cauliflower should be cut into florets. The plan is to have good contrasting texture and colour but not lots of little pieces, which would look awful. If in doubt, make the pieces bigger, not smaller.

Save at least ½ pint/300 ml of the water in which some of the vegetables were cooked; I actually cooked cauliflower, carrots and broccoli in the same water, one after the other, to make a good tasting vegetable water. (*Note:* it will *not* be good tasting if you overcook your vegetables).

Mix this vegetable stock with milk to make 1 pint/575 ml in all. Thicken slightly with several dessertspoons of arrowroot or cornflour, mixed to a paste with more milk.

If the flavour is not strong enough you might weaken enough to crumble in some chicken stock cube, no more than half I should think. Season with a little salt and pepper plus the cumin. Make it quite strong for it has a lot of vegetables to flavour.

When you are ready to serve, warm the pastry and heat the sauce. Turn the vegetables into the sauce and heat through. Do not let boil away or the texture will be quite spoiled. Spoon equally into the pastry shapes or into the split circle and serve.

Although not an advocate of cheese to finish dishes, this does benefit wonderfully by a sprinkle of a sharp cheese. Parmesan or Pecorino, of course, some mature Gouda or, if you are quite sure it really is mature and genuinely is Cheddar, some mature Cheddar would do nicely.

BURGUNDIAN GOUGÈRE CAKE

The best known version of gougère is a light ring of choux pastry flavoured with chunks of Gruyère cheese. This less well-known version is much heavier and more satisfying, delicious with a decent glass of wine as picnic food. Use Gruyère cheese, to be authentic, but you can also experiment as I did, with some mature Dutch Gouda.

Serves 4

4 oz/115 g *butter*	8 oz/225 g *Gouda cheese*
½ pt/300 ml *water*	1 *garlic clove, crushed*
8 oz/225 g *flour*	1-2 tsp *ground cumin or*
5 *eggs*	*cumin seed*
Salt	

Melt the butter in the water and when the mixture comes to the boil, mix in the flour all at once, stirring furiously. Keep stirring over the heat for 1 minute. Take off the heat and beat in the eggs, one by one – if you have a food processor this is considerably simpler and less wearing on the muscles. Salt quite well. Chop the cheese roughly – do not grate it – and flavour it well with garlic and cumin, then fold into the choux mixture.

Form the paste into a ring, spoonful by spoonful, on a greased baking sheet. Brush with extra beaten egg then put into a hot oven at 425°F/220°C/Gas 7 for 30 minutes.

Serve the gougère cake warm or cold.

CHESTNUT AND BLACK CHERRY PROFITEROLES

Canned purées of chestnuts and canned cherries, specially the black ones, are great cupboard standbys. I first combined them with cream and rum to make a sensational tower of profiteroles as a wedding cake (which the French call a 'croquembouche'). On another occasion I made a castle of profiteroles filled with different flavours of cream – some with orange flower water, some with rose-water, some with rum, some with brandy. They were stuck together with caramelized sugar to make a huge glistening ring and the centre was then filled with pounds and pounds of succulent summer fruits, raspberries, strawberries, currants and so on.

1 recipe *choux pastry*	*Dark rum or brandy (optional)*
8 oz/225 g *vanilla chestnut purée*	1 lb/450 net *canned black*
½ pt/300 ml *double or*	*cherries*
whipping cream	

Once the profiteroles are cooked, dried, cooled and split, mash up the chestnut purée. Whip the cream then fold it and the chestnut together. Flavour with rum or brandy if you wish. Actually if you are using rum or brandy, it is as well to start the day before by opening the cherries and soaking them in the liqueur then draining that off to flavour the chestnut cream.

Fill each profiterole generously with the cream. Then cut each cherry in half, if you are making small profiteroles, and place a half on the chestnut cream. Larger profiteroles can have a whole cherry stuffed into their mouths. These will stack well as long as you start with a complete layer of filled pastries rather than a circle.

Options For maximum wickedness melt some dark chocolate with a few teaspoons of water over medium heat and dribble that in rivulets over the profiteroles, whether stacked or not. Or melt and caramelize 8-12 oz/225-350 g of sugar and when it is a good golden brown spoon that over. Use a fork to spin some of it into long thin threads.

If you like a sauce with your puddings, then liquidize two more cans of black cherries with their syrup, heat and thicken only slight with a little arrowroot. Chill well then point the flavour with black rum. Serve a puddle of this on the plate topped by the profiteroles.

ENRICHED PUFF PASTRY

Although all the frozen puff pastry I ever buy performs admirably, noticably little of it is now made with butter. The switch to using vegetable fats is of advantage to both consumer and manufacturer; to the former it offers less cholesterol, to the latter less expense.

Thus adding butter to bought pastry gives you something that is almost home-made and, in taste alone, will be disguised from the shop-bought product. If you go one step further and add herbs or spices to the pastry as you refold it, the transformation will be complete and your pastry will be a star.

There is much puff pastry used in fine food these days, particularly for savoury first courses, and it is a simple matter to have prebaked some squares, rectangles or circles of puff pastry with are filled and surrounded by a delicious sauce at the last minute; for pudding, slices of fresh fruit layered into pastry with little but a liqueur flavoured cream or, say, a purée of raspberries will always be a winner and the contrast of the crunch of the pastry and the luscious texture of ripe mangoes or peaches a properly stimulating way to complete a meal.

The following is what I do to each 8 oz/225 g of defrosted puff pastry.

1   Gently roll out the pastry until it forms a long rectangle about one-third of its original thickness – you can make it thinner but the important thing is that the shape is as regular and straight-sided as possible.

2   Onto the bottom two-thirds of the pastry lay evenly 1oz/25 g of butter in very thin slices. The butter should be firm but not directly from the refrigerator. Use salted or unsalted butter (the latter is slightly better for pudding pastries).

3   Onto the butter sprinkle a flavouring, if you so choose – of a dried herb or a spice you will need about 1 teaspoon or enough to give a good covering. If you are using fresh herbs you will need at least 2 dessertspoons of most of them, in which case only strew half on at this stage.

4   Once the butter and flavouring are in place, fold down the top, unbuttered one-third of pastry, then fold up the bottom one-third. Give the pastry a quarter turn towards you so that the seam of the pastry you have folded up is on your right-hand-side. Pinch together the two short sides, either with your fingers, or by pressing firmly with your rolling pin, which entraps both the butter and the air and thus ensures a light, high pastry. Now carefully roll out the pastry until it is about the same size as before – don't force it if it has a mind of its own. Then repeat the buttering with a further 1 oz/25 g and strew on the rest of the fresh herbs if that is what you are using. You won't need any more spices or dried herbs. Repeat the folding, turning and rolling as above.

5   Then, without adding any more butter, fold, turn and roll, fold, turn and roll then fold once more. Use plenty of flour on the surface to ensure the pastry rolls evenly, then brush it off as you fold up the ends. Wrap the pastry in a piece of clingfilm then let it rest an hour or so in the refrigerator or a cool place.

6   Then proceed to roll and shape the pastry normally.

The first time I did this I used a commercially available mixture of ground ginger and dried orange peel and made an apple pie and some turnovers with the pastry. The apple had cinnamon and allspice and the overall effect was really marvellous. You would do equally well simply to grate fresh orange peel directly on to the pastry (doing it over the pastry ensures you collect the invaluable zest and oils) and lemon or lime would be equally good. The next recipe is a good example of this use, but first a few more tips about getting the best results from puff pastry.

Don't forget to allow the pastry to relax into shape before putting it to use. As you roll it out, constantly lift it from the table, which allows it to shrink back into its real shape. Once you have it approximately to shape, having loosened it from the surface, leave it a couple minutes before cutting out your final shape. Never pick it up in your hands to carry it, but roll it around your rolling instrument and transport it that way. These points should ensure you never have to endure the horror of shrunken pastry.

Puff pastry must also be cut only with something very thin and sharp, like a razor blade, and you should always ensure that any edge which is going to be exposed (the edge of the pastry, for instance) is protected from being squashed while you are making the pie etc. If the outside edge of a puff pastry is pinched or crushed it cannot rise.

Contrary to all received wisdom I get a better rise if the pastry is at a cool, room temperature when it goes into the oven. I never get good results if the pastry comes from the refrigerator, but perhaps that is a complication of the vagaries of temperature in my kitchen and the particular temperament of my oven.

Oh yes, and don't forget the tremendous kick you can give pastry by painting it with undiluted food colouring. Let the colours dry before you bake, and perhaps put an egg glaze on, too. Children love it; adults go wild for it.

Now, that recipe using pastry enriched with orange and butter.

ORANGE-CARAMEL APPLE PASTRY

One of the most fascinating and delicious puddings ever created has to be Tarte Tatin. For the uninitiated it is a simple confection of sliced apples baked with butter, sugar and caramel beneath a rich shortcrust pastry topping. Once baked it is inverted so the glistening apples now sit atop the crisp pastry.

In this version, which must be eaten very shortly after it has been cooked and as soon as it has been turned out, I have used puff pastry. But not just any old puff pastry – a puff pastry that has been rerolled with grated orange peel. The caramel is also made with orange juice, thus, once you have baked your pudding and turned it out, you have golden brown apple slices flavoured with orange and caramel on top of a floating, crisp base of orange pastry. Believe me, it is even better than it sounds. So good you can actually eat it without cream and not notice.

If you are firm, the recipe will feed six, but I warn you, the first one I made was eaten by just two people. At one sitting!

As with the Tarte Tatin, Golden Delicious apples are de rigueur.

Pastry	
8 oz/225 g *frozen puff pastry*	1 *orange*
2 oz/50 g *butter, unsalted*	

Caramel	
4 oz/115 g *white sugar*	6 tbsp *orange juice*

Filling	
2 lb/400 g *Golden Delicious apples*	Approx ¼-½ tsp *ground cloves*
	1-2 oz/25-50 g *butter*
1 oz/25 g *sugar*	

Once your frozen pastry is pliable, add the extra butter as explained in the previous section. Each time you add butter, grate finely some rind from a good, well-flavoured orange directly onto the pastry. Ensure that you include the gratings left inside the grater. If the orange is a decent size, about three-quarters of the rind is enough. Fold a few extra times then let the pastry relax and chill in the refrigerator.

Remember that unsalted butter varies enormously depending upon from which country it comes, and all have flavour added to the cream with which they are made. If you can find an unsalted Normandy butter that smells like cream, buy that, for this is what most food writers think they mean when they specify unsalted butter; what they really mean you to use is the virtually unobtainable sweet butter – butter made from cream that has been neither salted nor flavoured with a bacterial culture, which is what happens to the German, Dutch and Danish butters sold as unsalted. All will give good results, and so will salted butter, but it is better that you known what is what.

Next make the caramel. Put the sugar together with the orange juice into a heavy bottomed saucepan and cook together until a golden brown caramel forms. Do not be lily-livered about this. The caramel must be really brown and I find that the proper time to remove it is when I detect the very first whiff of bitterness and see the first puff of smoke. Before then the caramel is anaemic; after that it can be bitter. The caramel must be poured immediately and evenly onto the base of your baking dish, which should be at least 8 in/20 cm wide and a good 2 in/5 cm deep.

Quarter the apples, peel and core them then cut them into long, fairly thick slices. Toss the slices in the sugar as you go. Flavour lightly with the cloves.

Arrange the slices neatly on the caramel but do not be hysterical about making a beautiful pattern. As the apples cook and soften they crush together to make a pretty effect anyway. Dot the butter evenly over the top.

Roll out the pastry gently to form a circle that is slightly bigger than the dish. Lay it in gently then turn up the outside edges to allow the pastry to sit exactly inside the rim – saucer shaped. Use any leftover pieces of pastry to make squares that can be dotted over the top; once the pie is cooked and inverted they will give a greater sense of height, acting as extra supports.

Put the prepared pie into a 450°F/230°C/Gas 8 oven for 15-20 minutes, then reduce the heat to 375°F/190°C/Gas 5 for another 10-15 minutes, or until you are certain the pastry is fully risen and cooked right through. Let cool a few minutes then put a large flat plate over the pie, invert as quickly as you can, remove the dish and voilà! What a sight . . . indeed it is better to perform this act at the table so everyone can admire the effect and enjoy the great sensuous rush of orange-and-caramel steam.

ROUGH PUFF PASTRY

As with the choux pastry recipe, this is so simple and fast to make you will never understand what the fuss has been about once you have made your first batch. A batch is made in under 10 minutes and it takes only minutes more to double up so you have some to put in the deep freeze or refrigerator. Each recipe makes just over 1 lb/450 g of pastry.

8 oz/225 g	*strong white (bread) flour*	*soft*
4 oz/115 g	*lard, soft*	1 dessertsp *lemon juice*
4 oz/115 g	*butter or margarine,*	*Cold water (see method)*
		Salt (optional)

Sift the flour into a bowl. Both the fats should be at room temperature but not warm enough to be melting. Use your index finger and thumb to pull off knobs of both and drop these in the flour. When all in, toss gently to cover each piece of fat with flour. Put the lemon juice into a measuring jug then add very cold water to make ¼ pint/150 ml. If you are a salt freak you can add a pinch or two to the water. I never do.

Pour the liquid into the bowl all at once then, using a palette knife or something equally broad-bladed, carefully mix everything together until it looks as though it is generally holding together.

Tip the whole lot out onto a lightly floured surface, scraping everything out of the bowl, then gently pat into a brick shape.

Use whatever you like to roll, from Perrier bottle to broomstick, which is my favourite. My only caution is to use the lightest pressure you can and always to roll away from you, which gives the most even pressue. Roll into a rectangle anything between ¼-½ in/6-12 mm thick. Do not be alarmed at its appearance. If there is an excess of fat showing, sprinkle on some more flour without being excessive.

Fold up the bottom third of the pastry, then fold down the top third over that. Turn the rectangle a quarter turn clockwise, so that the seam which faced you is now on your left-hand side. Use the rolling instrument to tap this seam closed and do the same thing to the top and bottom edges of the pastry, thus trapping the air you have folded in. This is perhaps the most important part of the entire process. Ideally you should let the pastry rest just a few minutes now, and so if you are making two lots at once you would go on to the other. But, if not, nothing drastic will happen if you proceed with just the one batch.

Roll out the pastry as before, strewing flour if you think you really need it. It is very important that there is plenty of flour for the pastry to slide along when it is being rolled. Once you have another long rectangle, fold and turn it as before then seal the edges. If the underneath of the pastry is excessively floured when you fold it up, brush this away.

Roll and fold at least two more times. By the fourth time you will have pastry that is recognizable and which has a life of its own. Thus on this last rolling it may not wish to spread as far as it did at the start. Don't force it, but congratulate yourself on doing it right. The pastry will now look so good you may want to reward it by giving it a few extra turns. Once this is done, wrap it and let it relax and chill in the refrigerator.

This is superb for the pasta pies following, and lends itself admirably to being flavoured with herbs and spices as you fold and roll.

MACARONI PARTY PIE

Some years ago I remember a marvellous looking Italian woman winning a cooking competition in one of the Sunday colour supplements with an enormous pie filled with pasta. To make the stuffed tortellini, the sauces and the pastry took a whole day and so I didn't save her recipe, but the idea stuck with me and I developed two faster recipes, which turned out to be stunning.

For a 9 in/22.5 cm pie about 2 in/5 cm deep

12 oz/350 g *best minced beef*	2 *garlic cloves*
1 *small onion, minced*	6 oz/175 g *macaroni elbows (dry)*
6-7 tbsp *olive oil*	12 oz/350 g *puff pastry*
14-16 oz/400-500 g *canned plum tomatoes in their own juice*	4 oz/115 g *mature Cheddar or Parmesan cheese*
2 dessertsp *tomato purée*	4 tsp *dried oregano*
¼ pt/150 ml *strong red wine*	*Salt and pepper, to taste*
2 *dried bay leaves*	

Fry the meat and onion in 2-3 tablespoons of the olive oil until nicely browned then add the tomatoes, juice and all, the purée wine, bay, and garlic. Cook covered for 45 minutes by which time the meat will be very tender. Let cool.

Cook the macaroni until only just tender in masses of salted boiling water, drain and toss in just enough olive oil to lightly coat each shape.

When you are ready to put the pie together mix the sauce and the pasta. Do it earlier and too much of the sauce will be absorbed and the pie will turn out dry.

Use two-thirds or so of the pastry to line the baking dish then sprinkle in half the cheese and half the oregano. Add salt and pepper to the pasta and sauce mixture if you think it is needed then spread that evenly in the pie. Top with the rest of the cheese and oregano and sprinkle with some of the olive oil

Cover with the rest of the pastry and decorate if you wish. Paint with a beaten egg yolk if you would like a glazed effect.

Put immediately into a preheated oven at 425°F/220°C/Gas 7 and cook until the pastry is well risen, golden brown and cooked through. This pie is best eaten cold, or warm if you prefer, but it does not heat up very well.

TORTELLINI, ARTICHOKE AND WILD MUSHROOM PIE

Dried mushrooms from Italy, France or Poland give an unforgettable outdoor flavour to almost anything with which they are associated. This rich pie can be as lightly or as heavily perfumed with them as you can afford, and there is no need to stick with just one type. Use porcini or girolles, cèpes or morilles.

Tortellini is traditionally eaten with a cream sauce whether stuffed with a cheese or a meat mixture. Use whatever type you can buy. The ones you see dried and in cellophane packets are really quite good and perfectly suited to this pie.

Serves 4-6

1½ lb/675 g *puff or short pastry*	¾ pt/425 ml *milk*
At least ½ oz/15 g *dried mushrooms*	1-2 *garlic cloves, large*
	2 *fresh bay leaves*
½ pt/300 ml *dry white wine*	*Salt*
½ pt/300 ml *double cream*	1 lb/450 g *cooked tortellini*
1½ oz/40 g *butter*	6 oz/175 g *artichoke bottoms, canned*
1 *small onion, finely chopped*	
1½ oz/40 g *plain flour*	Approx ½ tsp *ground allspice*

You need a greater amount of pastry for this pie than the previous one as the filling is wetter and thus the casing must be more sturdy. So first prepare your pastry (rough puff is ideal – use 1½ times the recipe given), then leave it to chill while you make the filling which must also be cold before being enrobed with the pastry.

Put the mushrooms into a saucepan with the dry white wine (it really must be very dry); fino sherry is an excellent substitute. Simmer uncovered until the mushrooms have reconstituted and are tender, by which time the alcohol will have reduced to about half its volume. If you like to be exact simply pour it off and check in a measuring jug, and either continue reducing or top with some more of the same. Add the double cream and keep warm; it won't hurt if the mixture reduces a little more.

Melt the butter in a heavy-bottomed saucepan and soften the finely chopped onion in that. Then stir in the flour to make a roux and continue cooking gently for 2 minutes. Remove from the heat. Once the roux has stopped sizzling, pour the hot mushroom and cream mixture in all at once and whisk without ceasing until the sauce has thickened. Slowly add in the milk, crush the garlic and add that, throw in the bay leaves and leave to cook gently for 10 minutes. The sauce should be rich and unctuous, and flow well without being thin. Season with salt but do not add pepper. If you would like a little sharpness, a dash or two of brandy is the best bet, but do not forget that the tortellini stuffing will be a strong contrast to the sauce.

Remove the sauce from the heat, let cool a little then press clingfilm or aluminium foil to its surface and let it cool to room temperature or thereabouts but do not let it set solid.

Cook the tortellini in masses of boiling salted water. Note the weight required is that of the pasta *after* cooking. 1 lb/450 g of fresh tortellini gives about 1½ lb/675 g. The dried ones almost double in weight when cooked. Drain the pasta and leave to cool.

To prepare the pie, take two-thirds of the pastry and line a dish about 9 in/22.5 cm in diameter and at least 2 in/5 cm deep. Slice the canned artichoke bottoms thickly and stir into the mushroom sauce removing the bay leaves as they appear. Mix the sauce and the pasta together. If you cannot buy cans of artichoke bottoms, artichoke hearts will do. The rather earthy flavour of this vegetable neatly bridges the gap between the wildness of the mushrooms and the smoothness of the pasta.

Pour the filling into the pie then sprinkle generously with allspice – freshly ground is infinitely better.

Cover the pie with the remaining pastry and seal well. Prick through the cover with a fork or sharp-pointed knife rather than slashing the pastry.

Pop the pie into a preheated 450°F/230°C/Gas 8 oven for 15 minutes to give the pastry a really good start then reduce to 400°F/200°C/Gas 6 for another 30 minutes or until the pastry is well cooked, golden brown and delicious. Serve warm.

This, I assure you, is one of the best things you have ever tasted. At the risk of sounding like a food writer, it is best followed by a crisp salad. The flavour is solid enough to complement a red wine.

HADDOCK, LEEK AND ORANGE PASTRIES

This recipe just happened. Indeed it is a combination of leftovers and hand-me-downs. I had some pastry left over and I had been given some fish. Leeks were in the refrigerator because they were among the first of the new season's. It was simply a matter of combining them in the best possible way. You can make this for as many or as few people as you like. Here it is for one, and provided you can multiply you can take it from there. It is rather more filling than might seem the case.

For each serving

4-6 oz/115-175 g *puff pastry*	4-6 oz/115-175 g *haddock,*
4-6 oz/115/175 g *leeks, sliced*	*skinned and boned*
A little butter	1 *orange*
Salt and pepper	*A little grated nutmeg*

Roll out the pastry until it is 8 × 6 in/20 × 15 cm or thereabouts, then let it relax. The leeks should be sliced quite finely then rinsed and drained. Put them into a saucepan with no water and cook over medium heat until wilted and tender but still bright green. Stir from time to time to encourage all the liquid to evaporate. This method of cooking leeks ensures they retain all their goodness and flavour. Toss in a little butter, season, then spread on a plate to cool quickly.

Ensure the haddock is boned and skinned and cut into two or three pieces about half the length of the pastry. Grate about a quarter of the orange skin finely onto the fish and spread it evenly.

Pile the leeks in the centre of the pastry and spread them to form a bed for the fish. Flavour the leeks with nutmeg, layer the fish on top then dot with a few knobs of butter. Spread the mixture so it is thin rather than wide and stretches to within 1 in/2.5 cm of each short edge of the pastry.

Use a sharp knife to make even cuts about ½ in/1.25 cm deep all around the pastry edge. Then fold the two long edges up over the fish (they should not meet at the top but will at the sides), and overlap the two sides to seal the packet. You will have a mound that is open at the top and which has a flat border on the right- and left-hand sides. Ensure these stick together by adding a dab of water.

For a glazed effect paint the pastry with an egg yolk beaten with a teaspoon of water or milk.

Put into a preheated 425°F/220°C/Gas 7 oven for 20-25 minutes depending on how thick the fish was. Peep after 15 minutes and reduce the heat if the edge of the pastry is burning to 375°F/190°C/Gas 5. The butter on the fish will keep the top from drying out, but if it has been absorbed another dab would not go amiss. Serve hot.

BACON AND EGG PIE

Strictly speaking this isn't delicatessen food as all the ingredients can be bought from a supermarket. But it is something so simple that it soon becomes a standby of anyone who makes it and far more popular that 'quiche'. In New Zealand no picnic or beach trip is complete without a couple.

Serves 6-8

12-14 oz/350-400 g *puff pastry*
8 oz/225 g *streaky bacon*
Diced green peppers, slices of fried
    onion, or potato, green peas,
    sweet corn kernels (optional)

6 *large eggs*
Black pepper, be generous

Line a shallow 8-9 in/20-22.5 cm pie dish with 6 oz/175 g of the pastry. Coarsely dice the bacon and fry until the fat starts to run. Spread the bacon evenly over the pastry and some of the interesting extras if you have them; never mind if you don't.

Break the eggs over the bacon, encouraging the whites to join together by gently tilting the dish. Best plan is to have 5 eggs around the edge and 1 in the middle. Try not to break the yolks.

Pepper the egg yolks generously, cover with the remaining pastry, crimp the edges and decorate with any leftover bits and pieces. Glaze if you have an extra egg about.

Bake 25 minutes in a preheated 400°F/200°C/Gas 6 oven, then a further 15 minutes at 325°F/160°C/Gas 3. Serve warm or cold in slices.

WILD MUSHROOMS AND SNAILS IN PASTRY

Towards the end of writing this book I was able to clear out what had become my office and return it to its original function, that of dining room. Just as well, for I was due to entertain some generous and loyal friends generously. Of the main course, the less said the better. But the first two were quite memorable. First this feuilleté of wild mushrooms and snails, and then the Hot-Smoked Trout.

As with many of my recipes I really rather dislike giving exact quantities, for this seems unnecessarily daunting. Most of my recipes allow quite a variation; that is how it should be. Here is some guidance to making this sensational starter for six people.

Start by reconstituting about ½ oz/15 g of dried mushrooms in some very dry sherry. I used a mixture of girolles and cèpes. Leave the mixture simmering very gently indeed, adding more sherry or a touch of water if you think this is necessary. It takes 15 or so minutes for most dried mushrooms to be succulent and soft but some types benefit from a little more cooking. Once the mushrooms are done the liquid should only just cover them.

If you can also get some fresh wild mushrooms, rinse and dry them then toss in a little butter before putting into the warm sherry and dried mushroom mixture. If they need cutting, keep the pieces big and chunky. A very little salt might be added if you are absolutely certain it is needed. If you let this mixture sit around at room temperature for a few hours it improves enormously, thus it can be made in the morning for an evening's meal. Next you should prepare the pastry.

The most spectacular choice would be paper-thin phyllo pastry, which is increasingly available frozen throughout the country. The other choice is to use very thinly rolled puff pastry or to make millefeuilles from puff pastry. Let's start with the best.

The plan is to bake a separate top and bottom of layers of phyllo pastry for each serving. The phyllo curls and buckles as it is baked, giving the effect of great lightness and airiness. It is the ultimate puff pastry. For each serving you cut six pieces of phyllo pastry about 4 in/10 cm square. You make a pile of three of them, brushed with melted butter between each layer. Then make a similar pile of the other three but this time you cut a triangular pattern through the top layer with the tip of a sharp knife or with a razor blade. To avoid confusion I bake the six bottom piles and the six top piles quite separately. Put them into a preheated 375°F/190°C/Gas 5 oven for about 10 minutes or until they are risen and golden brown. You should be able to lift each layer separately. Do not overcook or the butter will burn and give a rather bitter flavour. These can also be made well in advance and reheated when needed.

To put everything together, reheat the mushrooms in their liquid then stir in ¼ pint/150 ml double cream. Open a can of 24 large, cooked snails, and put these into the mixture. Add just enough of the flavoured water in which they were packed to give you a well-textured and flavoured sauce. Heat through gently.

Put the bottom halves of the warmed pastry onto six small hot plates. Spoon the mushrooms and snails evenly onto them. Top with the other pastry pieces then spoon the sauce around the pastry to fill the plates. Serve at once. For a little extra bite some coarsely chopped parsley might be scattered on the pastry base which will also help prevent it becoming soggy too quickly.

To make this with puff pastry, you might like to imitate phyllo by rolling the pastry out as paper thin as you can. Best way is to ensure both sides of the pastry are well floured and then to roll it around your pin, so it rolls upon itself and spreads easily as it does. Then proceed as before.

Otherwise cut oblongs or squares of quite thick puff pastry, cook them through and then split them to remove any uncooked or soft contents. Reheat in the same way before serving.

SAVOURY FLANS

Believe me, I am by no means a purist, but the misuse and misunderstanding of what constitutes a quiche thoroughly depresses me. It is a losing battle to protest, I suspect, but why don't cooks know that a true quiche contains no cheese and no onion – a cheese quiche is a direct contradiction in terms.

The true Quiche Lorraine is simply eggs and cream, flavoured with a scatter of diced green bacon and perhaps some thinly sliced green of leek. It is baked in a pastry case (which is all the better for being precooked) until just set, and eaten when warm rather than hot. It is quite simply an unsweetened, slightly savoury custard tart.

A spinach flan, hot or cold, is a wonderful idea, of course. Yet how often is it swimming in its own juice atop drowned pastry? The answer to that problem is as startlingly simple as it is widely unknown. Take your raw spinach, wash it, tear it into pieces, then layer it with salt in a colander or deep bowl. Turn it from time to time over 2-3 hours, then drain, rinse in cold water and squeeze. Chop it as finely as you like and use it as you will – it will not produce further moisture.

For cheese flans I find it is best to mix cottage or curd cheese together with some harder grating cheese. Make it a very smooth mixture then add milk or cream and beaten eggs in the proportion of 1 to every ¼ pint/150 ml of mixture. When you are rich or want something that tastes so, start with cream cheese. In all cases sprinkle the mixture with both types of paprika and with nutmeg before baking.

The use of a soft cheese in these mixtures gives a most interesting texture and seems to minimize or delete the problems of such baked fillings creating moisture when baked. The following flans all use soft cheese in the mixture.

A reminder The basic recipe for a quiche or for the custard base of a savoury flan is 1 egg to each ¼ pint/150 ml of liquid. Fewer eggs will give a more *tremblant* finish, more will firm it more.

ONION, OLIVE AND ANCHOVY FLAN

Serves 6-8

10 in/25 cm *shortcrust base, precooked*	6 oz/175 g *cream or curd cheese*
1 lb/450 g *onions, peeled*	1 oz/25 g *butter*
½ pt/300 ml *milk*	4 *eggs*
1 *bay leaf*	12 *black olives, blanched*
	1 *small can anchovy fillets*

Finely chop the onions then cook in the milk with the bay leaf until really soft. Allow to cool a little then liquidize. Add the cream or curd cheese, butter and eggs and process briefly to mix thoroughly.

Pour the mixture into the pastry case, halve the olives and distribute around the edge. Cut each anchovy fillet in half lengthwise and arrange as spokes. Dribble the oil from the can of anchovies over the surface of the pie then bake in a preheated oven at 350°F/180°C/Gas 4 for 25 minutes.

This continues to develop its flavour over 2 or 3 days if you can bear to wait that long. Excellent chilled with a salad but perfectly wonderful if teamed with excellent, oily ratatouille. Also good scattered with a little freshly grated Parmesan cheese and ground black pepper.

LEEK AND MUSTARD FLAN

Serves 6-8

10 in/25 cm *shortcrust base,*
  precooked
1 lb/450 g *leeks, trimmed and*
  sliced
½ pt/300 ml *milk*
2 dessertsp *butter*

6 oz/175 g *curd or cream cheese*
2 dessertsp *lemon juice*
4 *eggs*
1½ desertsp *Dijon mustard*
  with seeds
Salt, to taste

Cook the sliced leeks in the milk and butter for 10 minutes or until the leeks are nice and soft, but before they start to lose brightness or colour. Purée leeks and milk and allow to cool somewhat before adding all the remaining ingredients. Mix thoroughly, pour into the pastry case and bake in a preheated oven at 350°F/180°C/Gas 4 for 30 minutes.

This is especially good with smoked fish and looks and tastes terrific with smoked salmon. For a fascinating contrast of flavour and texture, mix a little horseradish cream into soured cream and spread that atop the flan before serving.

CARROT AND GREEN GINGER FLAN

Serves 6-8

10 in/25 cm *shortcrust base,*
  precooked
1 lb/450 g *carrots, unpeeled*
½ pt/300 ml *milk or single cream*
1 in/2.5 cm *green ginger, peeled*
  and thinly sliced

1 *garlic clove (optional)*
6 oz/175 g *curd or cream cheese*
4 dessertsp *lemon juice*
4 *eggs*
½ tsp *ground cloves*

Scrub but do not peel the carrots, cut up roughly then cook until just tender in milk or single cream. Put the carrots and their cooking liquid into a liquidizer or food processor together with the green ginger. Add peeled garlic (if using), curd or cream cheese, the lemon juice and the eggs, then process until smooth.

Gently ladle the marigold-coloured purée into the prebaked pastry case, then sprinkle with the ground cloves.

Bake for 30 minutes in a preheated oven at 350°F/180°C/Gas 4 until set, but try not to brown the top. This makes a welcome splash of colour on an autumn buffet or luncheon table, or a sunny contribution to a picnic spread.

CELERIAC AND MINT FLAN

Serves 6-8

10 in/25 cm *shortcrust base, precooked*	1 *garlic clove*
1 lb/450 g *celeriac, trimmed weight*	6 oz/175 g *curd or cream cheese*
	4 dessertsp *lemon or lime juice*
¾ pt/425 ml *milk or single cream*	4 *eggs*
	Fresh or dried mint
	½ tsp *nutmeg or allspice*

Cube the trimmed celeriac quickly, keeping it in lemon juice or salted water to prevent it oxidizing and turning brown. Then cook until tender in the milk or cream. Pour the celeriac and milk into a liquidizer or food processor, add the peeled garlic, the curd or cream cheese, the citrus juice and the eggs. Process until smooth.

Line the prebaked pastry case with fresh mint leaves or sprinkle with a couple of teaspoons of dried mint. Gently ladle the celeriac purée into the pastry then dust the top with nutmeg or allspice.

Bake for 30 minutes in a preheated 350°F/180°C/Gas 4 oven or until set, but do not brown the top. Eat lukewarm or chilled, perhaps accompanied by a little Dijon mustard.

BRIE AND ARTICHOKE FLAN

This recipe presents Brie in a new way, combined with butter in a pastry case. The technique enhances the subtle flavour of the cheese and the flan itself is a stunning way to serve cheese after a summery meal or on a picnic. If you can replace the tinned artichoke hearts with slices of freshly cooked artichoke fonds directly from your garden or greengrocer so much the better.

Serves 6-8

8 oz/225 g *shortcrust pastry*	1 tsp *grated lemon or lime peel*
1 *egg, separated*	*French seed mustard, to taste*
14 oz/400 g net *can artichoke*	12 oz/350 g *Brie, just ripe*
hearts	6 oz/175 g *salted butter*
2-3 capfuls *gin*	

Sprinkle a board or table with wholemeal flour, roll out the pastry on that and line a baking dish about 9 in/22.5 cm diameter and at least 1½ in/4-5 cm deep. Let it rest for 15 minutes in a cool place, trim, prick all over then bake for 15 minutes in a preheated 350°F/180°C/Gas 4 oven until crisp and brown.

While the pastry is still hot, paint it with the lightly beaten white of the separated egg, which seals the base against early sogginess. Drain the artichokes well and then let them marinate in the gin and grated peel. If you can, leave them to marry for several hours as this dramatically improves the eventual flavour.

Once the egg white has set you can spread the base of the flan case with mustard, allowing for its strength and your preferences – remember this is not going to be cooked and so the strength you put in is what you will get when you eat. When you are ready to assemble the flan, slice four of the artichoke hearts and arrange them on the mustard.

The Brie used for this dish must not be runny or overripe – if anything it should be slightly underripe. Chop up the cheese, including the skin. Melt the butter over a low heat, then add the Brie. Stir until the cheese just begins to soften. The cheese must neither melt altogether or bubble.

Quickly turn the butter and cheese into a liquidizer or food processor, add the remaining artichokes and all the marinating liquid and peel and process until very smooth and homogenous. Pour evenly into the tart and sprinkle the top with a little nutmeg or more grated lemon or lime peel. Chill for 4 hours before serving in wedges; this should be enjoyed just slightly chilled rather than directly from the refrigerator.

Options   This is remarkably good if served with ripe pears, for Brie and pears have a wonderful affinity. Otherwise, you might consider replacing the artichokes in this recipe with pears, and use vinegar rather than citrus.

10 New Ingredients, New Ideas

The great delight of delicatessen shopping is the discovery of a new ingredient; the delight of cooking with delicatessen ingredients is the discovery of new uses for them.

This section is a collection of recipes which don't really fit into any category other than that of using something special. Coconut cream, pink and green peppercorns, and fresh ginger all offer delicious ways to cook chicken or duck, and Chinese-style mixed spices make belly of pork important enough for a banquet.

Once you have seen how to use these ingredients unexpectedly, you should feel secure enough to go off on paths of your own. Make the Cinnamon-Cherry Sauce with blueberries, now being grown in this country. Substitute veal for rabbit in the soured cream sauce, or change the vanilla for something else in the Soured Cream Soufflé. In the end the most special ingredient in any recipe is your imagination.

CHICKEN SATÉ

Although extremely popular in Thailand, this is really an Indonesian dish, something that becomes clear when you discover the peanut butter in the sauce, for peanuts are as integral to Indonesian cooking as onions seem to be to British.

The coconut milk called for here is easily prepared by using the blocks of coconut cream so freely sold now. These are dissolved in boiling water to make a cream or milk to whatever richness, texture and amount you need. Whatever portion of the solid cream you do not use will keep in the refrigerator. Don't try to melt coconut cream over heat or it will curdle.

The best skewers for saté are the long thin wooden ones. Saté is more a snack than a main course but it is delicious served hot with a crisp salad and this recipe would then serve four very generously indeed and certainly satisfy six for lunch.

2 lb/900 g *raw chicken flesh, boneless*	4 *garlic cloves, finely chopped*
	1 tbsp *curry paste*
2 in/5 cm *green ginger, peeled and finely chopped*	1 tbsp *ground coriander*
	¼ pt/150 ml *coconut milk*

Sauce

2 heaped tbsp *crunchy peanut butter*	1 tbsp *lemon or lime juice*
	1 tsp *salt*
½ pt/300 ml *coconut milk*	*Cayenne or chilli pepper*

Cut the boneless chicken flesh into long strips, no more than 1 in/2.5 cm wide. Put into a bowl and add the very finely chopped green ginger and garlic to lightly coat each piece. Then add the high quality curry paste (or powder in extremis), the ground coriander and the coconut milk (about the consistency of single cream). Mix together with your hands and slightly squash the pieces of chicken to open the strands of flesh and allow the marinade to penetrate. Leave in a cool place at least 2 hours – in a refrigerator at least 4 hours.

At some convenient time, make up the sauce by mixing together the crunchy peanut butter, the coconut milk, lemon or lime juice, salt and the dash of something hot – cayenne or chilli pepper would be most authentic. Adjust seasoning and peanut butter – you want a sauce that flows but which will easily cling. Do not chill.

The chicken can now be threaded onto long skewers and grilled, roasted or barbecued until cooked through, which won't take long and can be done in small batches if you like.

The sauce should be put into individual dishes, one for each guest and it is usual to put a little puddle of chilli sauce into the middle of each. A salad of cucumber is both usual and welcome as a freshener to the palate which stimulates you to want more. Don't make the sauce too hot or you will not be able to enjoy your saté or the other food which accompanies it.

MALLARD WITH FIGS AND PINK PEPPERCORNS

Before reading on, be warned – pink peppercorns are not peppercorns at all but the berry of something called Florida Holly. Many people are allergic to them and some countries have forbidden their import. However, if you are sure you are not allergic to them, they do have a haunting and delicious flavour which marries well with mallard, the most delicious of wild birds. Mallards are now being farmed, I understand, and thus may become more common.

Serves 2

2 *fresh limes*	1 *mallard duck*
4-6 *fresh black figs*	1 *garlic clove, crushed*
1 heaped tsp *pink peppercorns*	*Butter, softened*
¼ pt/150 ml *rich red wine*	

Cut the peel from half a lime and reserve. Slice the figs thickly and evenly into a shallow dish, squeeze on the juice of 1 lime, sprinkle with the pink peppercorns, then cover with the red wine. Leave covered in a warm place at least 1 hour.

Prepare the duck for cooking by rubbing it well with the lime juice from the second lime. Cut up that lime and put into the bird's cavity with the crushed garlic clove. Smear the bird with a little softened butter, then roast in a preheated 425°F/220°C/Gas 7 oven for 30-40 minutes, depending on how rare you like the flesh. Remove from the oven, turn on its breast and keep warm. It will continue to tenderize for almost 20 minutes.

While the duck is roasting, or at any previous time, slice the peel from the half lime into the finest julienne strips, even going to the trouble of removing some of the pith from the peel first. Blanch these strips in boiling water until softened, but do not let them turn yellow. Rinse well under cold water and reserve.

Pour most of the fat from the roasting pan, add the juice only from the marinade, scrape up any crustings then reduce the liquid by half either in the pan or in a separate saucepan.

Cut the duck in half, and put onto warmed plates. Add the sliced figs and pink peppercorns to the sauce, heat through then pour around the duck. Scatter the sauce with the blanched lime peel.

If you are adept with sharp knives and hot food, the presentation is much better if you can quickly carve the two breasts off the bone in one piece. Serve them alone, leaving the legs for second portions. The plates will look neater and more elegant before and after you eat.

DUCK SUPREMES WITH LIME AND GREEN PEPPERCORN SAUCE

Green peppercorns are now seen everywhere. As they offer the cook an opportunity to give food a little heat combined with a lot of flavour, they are a more interesting adjunct to your repertoire than other hot spices.

Serves 2

4 lb/1.8 kg *duck, cleaned weight*	1 tsp *green peppercorns,*
6 fl oz/175 ml *rich red wine*	*lightly crushed*
4 fl oz/115 ml *vodka*	1 oz/25 g *butter*
2 *juicy limes*	

Remove the breasts in one piece from the duck; this is easiest if you first trim away the neck skin and cut out the wishbone. Use a very sharp knife and angle it always towards the carcass and solid pieces of flesh will come away easily. Trim into a neat shape. The remaining wings, back thighs and legs are just right for Chinese Salted Duck (see Chapter 3).

Using the same very sharp knife cut an even criss-cross pattern through the skin and the fat of both supremes. Put these into a small shallow dish in which they can lie flat side by side. Add the wine, vodka, the juice of the limes and the lightly crushed green peppercorns. Leave in the marinade in a cool but not cold place for 12 hours or more, turning the breasts from time to time.

At some stage, take the peel off one of the limes very thinly and cut into the thinnest possible strips. Throw these into boiling water for just 2 minutes, less if they seem about to lose their essential greenness. Put them under running cold water to cool rapidly.

When you are ready to eat, pour the marinade off the duck

and into a small saucepan, then reduce it until only 3 or 4 dessertspoons remain. Keep warm.

Have your grill at maximum heat. Put the supremes under it skin side down until the unprotected flesh is sealed, then turn over and cook at high heat until the squares of skin sizzle at the edges. Turn down the heat and continue to cook another 10-12 minutes. If the flesh is not served rare it will be tough.

Put the breasts to one side to settle for at least 5 minutes. They will not cool unduly and will develop extra tenderness.

Reheat the reduced sauce then whisk in the butter piece by piece. Quickly slice the breasts crosswise into four or five pieces each. Divide the sauce between two plates, place the duck atop the sauce and scatter the dish with the green lime peel. Vegetables or a salad should be served on a separate platter.

GREEN PEPPERCORN AND CORIANDER TUNA

Most of the recipes in this book are new ones, but there are some from previous books I must include. This is one of them, deserving a place in any book for its really original flavour. The fresh coriander leaf is quite important but if you really do not like the bitter flavour, parsley is nice enough.

This recipe would serve six to eight people as a starter or twice that many as part of a buffet. Because the fish is uncooked, take care to keep it as cool as possible and do not let it sit around in a warm kitchen but serve it directly from the refrigerator.

1½ lb/675 g *fresh or frozen tuna*	*in brine*
6-8 *fresh limes*	1 *bunch fresh coriander leaves*
1 *small can green peppercorns*	¼ pt/150 ml *dry white wine*

The weight of tuna is that of flesh devoid of all bone, skin and so on. Ideally it should be in two fillets prepared by your fishmonger, but, as fresh tuna is usually sold frozen, you may have to take it home and butcher it yourself later. It is easier to do when only half defrosted for the firmness of flesh means you can cut it thinly and accurately.

Either way, cut each fillet in half lengthwise, then cut each of those across their middles making four approximately even pieces. Trim neatly. Using a very sharp knife and much patience, cut thin slices from each piece along its length. Once this is done to all the fish, take an earthenware dish that will hold them all, and make a first layer of the tuna slices.

Squeeze juice from the limes over them, sprinkle with some of the flavoured brine from the can of peppercorns, crush half a dozen peppercorns and distribute them and then cover lightly with roughly chopped coriander.

Make another layer of fish, at right angles to the first one, which allows the marinade to penetrate and flavour as before. Continue layering until all the fish is used. Pour in white wine so the marinade (essentially a mixture of lime juice, peppercorn brine and wine) just covers the fish. Cover and refrigerate for at least 10 hours, then drain off the liquid and arrange the tuna on chilled plates with just a little brown bread and butter, a sprig of coriander and a thin slice of lime if you have any left over.

Because this is marinated in acid, the flesh will be opaque, unlike in salt-pickled recipes where the flesh retains its translucency.

In the half dozen times I have made this I have varied the peppercorns or the amount of lime juice according to what I felt like; you can do the same simply by putting your finger into the completed marinade and adjusting it, something you could never do for a marinade that included raw meat.

SOURED CREAM

Soured cream brought commercially is homogenized single cream that has been thickened and soured by the action of a carefully controlled culture. Never substitute double or single cream that has soured in your refrigerator, or elsewhere, as there is no knowing what sort of bacteria has caused the changes.

Soured cream can be used in any course of a meal, mixes with most vegetables and, when sprinkled with sugar, with most fruits as well. Use as a substitute for cream in any dish that requires its addition to finish a sauce. You'll find it popping up in a number of recipes throughout this book, but here are some special ones.

BAKED FISH IN SOURED CREAM

Serves 4

1½ lb/675 g *potatoes*
At least 1 oz/25 g *butter, melted*
1 *garlic clove, finely chopped*
3 tsp *dried dill weed*

1½ lb/675 g *haddock or cod, cubed*
Salt and freshly ground black pepper
½ pt/300 ml *soured cream*
Mixed hot and sweet paprika powder

Peel the potatoes and place in a pan of cold, salted water. Bring to a boil and cook for 20 minutes.

Drain and slice the potatoes thickly. Butter the base of a shallow casserole dish and place the potatoes in a layer on the base. Pour over the melted butter, sprinkle over the garlic and half the dill. Place the fish on top and sprinkle over the remaining dill. Season with salt and freshly ground black pepper. Cover with soured cream and sprinkle generously with paprika. Bake at 350°F/180°C/Gas 4 for 25 minutes or until fish is just cooked through.

CHICKEN WITH SOURED CREAM AND OLIVES

Serves 2

2 *boneless chicken breasts*
Olive oil (see method)
3 dessertsp *lemon juice*
1 tsp each *cumin, coriander and*

hot paprika
12 *green olives*
¼ pt/150 ml *soured cream*

Marinate the chicken breasts (ask for supremes) in 3 dessert-spoons olive oil, the lemon juice and spices for 2 hours.

Pit, blanch and halve the green olives. Sprinkle over the marinated chicken. Cover with soured cream and dribble over about 1 tablespoon of olive oil. Bake at 350°F/180°C/Gas 4 for 15-20 minutes.

Option   Black olives are just as good in this dish, which I based on an idea from Morocco. Serve each breast on a bed of rice, which should be buttery and well flavoured with much saffron.

RABBIT IN SOURED CREAM AND MUSTARD

The combination of soured cream and a fairly strong mustard counteracts the rather sweet taste of rabbit flesh. The mustard's power cooks out amazingly quickly, so if you find you've added too much, just let the combination cook on a little longer.

Serves 4

1½-2 lb/675-900 g *rabbit meat, boneless*	¾ pt/425 ml *chicken stock, wine or cider*
Flour, seasoned	4 *fresh thyme sprigs*
Olive oil	4 tbsp *moutarde de Meaux*
Butter	¼ pt/150 ml *soured cream*

Cut your rabbit in nice chunks, then toss it in some seasoned flour. Brown slightly in equal generous quantities of oil and butter (remember there'll be no fat on the rabbit), then add the stock, wine or cider or a combination of the stock and alcohol (this really isn't as nice if made with stock-cube stock, but it's still very good). Lie the sprigs of thyme on top, cover and simmer for 45 minutes, stirring from time to time.

Five minutes or so before serving, remove the thyme and stir in the mustard and soured cream. Bring back to simmering point and cook gently until the sauce is lovely and creamy and shiny. Check for flavour and consistency; you might need more mustard. This can be kept hot beautifully, if covered, and tends to improve if anything. It's extra good with a crisp baked potato on the side and one bright green vegetable.

SOURED CREAM SOUFFLÉ

Serves 6

¾ pt/425 ml *soured cream*	1 tsp *vanilla essence*
6 *eggs, separated*	3 oz/85 g *sugar*
2 oz/50 g *flour*	

Beat the soured cream until frothy. Gradually beat in the egg yolks, flour, vanilla and sugar. It will look suspiciously runny, but this is normal. Whisk the egg whites until stiff but not dry. Fold into the soured cream mixture and turn into a buttered 2-2½ pint/1.1-1.4 litre soufflé dish. Cook at 375°F/190°C/Gas 5 for 45 minutes when the soufflé will be well risen but deliciously creamy in the centre.

Served traditionally in the Ukraine with sweetened cream, I think that a warmed fruit purée might be more acceptable to most people. This is easily done by melting jam sharpened with brandy, lemon or orange juice. Either way this really is fabulous.

BAKED LIVER WITH MUSTARD AND LEMON

Seedy mustards, particularly those made with wine, are wonderful complements to a great number of foods. When cooked the heat tends to dissipate leaving complicated but soft flavours. Use mustard with fish too; puréed with leeks it makes a stunning sauce for fish.

Serves 4

2 lb/900 g *liver, in one piece*	1 *fresh thyme sprig*
1 oz/25 g *pork fat or lard*	2 *lemons*
3 oz/85 g *butter*	1 dessertsp *Dijon seed mustard*
2 *onions, chopped*	*Lemon and parsley, to decorate*

You can use cheap pigs' liver for this recipe, in fact it was recommended to me. I generally find it too strong unless it has been soaked for some time in milk – overnight even. It is a technique which improves even the milder livers like lambs'.

Pat the liver dry. Melt the fat and butter in a heavy casserole big enough to take the liver in one piece. Brown the onions well. Add the liver and brown on all sides.

Scrape the onions all together to form a layer on the base of the casserole. Rest the liver on this bed of onions and sprinkle with the leaves from the thyme. Cover and put the casserole in a 350°F/180°C/Gas 4 oven and bake 30-40 minutes depending on how pink you like liver to be.

Meanwhile, peel one of the lemons very thinly, cut the peel into strips and blanch these in boiling water for 5 minutes. Drain.

Squeeze the juice from both lemons. Once the liver is cooked, take it out and rest it on a warm serving dish back in the oven (with the heat off, of course).

Add the lemon juice, the blanched peel, and the mustard to the contents of the pan and cook over heat for 3 minutes. Pour the sauce around the liver and decorate with more lemon and parsley. Slice at the table and serve with boiled or mashed potatoes.

CHINESE PORK WITH GOOSEBERRY SAUCE

The one thing the Chinese are fanatical about is using fresh seasonal vegetables, and they are also very keen on the use of spices with meat.

This recipe should only be made for the few weeks of the year when gooseberries are available, but it is so remarkably good that I break my rules and make the sauce with frozen goose-berries when fresh ones are out of season.

Serves 4-6

2½ lb/generous kg *belly of pork* *(gross)*	1 tsp *ground allspice*
	1 tsp *ground cinnamon*
3 tbsp *soya sauce*	½ tsp *ground cloves*
2 tbsp *fresh lemon juice*	1 *large garlic clove*
2 tsp *chili sauce*	

Sauce

¼ pt/150 ml *bone stock*	1 lb/450 g *gooseberries, topped*
1½ tbsp *white sugar*	*and tailed*

Trim the bones and sinews from the meat to give you about 2 lb/900 g net weight, and save them. If the skin of the pork has not been scored, do so, deeply.

Make up a marinade by mixing together the liquids and spices, including the garlic. Pour this over the pork in a shallow dish and make sure the liquid gets into the scoring. Leave in a cool place for most of the day or overnight. Meanwhile, start preparing the sauce by boiling up the bones of the pork, even-tually reducing the liquid to a bare ¼ pint/150 ml.

Sit the meat on a rack in a roasting tray and put into a preheated 425°F/220°C/Gas 7 oven for 10 minutes then reduce to 350°F/180°C/Gas 4 for 30 minutes, plus an extra 5 minutes if the meat came directly from the refrigerator.

Once the meat is in the oven, rinse out the marinating dish with the pork stock so that it collects every bit of flavouring that remains. Into a saucepan put the white sugar and melt it over a gentle heat until a golden brown – do not let it really darken or it will be too bitter. Add the strained stock and keep warm.

Once the meat is cooked, put it on a warm plate, and add all the pan juices and brownings to the stock. Add the gooseberries and cook until starting to soften – just a couple of minutes. Push through a sieve and it is ready to serve.

Cut the meat along the scoring marks and serve with the sauce on the side.

SPICED MONKFISH

The use of red vermouth and spice with fish is something I pondered a long time, but when I first served it the vote was 'a triumph'. It works better if you can buy small tails, of only 8 oz/225 g each.

Serves 6

1 pt/575 ml *water*	½ *carrot*
4 *allspice berries*	½ *onion*
12 *coriander seeds*	*A handful of parsley stalks*
12 *white peppercorns*	3 lb/1.3 kg *monkfish tails*
2 *fresh bay leaves*	

Sauce

1½ oz/40 g *butter*	¼ pt/150 ml *double cream*
2 tbsp *flour*	4 oz/115 g *cap mushrooms,*
¼ pt/150 ml *red vermouth*	*very thinly sliced*
¼ pt/150 ml *white wine*	*Butter and nutmeg*

Simmer the water with the spices, bay, carrot, onion and parsley to start extracting their flavours. Prepare the monkfish by cutting off the discoloured membrane that surrounds the firm white flesh. Be brutal for the sake of the final appearance. Place the prepared fish in the well-flavoured stock, bring gently back to the simmer and poach 6-8 minutes; when the fish is cooked you will see the single central bone in the tail start to bend and come away from the flesh. Remove the tails and drain. Reduce the stock until just ¼ pint/150 ml.

If you have small monkfish tails, cut in half along the bones, giving two nicely shaped pieces, like giant scampi or Pacific prawns. Otherwise, cut large tails into generously sized portions. Put them to one side while you make the delicious sauce.

Melt the butter, stir in the flour and cook gently for a few minutes. Then stir in the ¼ pint/150 ml fish stock, the vermouth, wine and cream. Cook for 10 minutes at least, as this will improve the flavour even more, but do not let it reduce. Add the monkfish tails and the thinly sliced mushrooms.

Once the fish has been heated through in the sauce, check for flavour and consistency. A touch more cream will thicken the sauce; it is unlikely to be too thick as juices from the mushroom will have some diluting effect.

Serve the monkfish pieces onto warmed plates, then quickly beat a knob of butter into the sauce. Pour this around each portion and sprinkle with the merest dusting of nutmeg.

SPICED PLUM SAUCE

To make about 8 lb/3.6 kg

10 lb/4.5 kg *red-fleshed plums*	1 oz/25 g *ground allspice*
2 pt/generous litre *red wine vinegar*	1 oz/25 g *crushed black peppercorns*
2 lb/900 g *muscovado sugar*	¼-½ oz/7-15 g *ground ginger*
1 oz/25 g *ground cloves*	¼-½ oz/7-15 g *cayenne pepper*
2 *large onions chopped*	5-6 oz/150-175 g *salt*
1 oz/25 g *fresh garlic (optional)*	

The plums should be fully ripe and flavourful but avoid those that are softening too much. Chop them up roughly, but don't discard the stones and skins. Put all the ingredients into a preserving pan with the smaller amount of salt. Bring slowly to the boil and simmer for about 4 hours until well reduced.

Let the mixture cool somewhat then strain it through a colander (not a sieve), which will get rid of the stones but leave you with some texture, which I think is important.

Then taste and add extra salt, ginger and cayenne if you think this is necessary. Bottle whilst warm.

Option There is a remarkable French version in which you use two-thirds plums and one-third tomatoes; otherwise the proportions and ingredients are the same.

CINNAMON-CHERRY SAUCE

Now that imports and new varieties mean the cherry season is so much longer than it used to be, it is nice to have some different ways to enjoy them. This sauce is especially good with duck, chicken or ham or cooked bacon and, if you were to find some well-flavoured cherries at Christmas time, would be a welcome accompaniment to the turkey or goose.

To make 4 servings

¾ pt/425 ml *red or white wine*	1 *fresh bay leaf*
2 in/5 cm *cinnamon stick*	1 lb/450 g *red cherries, pitted*
2 *whole cloves*	2 level tbsp *cornflour*
1 tsp *grated orange or lemon rind*	*Sugar or redcurrant jelly, to taste*

Put the wine, spices, citrus rind and bay leaf into a small saucepan and simmer covered for 5 minutes. Then let cool, covered, for another 15 minutes. Meanwhile pit the cherries – do this over a bowl so that you catch the juice.

Strain the spiced wine, add the cherry juice then mix the cornflour to a paste with a few spoonfuls of the liquid. Bring the liquid back to the boil, remove from the heat then whisk in the cornflour and heat gently until thickened and smooth. Cook gently for 2 or 3 minutes until the floury taste has disappeared, then add the cherries and heat through just enough to soften them without destroying the colour of the skins.

Now taste and if it is too sharp, add a few teaspoons of sugar or of redcurrant jelly, which is a nice addition. For something more special, brandy or black rum might also be stirred in, and some knobs of butter will enrich it marvellously. I think this is better for being served warm rather than piping hot.

Options   For greater richness of flavour, it might be made with a Cyprus port type of wine or a cheap port wine – even a mixture of wine and port would make an appreciable difference.

If you can only buy the sweeter and blander black cherries, you may find you need more citrus or a dash of brandy.

YOGHURT SAUCES AND SUBSTITUTIONS

So much is being written on cooking with yoghurt I am loathe to add further to the deluge. Suffice to say that it will naturally reduce your calories and cholesterol intake if it is substituted for cream, more so if made from low-fat milk. It is seen more and more often in salad dressings, which seems perfectly extraordinary to me.

The most important uses of yoghurt I have discovered are the following.

To make a less dangerous substitute for double cream, for savoury or fruit dishes, smooth the lumps from cottage cheese by sieving, then fold in an equal amount of plain yoghurt. (To make a substitute for single cream, mix de-lumped cottage cheese with milk until the consistency is as you wish.)

If you insist on using yoghurt in hot sauces and, naturally, wish to avoid the yoghurt clotting and curdling, first whisk in to liquify it, then mix in a little dissolved cornflour and heat, stirring constantly. This is usually known as stabilizing and is a much more reliable method than the use of egg.

II Salads and Mayonnaise Sauces

Few delicatessen customers could exist without relying at some time on the contents of the chilled salad counters. There seems no end to the relentless creativity of the manufacturers of these standbys, no ingredient that has not been combined with some other in the hope of catching your eye. But in the end these salads are limited by the need for them to stay crisp, fresh and good tasting for several days or more. Many expensive or subtle ingredients are not suited to these demands, in other salads an insistence on the inclusion of onion means that after 24 hours most of them taste the same.

One of the best ideas of all in this book is the first set of salads, based on canned beans. Instead of the eternal combination of several contrasting types, I have used a purée of one sort as the sauce for another. Excellent as a salad, a main course or a dip.

A terrific way to disguise your reliance on the delicatessen counter, if indeed you hanker for subterfuge, is to buy a portion or two of a complicated and colourful salad and then to dilute it by mixing it into cold pasta, a potato or a rice salad. It will look and taste far more fabulous than you could have run up from scratch for the same cost. And talking about potato salads, whatever you do and however you like them, always toss the potatoes in a little oil and vinegar while still warm; you can even add garlic at this stage. Then once cold they will taste terrific, whether mixed with soured cream or mayonnaise.

Canned potatoes are good for salads, but few other canned vegetables are really suited for salads. Some exceptions are artichoke bottoms and hearts, hearts of palm, whole kernel sweet corn, red peppers and, for good contrast of texture and crunch, Chinese bamboo shoots or water chestnuts. Far better to use frozen vegetables, of which haricots verts are the best.

Fresh or frozen vegetables which have been only lightly cooked in a little chicken stock, mixed into a thick, rich mayonnaise, perhaps with some herbs, and then topped with cold turkey will make Boxing Day's leftovers worth waiting for.

MIXED BEAN SALADS

Although they are always delicious, salads of contrasting beans have become rather too common to be special. Here is an orginal way to combine two or more types of cooked bean – you purée one of the types and use as a sauce for the others. All the cans specified in these recipes are 1 lb/450 g or thereabouts; a small variation will not matter.

CHICK PEAS WITH SPINACH TUNALLENI SAUCE

Serves 4

1 can *cannellini beans, drained*	*drained weight*
8 oz/225 g *canned tuna, drained*	*Salt*
Olive oil (see method)	1 tbsp *lemon juice*
2 *garlic cloves*	1 can *chick peas, drained*
4 oz/115 g *spinach, cooked and*	*Nutmeg*

Put the drained cannellini beans, the tuna, 2 tablespoons of olive oil, garlic and very well-drained spinach into a liquidizer and blend extremely well. If you have a little trouble getting the purée to start forming, add a spoon or more of oil.

Add salt and lemon juice to taste. For the sake of presentation, do not mix the chick peas into the sauce, but spread the sauce and arrange the chick peas in the centre. Sprinkle with nutmeg, and a little more olive oil.

Options   You might use canned pink salmon instead of tuna, in which case only use 1 clove of garlic and sprinkle with fresh thyme.

To extend this delicatessen dish further, some tuna or salmon could be mixed with the chick peas too.

RED ON RED CHILI SALAD

Serves 4

2 cans *red kidney beans, drained*	1 dessertsp *red wine vinegar*
Olive oil	*Lemon juice*
2-3 tsp *chili seasoning*	1-2 *fresh chilli peppers (optional)*
½ tsp *salt*	

Purée 1 can of beans with 1 tablespoon olive oil. Add the chili seasoning (check the label to ensure it is a mixture of chilli, cumin and other ingredients and not just cayenne or chilli pepper). Complete flavouring with salt and red wine vinegar.

Toss the drained contents of the other can of beans in a little more olive oil and lemon juice plus, if you like, some very finely chopped and seeded fresh chilli peppers.

If you find you have made this too hot, top with soured cream. Cubes of smoked sausage such as kabanos, or of smoked ham, would extend the top layer nicely.

PAPRIKA AND BEAN SALAD

Serves 4

1 can *red kidney beans, drained*	*Lemon juice*
2 tsp *sweet paprika*	*Salt, to taste*
1 tsp *hot paprika*	1 can *cannellini beans, drained*
1 small can *red peppers, drained*	*Olive oil*
¼ pt/150 ml *soured cream*	

Purée the red kidney beans with the paprika powders, red peppers and soured cream. Complete flavouring with 1 dessertspoon lemon juice and salt.

Toss the cannellini beans in olive oil and a further squeeze of lemon juice and arrange on top of the sauce. You could add parsley to the sauce for colour and extra flavour.

CHICK PEA AND FETTA SALAD

Serves 4

2 cans *chick peas, drained*	1 tbsp *lemon juice*
3 tbsp *olive oil*	6 oz/175 g *fetta cheese*
2 *garlic cloves*	*Dried oregano*

Purée 1 can of chick peas, oil, garlic, lemon juice and 2 oz/50 g of the cheese. Mix the other can of peas with remaining crumbled Fetta, olive oil and lemon juice and sprinkle with oregano.

THUNDER AND LIGHTNING SALAD

Whereas Cornwall has a pudding of this name with includes molasses and creamy custard, the Italians have a salad which mixes chick peas and pasta. My version is rather more fun, I think, and can be multiplied as much as you like.

Serves 4

4 oz/115 g *pasta shapes,*	*Black pepper*
dry weight	1 can *chick peas, drained*
1½ tbsp *lemon juice*	1 *garlic clove*
4½ tbsp *olive oil*	1 oz/25 g *grated Parmesan cheese*
Fresh herbs (see method)	

Cook the pasta in plenty of boiling salted water, drain and then pat dry in a towel. While still warm, toss in about ½ tablespoon each of lemon juice and oil, and lots of fresh herbs – whatever you have handy, even simple parsley – and some black pepper.

While it is cooling, purée the chick peas with the remaining oil and lemon juice, the garlic and grated Parmesan cheese. Chill well. Serve the pasta shapes on a bed of the chick pea and cheese purée.

Cold chicken, pink salmon, fingers of ham or tongue or some mixture would all feel at home in the pasta part of this. This is nicer cold than hot, when it is very bland.

LENTIL AND BUTTER BEAN SALAD

Serves 4

1 can *lentils, drained*	1 can *butter beans, drained*
3 tbsp *olive oil*	1 can *frankfurters, drained*
1½ tbsp *lemon juice*	½ tsp *dried sweet basil*
1 *garlic clove*	

Purée the lentils with 2 tablespoons of the oil, 1 tablespoon of the lemon juice, and garlic. Toss the butter beans and frankfurters, sliced diagonally, with remaining olive oil, and lemon juice and the sweet basil. Spread the lentil sauce across a plate, and pile the beans and frankfurters in the middle.

COLESLAW SALADS

You don't need a recipe to make coleslaw, just some decent cabbage, a sharp knife and some mayonnaise spiced up with mustard and/or garlic.

But that simple combination of coleslaw bought from shops can easily be made your own. Do try to persuade your delicatessen only to sell coleslaw that does not contain raw onion, for this quickly sours and taints the salad. If you like an onion flavour then toss in some finely chopped chives at the last minute, which at least has the excuse of improving the salad's appearance.

The best improvements to bought coleslaw, which is sweet and fresh, are:

More mayonnaise, for yours is bound to be a better quality than that used (do I need to say never to use salad cream – for anything?); soured cream; grated orange peel; very finely chopped juniper berries or finely chopped or crushed pineapple perhaps combined with some gin which enhances the flavour of both; a little chili sauce; currants and toasted nuts; a touch of vinegar and some caraway seeds; grated carrot and/or celery; beansprouts to lighten the texture and currants, raisins, nuts and carrot for appearance and contrast of texture; finely chop equal quantities of garlic and green ginger with chili sauce, or some soya; a few prawns, mussels or baby clams plus cucumber; or cubes of smoked or garlic sausage, such as kabanos.

MAYONNAISE SAUCES

A quantity of mayonnaise, bottled or home-made, is an excellent thing to have in your refrigerator at all times, for it is the basis of many simple sauces and garnishes throughout the year. There are now some flavoured versions of the commercial mayonnaises, which indicate how easy it is to give a twist to simple foods with mayonnaise.

In all these recipes, please be careful when adding liquid ingredients, for although it is sometimes nice to have rather runny, mayonnaise-based sauces, this is only fine when you have planned it that way. Mayonnaise can differ so violently from maker to maker that the following proportions are simply a guide to what I could do to the rather thick version I make; with commercial varieties you will certainly have to proceed with caution. However, you will always arrive at something worthwhile.

After the basic flavouring of mayonnaises, I list some of the sauces I have made recently; each will make between ½ pint/ 300 ml and ¾ pint/425 ml, but don't be afraid to add more mayonnaise or more of another major ingredient to get a texture you like, for these are simply guides to things that go together.

Other flavoured mayonnaises will be found in the salad sections, especially poultry and seafood salads.

OIL, VINEGAR AND STORE-CUPBOARD MAYONNAISE

In the same way olive oil is used to give flavour and sumptuousness to mayonnaise made with cheaper blander oils, you should consider using some of the rarer nut oils to give individuality. The magical affinity of tomatoes and walnuts is enhanced by serving them topped with mayonnaise flavoured with walnut oil, and perhaps stirring in some very finely chopped nuts, too.

Hazelnut oil and virgin-pressed almond oil can also give an extraordinary but subtle lift to a mayonnaise even if served with something as simple as cold French beans, artichoke or asparagus.

Remember when you are making mayonnaise you can increase the eventual quantity dramatically by diluting with water or vinegar or wine as you proceed: when the mayonnaise is very thick, keep beating, but dribble in water until it is much softer then, if you like, add a little flavoured vinegar or citrus juice. Proceed with more oil. There is no reason why you should not substitute wine, vermouth or some spirit or liqueur, or a balanced mixture, for the water.

It is extraordinarily simple to flavour mayonnaise with spices or herbs, but ensure you first heat the spices somewhat to encourage the flavours to develop and that you leave herb combinations to blend for some hours, preferably out of the refrigerator. To start you off on this exciting road, I suggest you use an Eastern Mediterranean combination of equal parts of ground cumin, coriander and cinnamon, which is also a revelation upon hard-boiled eggs.

CUCUMBER AND GREEN GINGER MAYONNAISE

¼ pt/150 ml *mayonnaise*	*yoghurt*
½ *cucumber, small to medium*	1 oz/25 g *green ginger*
2½ fl oz/75 ml *soured cream or*	*Salt and pepper*

Peel the cucumber, cut it in half lengthwise, scoop out the seeds and cut the two halves into slices, which will give you half-moons of flesh. Cook these in boiling water until just starting to soften then plunge into very cold water, when they will turn green and translucent. Drain well. Stir the soured cream or thick yoghurt into the thick mayonnaise. Peel the green ginger, cut it up roughly and press its juice out through a garlic press into the mayonnaise until well flavoured. Add salt and pepper and fold in the cucumber.

Good with cold fish, with potatoes and vegetables.

MINTED VERMOUTH MAYONNAISE

½ pt/300 ml *mayonnaise*   4 tbsp *mint leaves*
4 tbsp *white vermouth*   *Black pepper*

Add the white vermouth and fresh mint leaves plus a little black pepper to the mayonnaise. A small squeeze of garlic is also good and you might need to sharpen the flavour with some lemon juice or tarragon vinegar.

Good with fish, excellent with eggs and tongue or chicken.

RED PEPPER AND OLIVE MAYONNAISE

¼ pt/150 ml *mayonnaise*   ½ small can *red pimentoes*
4 oz/115 g *olives*   *Tabasco or chili sauce*

Make a purée of half the olives – green or black or a mixture – and the drained red pimentoes. Finely chop the remaining olives. Fold both into the mayonnaise and, if you like, spike with a tiny drop of Tabasco or rather more of a milder chili sauce.

Good on barbecued lamb and, especially, hamburgers.

RASPBERRY MAYONNAISE

¼ pt/150 ml *mayonnaise*   *(see Chapter 12)*
3 tbsp *raspberry vinegar*   4 oz/115 g *raspberries*

Reduce the raspberry vinegar to just 1 tablespoon. Blend into the mayonnaise together with the fresh raspberries which have been lightly crushed. (If you have to use frozen raspberries, ensure they are very well drained indeed.)

This simple sauce is superb with ham and poultry, extraordinarily good with green beans or blanched heads of cauliflower. It is changed but enhanced by adding ground hazelnuts or walnuts, too.

Options   Naturally blackberries or currants can also be used, particularly if you use vinegar flavoured with them.

WALNUT MAYONNAISE

¼ pt/150 ml *mayonnaise*
2 oz/50 g *ground walnuts*
2 tbsp *walnut oil*

1 tbsp *vinegar (see method)*
1 *garlic clove*

Fold into the mayonnaise the ground walnuts, walnut oil, a sympathetic vinegar (say, tarragon, cider or raspberry), plus the juice of the medium clove of garlic.

Although wonderful with veal or chicken, one of my experimenters found it specially good on cold cooked vegetables, particularly cold sliced fennel. I imagine it is quite as good on the raw ones. I also think this would be nice with the addition of some grated orange rind.

CELERY AND TOASTED HAZELNUT MAYONNAISE

¼ pt/150 ml *mayonnaise*
8 oz/225 g *celery, canned*
2 oz/50 g *hazelnuts, toasted and*

crushed
1 *garlic clove*
Black pepper

Drain the celery, purée it, and then strain. Mix with the toasted crushed hazelnuts, garlic and a little black pepper, and then fold into the mayonnaise. You could add extra mayonnaise or some lightly whipped double cream to increase the bulk if needed.

Naturally good with fish and chicken, this is also a winner on cold pasta.

KIDNEY BEAN BARBECUE MAYONNAISE

At least ¼ pt/150 ml *mayonnaise*
1 lb/450 g *red kidney beans,*
    canned

1 tbsp *red wine vinegar*
1 tbsp *lemon juice*
2-3 tbsp *chili seasoning*

Drain the red kidney beans then mash or purée together with the red wine vinegar, lemon juice and chili seasoning (*not* chilli powder which is simply cayenne pepper). Fold into the mayonnaise.

WALDORF MAYONNAISE

¼ pt/150 ml *mayonnaise*
8 oz/225 g *Bramley apples,*
       trimmed, cored and peeled
1 tbsp *water*

2 tbsp *walnut oil*
Sugar
1 tbsp *fresh mint leaves, chopped*

Cook Bramley apples with the water and walnut oil until soft and fairly dry. Strain, then add up to 1 dessertspoon of sugar, if you think this is necessary. Mix with the chopped mint leaves and fold into the thick mayonnaise.

Very good with cold poultry, especially turkey. Some toasted, flaked almonds would be a good garnish.

CLAM MAYONNAISE

¼ pt/150 ml *mayonnaise*
3-5 oz/85-150 g *clams, canned*
4 tbsp *double cream*

1 *garlic clove, crushed*
1 dessertsp *brandy*

Fold the drained clams into the mayonnaise with the double cream, garlic and brandy. Some chopped parsley could be added and so could the slightest dash of Tabasco.

This is good on tomatoes or on pasta, hot or cold.

PEAR MAYONNAISE

¼ pt/150 ml *mayonnaise*
6 oz/175 g *pears, peeled and cored*
1 tsp *tomato purée*

1 tsp *tarragon vinegar*
½ *garlic clove (optional)*

Mash the net weight of ripe pears with the tomato purée, tarragon vinegar and, if you like, a very little garlic. Fold into the thick mayonnaise.

Wonderful with almost anything, and could be given texture by the addition of chopped walnuts.

YOGHURT OR SOURED CREAM MAYONNAISE

A simple lift of flavour can be given by folding yoghurt or soured cream into mayonnaise. This may be served just as it is or flavoured in most of the ways above. Dill weed always goes well with the combination, as does chopped mint. Even the subtle addition of horseradish cream will give interest – try a soured cream and horseradish mayonnaise on hot or cold beetroot, or on cold smoked trout, or on hot-smoked trout (see Chapter 2).

YOGHURT CHILI DRESSING

4 dessertsp *plain yoghurt*	1-2 tsp *chili sauce*
4 dessertsp *mayonnaise*	Salt
1 tsp *chili seasoning*	

Lightly mix the yoghurt and mayonnaise, add the chili seasoning and sauce, then a pinch of salt if you think it needs it. Be most careful that you use chili seasoning and not just chilli pepper or cayenne; chili seasoning includes cumin and oregano (look on the side of the packaging for confirmation).

This hot-cool dressing was invented for a mixture of tomato and orange slices on a bed of crisp chicory, but would be nice on a simple salad of thickly sliced, rich red tomatoes.

RASPBERRY GINGER DRESSING

Not a hint of mayonnaise in sight, but this is very special!

3 dessertsp *mild salad oil*	½ in/1.25 cm *peeled ginger root*
1 dessertsp *raspberry vinegar*	Salt
(see Chapter 12)	

Mix the oil and vinegar and crush the juice *only* from the ginger directly into the mixture. Finish with a little salt.

Use on cucumber, sprigs of raw cauliflower, or a mixture of sliced strawberries and cucumber.

Red wine vinegar or strawberry vinegar might be substituted for the raspberry vinegar.

COLD MEAT AND POULTRY SALADS

When faced with wanting to do something interesting with a cold chicken, turkey, ham and so on, rather than arrange bits and pieces around a plate, mix them all together and bind with mayonnaise.

Almost anything that would appear together on a plate can be combined in such salads. By substituting some of the mayonnaise binding for whipped cream or good, plain yoghurt, you can add even more individuality.

Whether ham, chicken, turkey, tongue or smoked sausage, the basis for making any salad bound with mayonnaise is the same. The flesh must be in big pieces, so ask your delicatessen to slice ham, for instance, at least ½ in/1.25 cm thick. Thicker is even better, then you can make generous chunks. A proportion of 1-1½ lb/450-675 g meat to ½-¾ pint/300-425 ml mayonnaise is a good basis for planning your shopping list.

Choose ingredients on the basis of a contrast of texture and flavour. Nuts always finish such a salad marvellously, especially if they have been lightly toasted.

Neither should you be shy about including a little alcohol in the mayonnaise. If you were to make a salad from cold pork, mixed with a little apple, celery and chopped walnut, dash in some Calvados. A salad of prawns, cucumber, chicken and avocado would only be improved by brandy, doubly so if there were cream in the dressing.

Fruit juice can also be used. Some unsweetened pineapple juice would certainly help a salad of cubed ham, pineapple pieces, some kernel corn and small amount of green or red pepper.

Tongue is very good with orange; a refreshing and unusual salad is made by mixing cubes of tongue with some ham or chicken, some peeled and seeded very ripe tomato, some segments of orange. Add a little grated orange rind to the mayonnaise and just enough chili sauce to add a bite rather than to reflavour.

TARRAGON PEAR CHICKEN

Serves 4-6

---

12 oz/350 g *ripe pears*   ½ pt/300 ml *mayonnaise*
⅛ pt/75 ml *tarragon vinegar*   1-2 *garlic cloves*
1-1½ lb/450-675 g *cold chicken*

Peel and core the pears then slice them neatly lengthwise. Cover with the vinegar, ensuring all faces are moistened. Pull the chicken flesh into generous, meaty pieces.

Drain the vinegar from the pears and stir 2 tablespoons into the mayonnaise (reserve any that is left over, or add extra vinegar if the pears have absorbed too much). Squeeze the juice of the garlic into the mayonnaise. Gently fold the pears and the chicken into the flavoured mayonnaise then leave at least 4 hours for the flavours to develop.

If after that time the tarragon is not quite noticeable enough, dribble in more vinegar, using that reserved if there was some.

Serve with lots of bay flavoured cold rice. If you have a garden full of herbs, scatter the lot with some roughly chopped fresh tarragon, basil or lemon balm.

This recipe is also good made with turkey, and as you usually have rather more of this meat left over, double the above quantities with equanimity.

CHICKEN AND AVOCADO IN CHILI MAYONNAISE

Serves 4-6

8-12 oz/225-350 g *avocado flesh*   ¾ pt/425 ml *mayonnaise*
8-12 *orange segments*   *Chili sauce, to taste*
1 or 2 *garlic cloves*   1-1½ lb/450-675 g *cold chicken*

The peeled and stoned avocado halves should be cut into slices lengthwise or across, according to your aesthetics. When peeling them, do try to include as much as possible of the brilliant green layer immediately under the skin. Ideally, peel the avocados by simply pulling the skin back. Otherwise use a knife as sparingly as possible.

Keep the orange segments whole but remove as much of the membrane as possible. Mandarins, tangerines and other small citrus fruits you have on hand would do as well.

Squeeze the garlic into the mayonnaise then add chili sauce. These sauces vary enormously, so try to use one which includes plums as they have much more flavour than those exclusively of chilli pepper, which is unadulterated cayenne pepper. 1-2 dessertspoons might be more than enough sauce for most people. Fold in the other ingredients, check again for flavour, then chill for 4 hours.

Although a rice salad would be good with this, it might be simpler to serve a plain white bean salad, and the blandness would certainly help if you had overdone the chilli.

CHICKEN WITH MANGO IN A GREEN PEPPER SAUCE

Serves 4 as a main course; more as a starter

¾-1 lb/350-450 g *cold chicken*	1 or 2 *mangoes*
12 oz/350 g *green peppers, whole*	¼ pt/150 ml *mayonnaise*
1 or 2 *fresh chilli peppers*	¼ pt/150 ml *soured cream*

The chicken should be denuded of skin and pulled into long generous pieces. Cut the stalks from the green peppers and discard the seeds. Slice thinly and plunge into boiling water until they soften but still remain a very bright green. Drain and, while still warm, put into a food processor or liquidizer and make into a purée with the fresh chilli peppers. I recommend you remove the seeds from these small peppers first or the results will be too fiery for most – use rubber gloves so you do not run the risk of getting the painful oils in your eyes. If the peppers are not making a nice purée, add a touch of white wine of milk or some of the sauce ingredients. Force the purée through a sieve for the best possible texture.

Slice the mangoes into strips or into cubes and gently mix with the chicken flesh. Fold the mayonnaise and soured cream together then blend in the green pepper sauce. Pour over the chicken and mango and leave in a cool place for 2 hours; serve chilled but not directly from the refrigerator.

PEACH CHICKEN

Serves 4-6

2 tsp *cumin powder*	6-8 oz/175-225 g *peach chutney*
2 tsp *ground coriander*	1-1½ lb/450-675 g *cold chicken*
¾ pt/425 ml *mayonnaise*	2-3 *fresh peaches*

Warm the spices and mix lightly into the mayonnaise. Stir in the chutney then the chicken pieces. Plunge the fresh peaches into boiling water for a minute, then peel and slice evenly and thickly. Fold quickly into the mixture. Chill for 4 hours.

This lends itself especially to the inclusion of yoghurt or whipped cream in the dressing and/or a sprinkle of toasted hazelnuts or almonds on top. If you serve cold rice, make sure it is cooked with several bay leaves.

SEAFOOD SALADS

A salad of seafood and mayonnaise alone will be rather expensive but such accompaniments as avocado, cold pasta, potato, poached cucumber, raw or cooked red and green peppers, tropical fruit, eggs and fresh herbs can all expand the quantities. When using seafood from cans, reserve the brine and incorporate some of that into the mayonnaise. Many of the previous meat or poultry salads could also include or feature seafood.

SALADE PANACHE

1 lb/450 g *large prawns,*	2 *fresh limes*
fresh or frozen	¼ pt/150 ml *double cream*
At least 12 *quails' eggs*	½ pt/300 ml *mayonnaise*
3-4 *Kiwi fruit*	2 dessertsp *dill tips*

Defrost the frozen prawns overnight in their bag in the refrigerator. If the quails' eggs have been bought ready prepared, so much the better. If they are fresh, cover them with cold water, bring slowly to the boil, turn off the heat, leave exactly 1 minute, then cool them under running water. When quite cold, shell, then cut in half lengthwise. Peel the kiwi fruit, cut into segments lengthwise and bathe in lime juice.

Whip the cream lightly and fold into the mayonnaise. Drain the prawns well. Fold them and the kiwi fruit into the dressing together with the dill. Taste and adjust the lime and dill flavours then carefully incorporate the quails' eggs. Leave to chill for 4 hours.

Serve on leaves of bright red radiccio or on raw spinach or on some other combination. Of course, if you have, or can afford more eggs, they would make a fabulous garnish or could also be incorporated.

If you have had the time to prepare them, serve this salad in or on pastry cases or sandwiched into feuilletés.

PINK PRAWN AND POTATO SALAD

1 lb/450 g *small new potatoes*	½ pt/300 ml *soured cream*
1 dessertsp *white wine vinegar*	3 tsp *creamed horseradish*
3 dessertsp *olive oil*	2 tsp *tomato purée*
3 dessertsp *chopped fresh dill*	*Salt, to taste*
(or half as much dried dill)	4 oz/115 g *peeled cooked prawns*

Scrub the potatoes but do not peel them. Cut in half lengthwise and cook in boiling water until just tender. Drain then turn in the vinegar, oil and dill, and leave to cool and absorb the flavours.

Mix together the soured cream, horseradish, and tomato purée and add salt to taste. Stir in the potatoes, then the prawns. Pile high on a platter or in a serving dish and serve good and cold.

For a pretty contrast of colour, add some hard-boiled quails' eggs, sliced in half lengthwise, or some arcs of poached cucumber, or both. A soupçon of garlic would only be a good thing.

12 Oils, Vinegars and Pickles

HERB-FLAVOURED OILS

Although we are all being persuaded to use low-cholesterol oils instead of butter for cooking and are told that safflower or sunflower oil are best from this point of view, these oils and many others recommended to us for our health's sake are, frankly, bland. Their unaggressive presence, with the exception of corn oil which is always obvious, can be used to your advantage only when the full throatiness of olive oil or of a nut oil would be too overpowering for some specially delectable salad or dish; then you can simply flavour the lesser oil with the greater – a good tip to save expense when making mayonnaise. With little trouble these faint oils, and the more robust ones, too, may also be flavoured by marinating herbs, garlic or onions in them.

Oils do not take well to being exposed to the sun or to warmth and thus they will take a month or so in a cool cupboard to absorb all the goodness of most herbs. But you could cheat by warming a good handful of the herbs in some of the oil and keeping it just bearably warm for 10 minutes or so to encourage the transfer of flavour. Rosemary, basil, thyme, oregano or garlic all work well and you can use dried herbs to help or to replace fresh ones, but remember that dried basil even of the highest quality, tastes quite different from fresh. From my experiments with marinating cheeses in flavoured oils, I found that a couple of pieces of lemon peel was an excellent addition.

As you would tend to use rather less of a flavoured oil, you might make them in small quantities and have a variety on hand, which makes it simpler to experiment and to make the most of dried herbs or mixtures of herbs. If you have a cool shelf in the kitchen, they make a nice display, too.

Just as a last thought, I reckon crushed juniper berries perhaps with a little garlic would make a superb oil for helping with game dishes or for flavouring the vegetables to accompany them. You might add a little orange peel, too.

FLAVOURED VINEGARS

Red or white vinegars flavoured with the sun-enhanced summer essences of fruit, flower and herbs are one of the trademarks of modern chefs, but like purées of vegetables and sauces of reduced cooking liquids they are actually reincarnations from earlier cuisines – little is genuinely new in the kitchen.

Once you have tasted and used these vinegars you will wonder, as I have, why we ever stopped using them. They are more and more available commercially throughout the country but are so simple to make any serious cook can have a variety of fascinating vinegars in the store cupboard.

The most common use of flavoured vinegars is to finish sauces of reduced cooking liquids, in which case you often also reduce the vinegars themselves. They are used for swishing out pans in which meat or fish has cooked and while absorbing the flavour of any solids from the pan, the vinegar will reduce in volume increasing the intensity of its flavour.

I also reduce these vinegars to add flavour to mayonnaises without affecting volume; and I have even found they can replace lemon or orange juice in fruit dishes. A teaspoon of reduced raspberry vinegar magically enlivened a sorbet of fresh tamarillo (the New Zealand tree tomato) for me once, and it would certainly do the same for a raspberry or strawberry cream or fool. Elderflower vinegar, well reduced, would unquestionably make a gooseberry fool to be remembered forever.

Here is some guidance.

FRUIT VINEGARS

First, a suggestion. Many Victorian recipes for these suggest fruit-flavoured vinegars be boiled and then sweetened. My advice is to forget that; the first destroys the freshness of flavour, further lost by the boiling needed for reductions, and the second restricts the use of the vinegar to the base of a summery drink. The combination of boiling and sweetening gives a flavour of jam rather than of summer.

The usual technique for making a fruit vinegar is to macerate 1 lb/450 g of fruit in 1 pint/575 ml of vinegar. Red or white wine vinegar or cider vinegar gives the best results, I think, but champagne vinegar just about justifies the extra expense.

You simply mix the fruit and the vinegar and store them in a glass jar somewhere sunny and warm for a week or two, giving an encouraging shake from time to time. Then you strain and bottle it. A touch of sugar might be added to strengthen the fruit flavour, but don't add so much that the sugar cancels the sharpness of the vinegar. If you have masses of suitable fruit, replace the initial lot once or twice during a month and get really intense flavour and colour. If you can't get fresh fruit when you want to make such vinegars, frozen currants and raspberries work very well, but cost you a lot more.

Raspberry vinegar

This is both the easiest to buy and the most popular. I am constantly amazed at the number of ways in which it can be used. Just a little gives extraordinary lift to any vinaigrette, especially one made with a nut oil. It is sensational when used for a sweet and sour sauce for poultry or game and in a mayonnaise (see the previous chapter).

Its special affinities are green beans and raw cauliflower; it is pretty wonderful to serve a bowl of bright white florets of the latter with a saucer of raspberry vinegar as a drinks snack. No one will try it at first, then everyone will want more.

If you make or buy raspberry vinegar, make some of it quite sweet and use that as a syrup for long cooling summer drinks, topped up with sparkling water or even lemonade. Immensely refreshing.

Strawberry vinegar

This is quite as good as raspberry vinegar but harder to get right – you need very fragrant strawberries with a good balance of flavour and acidity. The red-fleshed varieties which tend to come later in the season are best to my mind. A proportion of alpine or wild strawberries would help a lot. I like this vinegar on green salads which are to go with tongue or ham.

Blackberry vinegar

You probably know that blackberries make a marvellously flavoured gin. So, a teaspoon or two of blackberry vinegar in a glass of gin makes a sensational cocktail which I call a Fruitini. Try also a dash of raspberry or strawberry vinegar in gin or vodka. If you have not sweetened your vinegar you may want to add a grain or two of sugar.

Pears, peaches, plums, apples, etc
All these make delicious and useful vinegars, but I think that vinegar made with sliced pears is the best by far. If you use peaches or apricots, include one or two of the crushed kernels from the stones. They both enhance the flavour and give a haunting almond-like overtone.

Cherry vinegar
Whether made with red or black cherries this vinegar is about as flexible in use as the raspberry version. Use plenty of crushed stones and kernels to dramatize and intensify the flavours of the cherries. Particularly good with pork, chicken or veal dishes, or in them, to sharpen a casserole, for instance.

FLORAL VINEGARS

The simplest to make is elderflower vinegar for somewhat fewer flowers are used. Rose vinegar is also easy enough to organize, but some of the other delicious flavours possible, such as violet, clover or cowslip, are fraught with the double-trouble of first finding enough of them and then ensuring they have the right fragrance. In fact, the more fragrant the bloom, the less you will need and the simpler your harvesting. Any fragrant flower that is safe to eat and which has not been sprayed with something lethal will make you a fabulous vinegar, and there is no reason why you should not mix several flavours.

Generally the amount of petals you need is reckoned to be equal in volume to the amount of vinegar. Thus for 1 pint/ 575 ml of vinegar, you would need to gather enough blooms to fill a pint/575 ml container.

If you are going to use elderflowers they may be measured with a very casual eye, and before you have taken off the green stalks, but it is only the blooms you need. Ensure you have checked each head of blossom for the occasional rogue which smells like a tom-cat's urinal. The perfume should be that of honey and muscat, so there is little chance of a mistake. You should not collect them from beside busy roads, either, as they absorb huge amounts of lead.

For roses, cut off the bitter white bottom of each petal. Rose vinegar is specially good on plain green salads, which could also be topped with a few more rose petals. They are good to eat if they are very fragrant and chemical-free. Sweetened floral and fruit vinegars are very good on ice cream.

HERB VINEGARS

I have left these to the last because they are the best known; but they are far from being the least valuable. You make them in the same proportions as that for floral ones, that is 1 pint/575 ml of vinegar to 1 pint/575 ml of herbs, but for the more pungent ones, such as rosemary or thyme you can get away with fewer.

The most commonly used herbs for vinegar are thyme, tarragon and dill, but I also like to use basil, mint, rosemary, bay, lavender, marjoram and chive. Each of these, but especially the smoky lavender version, is perfect for finishing fish sauces and for underpinning the flavours of salads that include fresh herbs.

PIQUANT VINEGARS

Very piquant vinegars are made using fresh or dried chilli peppers or using cayenne pepper (which is largely flavourless) and other ingredients, notably garlic and/or horseradish. Any of the great range of fresh green or red chilli peppers can be used for making vinegar. Remember the smaller the chilli the hotter it usually is. If you remove most of the seeds, you will get more flavour and less heat, which is to be encouraged. Wear rubber gloves when working with these peppers to avoid getting on your fingers the intensely hot oils which are difficult to wash away and can cause violent irritation if accidentally rubbed anywhere near the eyes.

A good hot vinegar is made by adding to 1 pint/575 ml of cider vinegar, ½ oz/15 g dried, or 1 oz/25 g fresh chilli peppers. A rather more flavoursome effect is obtained by putting into the same amount of vinegar about 1½ oz/40 g of grated fresh horseradish, 1 oz/25 g grated onion and a couple of pinches of cayenne pepper.

Both these vinegars need at least 2 weeks to mature and the

vinegar should be strained through scalded muslin or a coffee filter. Garlic makes either better, as it also does most of the herbs mentioned above.

Note Many of the above vinegars – fruit, flower, herb or piquant – will become cloudy if you squash of squeeze them when you strain them. It may not matter to you. If it does, straining them through scalded muslin or a coffee filter will generally sort this out. If you have neither to hand, treat the vinegar like a stock. Beat in an egg white and the clean, crushed shell of an egg. Heat slowly, simmer a few minutes until the crust of egg white has formed then strain very gently through that foam. You sacrifice some of the freshness of flavour for clarity of colour, of course.

And what if you make a mistake and use too little of your chosen herb or flower or fruit? Easy. Add more and let stand longer. If you use too much, which can be easy with something as fragrant as elderflower, then simply dilute it with more of the same vinegar or oil. Honestly you can't lose.

TWO SPICED CREOLE VINEGARS

Excellent when making pickles and sauces and perfect for bottling up as Christmas presents. Or use to make Creole Tabasco, a recipe which follows.

---

1 lb/450 g *sugar*
1 gallon/4.5 litres *cider or white wine vinegar*
1 oz/25 g each *whole cloves,*

allspice berries, mace, celery seeds and mustard seeds
Generous 1 oz/25 g each *black peppercorns, dried ginger root, ground turmeric*

First dissolve the sugar in the excellent cider or white wine vinegar, then add the whole cloves, allspice berries, mace, celery and mustard seeds. Then measure out rather more each of black peppercorns, dried ginger root and ground turmeric. Place all in the vinegar in a stoneware or earthenware container, or you could divide it evenly between big glass jars if that were easier. Cover tightly and keep for 3 weeks or more before straining off the spices. Of course you can leave the spices in there as long as you like.

2 pt/1.2 litres *cider or white wine vinegar*
1 tbsp *sugar*
2 *small onions, finely chopped*
2 *garlic cloves, chopped*
1 tsp *black peppercorns*

1 tsp *grated nutmeg*
½ oz/15 g *dried mint, at most*
1 oz/25 g *fresh parsley stalks*
Approx 1 tbsp *brandy*
Salt, to taste

To each 2 pints/1.2 litres of cider or white wine vinegar add all the ingredients listed. Let it stand at least 3 weeks then strain and use on salads.

CREOLE TABASCO

We cannot get the special Louisiana Tabasco peppers, which are large and red and full of flavour, but can make do by combining sweet red peppers and large chilli peppers; the use of chilli peppers alone will give mainly heat and little flavour.

8 oz/225 g *sweet red peppers*
8 oz/225 g *chilli peppers*
Water

1-2 *garlic cloves*
Creole vinegar, as required

Chop the peppers roughly, just cover with water, and add the garlic. Simmer until very tender and let the liquid reduce until it is just visible. Make a purée of the peppers, using a little of the remaining water to help. The purée must be strained carefully which will give you a fairly thick paste.

Dilute by beating in some Creole vinegar (previously brought to the boil) until the consistency is like unwhipped double cream. Bottle it up and use it with discretion as you would the commercial variety.

VINEGAR-POINTED SAUCES

Just in case the revived technique of making sauces without a butter and flour base has passed you by, this is how to do it. These can also be called a 'mounted' sauce.

You reduce cooking liquids or pan juices down to only 1 or 2 tablespoons of somewhat syrupy liquid per serving. Then you add cream or butter to that whilst beating intently, which all emulsifies and increases in volume and unctuousness. The flavour and the texture can then be pointed with a special vinegar, either as is or also reduced – indeed the vinegar itself may be the pan liquid. For instance, if you have cooked some lamb or calf's liver in a pan, you would remove the liver then swish the pan around with blackcurrant vinegar and keep heating and swishing until the syrupy texture had been reached and then beat in a little butter, which in this case also acts to balance the sharpness of the now reduced vinegar. Add some fresh or frozen blackcurrants if they are to be had then quickly pour the sauce and fruit neatly onto a plate and place the slices of liver on top. A garnish with fresh mint leaves would be right with this dish.

PICKLES

FRUIT-VINEGAR PICKLED FRUIT

A few small bottles of spiced summer fruits, kept chilled in the refrigerator, take little time to make and are an excellent adjunct to meals both simple and super. Although I've specified fruit vinegars in the recipes, wine vinegar would give equally interesting results and cider vinegar is particularly good in this sort of thing. It is important to leave on the skins as they impart a pretty colour to the preserving liquid.

1 lb/450 g *firm peaches, plums or pears*	1 *cinnamon stick*
8 dessertsp *white sugar*	½ pt/300 ml *raspberry or strawberry vinegar*
2 dessertsp *pickling spice*	

The fruit should be only just ripe and nicely firm. Rinse them under running water. Dry then cut into four, six or eight segments according to how big they are.

Put the other ingredients into a pan and bring to the boil very slowly. Simmer covered for 10 minutes. The spices can be strained out now but I rather like to leave them in. Add the segments to the pickle, bring slowly back to the boil, simmer for 5-8 minutes (depending on firmness), and leave to cool slowly.

Spoon the fruit into a screw-top jar, then pour in the liquid and spices. Store in the refrigerator for at least 3 days. These have continued to improve in flavour and appearance for as long as 4 weeks – after that they had all been eaten. Serve them solo or as a fascinating addition to salads and mayonnaises.

Options If you want the fruit to last longer, cook them for only 3 minutes, which keeps them firmer, of course. You will need to wait 3 weeks before eating them but they will stay firm for some months – longer in the refrigerator.

Some vodka, brandy or peach brandy added to the cool pickle would also prolong the fruit's potential life, but add so much extra pleasure they may be eaten even sooner!

GREEN-GINGER PICKLED STRAWBERRIES

Sweet fruit pickles make a delicious addition to simple meals, salads and buffets; they also make a pretty and individual gift at Christmas time. The usual spices are just cloves and ground cinnamon, but here I have made use of the affinity good strawberries have with fresh ginger root. Use firm, full-flavoured, red-fleshed strawberries or your pickle will be only a pale shadow of what it might be.

The recipe can easily be quadrupled.

Fills a 1 lb/450 g jam jar

1½ lb/675 g *firm, small, just ripe strawberries*	12 oz/350 g *white or golden granulated sugar*
2 in/5 cm *fresh ginger root*	½ pt/300 ml *fruit vinegar or red wine vinegar*
2-3 tsp *ground cinnamon*	
12 *whole cloves*	

Wash and dry the strawberries only if absolutely necessary. Then remove the green calyx. Peel the fresh ginger root and slice thickly. Layer the strawberries in a clean glass jar or two and as you do, layer the ginger slices and sprinkle in the ground cinnamon and the cloves. There is no need to be too careful about evenness or indeed about exact quantities.

Combine the sugar and the vinegar in a saucepan and boil gently for 5 minutes. A fruit flavoured vinegar – strawberry or raspberry – is best, otherwise the order of preference is red wine vinegar or cider vinegar. The latter gives excellent flavour but it is an advantage to have the colour that a red vinegar gives.

Pour the boiling vinegar syrup over the strawberries. Close the jar and leave for 24 hours, turning the jar from top to bottom from time to time to prevent the fruit crunching itself up. Then pour the syrup off and boil again for 5 minutes. Put back onto the fruit and leave another 24 hours. Don't worry that the fruit looks pale and flabby at this stage.

Then put fruit and syrup into a saucepan and bring to the boil and simmer slowly for 15 minutes if your fruit is quite small, up to 25 minutes if it is larger. You can also add extra sliced ginger, too, but cut rather more thinly than before. The point is to reduce the syrup so that it just covers the strawberries. If the proportion of syrup formed looks vastly excessive, you would do better to pour off most of the syrup, reduce separately and then add the strawberries and simmer. By the time you have finished the strawberries will be quite red again but their bulk will be about half the amount you started with. Let the mixture cool for at least 15 minutes before bottling, as this will prevent the fruit floating to the top.

Best left a couple of weeks before being eaten. A perfect wonder to serve with ham at Christmas time.

PENNSYLVANIA DUTCH PEARS

These are intended for use with cold meats and poultry, but are so delicious I serve them with cheese as a pudding.

The quantity made will depend on the size you choose – whatever that is, ensure they are uniform so they are cooked to the same state at the same time.

3 lb/1.3 kg *white or brown sugar*	1 tbsp *whole cloves*
¾ pt/425 ml *cider vinegar*	3 *cinnamon sticks*
½ pt/300 ml *water*	7 lb/about 3 kg *firm, ripe pears*

Combine the sugar, vinegar, and water. The cloves and cinnamon sticks – which should be broken into pieces – may either be added as is or put into a muslin bag. Simmer all together for 30 minutes from the time the syrup comes to the boil. Taste carefully and add more cinnamon if your sticks were not as strong as you thought – remember the flavour is going to be very diluted by the addition of the pears.

While the syrup is simmering, peel the pears but keep on the stems and do not core them. Brush them with a little water and lemon juice to keep them white if you are using white sugar, otherwise a little discoloration can be overlooked.

Put the pears into the syrup and cook gently until tender but still firm. Spoon the pears carefully into sterilized containers and cover but do not seal. Boil the syrup fairly rapidly for 30 minutes, pour carefully over the fruit, then seal. I would leave these a couple of weeks before eating them.

Option Thick slices of fresh ginger root would be a delightful addition to this fairly simply flavoured recipe; indeed, one day I intend to use masses of ginger as the only flavouring.

PICKLED GREEN WALNUTS

Although everyone seems to know about pickled walnuts, few people now seem to have eaten them. Just in case you have a walnut tree about, I give two ways in which to make pickles, and also something I find even more scrumptious, a walnut ketchup.

Fast Method
It is essential that walnuts for pickling have not the slightest hint of a shell formed – you must be able to pierce each one right through with a pin or the eye end of a needle.

Pick such walnuts and pierce both ways – from side to side and from tip to bottom. Make enough brine to cover them, in the proportion of 6 oz/175 g salt to 2 pints/1.2 litres water. Boil together and cool. Leave the walnuts in the brine for 12 days, drain them, then spread in a single layer to turn black. Place in wide-mouthed glass jars. Make a vinegar pickle (below) and pour onto walnuts when boiling hot. Leave 2 weeks before eating.

Traditional Method

The more traditional method of pickling green walnuts differs from the above in that the nuts are not pricked and the vinegar is used cold, both of which techniques mean the walnuts require very much longer to absorb the flavours of the vinegar and spices. Of course it is precisely the long slow process of ageing that gives them the special flavour so admired.

In this case you wipe the walnuts clean and cover with a brine made in the proportion of 6 oz/175 g of salt to 2 pt/1.2 litres water, as above. Ensure the walnuts are continuously immersed by weighting slightly with a wooden board or plate and turn them over gently each day with a wooden spoon.

After 6 days, boil up and cool another brine of the same strength. Drain the walnuts and put into the new brine. Leave for 3-6 days, depending on how busy you are. Choose a nice sunny day and spread the walnuts out in a single layer covered with sacking and turn them very gently a few times until they are evenly blackened.

Make up enough of the vinegar pickle below and let cool thoroughly. Take out the large pieces of ginger at least, and either leave the rest or strain them out.

Put the walnuts into wide-mouthed jars and pour on the vinegar to cover them completely. Tie down with greaseproof or brown paper, and as the vinegar is slowly absorbed, top up with ordinary vinegar as they must always be fully immersed.

They will be ready in 3 months but if you leave them longer they will be even better.

VINEGAR PICKLE

The ingredients listed are the basic proportions and you need enough to cover the walnuts – measure the amount of vinegar you need by covering with water, draining and measuring, then progress from there. The amounts are not critical and may be reorganized according to what you have or what you like.

4 pt/2.3 litres *vinegar*
2 oz/50 g *dried ginger root*
2 oz/50 g *black peppercorns*
8 *blades of mace*

2 oz/50 g *mustard seeds*
12 *cloves*
4 *onions, sliced*

Simmer everything together for 10 minutes then use hot for the green walnuts or cold for the traditional ones.

Rather than going to the trouble of buying the separate spices, you might simply purchase 6-8 oz/175-225 g of a pack-aged pickling spice mixture from your delicatessen or super-market. Brown or white sugar can be added to make sweet walnut pickles.

SWEET AND SOUR CUCUMBER PICKLE

Small immature cucumbers, each about 4 in/10 cm long, are best for this and the following recipes only because they look so good in the jars. They've been so difficult to find in the shops but now the Dutch are growing them specially for the UK market. If you grow cucumbers then you can pick them when they are the size you require. However, even if you don't grow them and can't buy small ones, the large salad cucumber is fine. It just needs cutting into manageable pieces.

6-8 immature (or 1 large)
    cucumber
2 oz/50 g *salt*
1 pt/575 ml *vinegar*

8 oz/225 g *granulated sugar*
1 tsp *mustard seeds*
2 tsp *whole mixed pickling spicies*

Wipe the cucumbers, cut them into 3 in/7.5 cm lengths, then into quarters lengthways. Dissolve the salt in 1 pint/575 ml cold water and soak the cucumber pieces in this brine for at least 12 hours. Bring the vinegar to the boil with the sugar and spices, remove the pan from the heat and let the mixture cool. Drain and rinse the cucumbers under running cold water then drain them well. Pack the slices into jars and pour on the cold spiced vinegar to cover them. Even within one day, the pickle is good to eat and it improves with keeping.

CUCUMBERS IN BRINE

2 large or 12-14 immature
   cucumbers
Vine leaves
12 *dill sprigs*

2 *garlic cloves*
4 oz/115 g *salt*
½ tsp *peppercorns*
6 *whole allspice berries*

Wipe the cucumbers and cut them into 3 in/7.5 cm lengths, then into quarters lengthways. Put a few vine leaves at the bottom of the jars then pack in the cucumber slices with the dill sprigs among them. Peel and slice the garlic cloves and put them in a pan with the salt, 2 pints/a generous litre cold water, the peppercorns and allspice. Bring to the boil, then simmer the brine for 15 minutes. Allow it to cool before pouring it into the jars to cover the cucumbers. Pack more vine leaves at the top of the jars. Use a week or so after bottling because cucumbers in brine do not keep well for more than a few weeks.

If you cannot find dill, use fennel sprigs instead.

DILL-PICKLED CUCUMBERS

2 large or 12-14 immature
   cucumbers
Salt
12 *dill sprigs*

2 tsp *dill seeds*
2 tsp *coriander seeds*
2 tsp *white peppercorns*
2 pt/generous litre *white vinegar*

Wipe the cucumbers and cut them into suitable lengths for your jars. Dissolve 4 oz/115 g salt in 2 pints/a generous litre cold water and cover the cucumber pieces with this brine. Leave for about 6 hours, making sure the pieces are completely submerged (put a small saucer or plate on top to keep them under the liquid). Drain and rinse under running cold water then drain again well. Pack the slices into jars sprinkling the dill sprigs, seeds and peppercorns among them. Boil the vinegar with 4 teaspoons salt, cool the mixture then pour it over the cucumbers to cover them. This pickle is best if kept for a month before opening and it keeps well for 3 months.

If you prefer to have a sweet rather than a sour pickle, dissolve sugar in the vinegar, allowing 4 oz/115 g to each pint/575 ml.

13 Cakes and Cheesecakes

In New York a delicatessen is a place where you go to have sandwiches and salads made, and thus cheesecakes and speciality cakes are always part of their wares. During the last 10 years, cheesecakes, chocolate and carrot cakes have become familiar to most of us.

This section concentrates on cheesecakes with recipes from around the world and here and there you will find some interesting crossovers such as the carrot cheesecake, which I put together for people who wanted to make cheesecakes, but who either could not afford to buy large quantities of cheese, or who wanted to eat less cholesterol.

CARROT CAKES

There has long been a tradition of carrots in baking throughout Europe, and in times of poverty and hardship they were used as a substitute for eggs in a great variety of puddings and cakes. In fact their sweetness, and the lightness they added, was used just as much in times of plenty simply for the pleasure given.

It is now a favourite dessert in hamburger restaurants, and therefore has become a stock requirement in delicatessens which serve the same sort of people. In all these venues it is usually sold as Passion Cake but I cannot imagine – or ascertain – quite why this should be. It is rarely good enough to excite one and has nothing to do with Easter.

The first recipe is pale and interesting, the second rich, dark, moist and provocative. Indeed, the first time I made it, it was christened Butch Carrot Cake.

PALE PASSION CAKE

**To fill 3 × 9 in/22.5 cm sandwich tins or
1 × 11 × 15 in/27.5 × 37.5 cm roasting tin**

8 oz/225 g *butter*	4 *eggs*
1 lb/450 g *sugar, white or demerara*	8 oz/225 g *grated carrot*
	3 oz/85 g *walnuts, chopped*
1 tsp *ground cinnamon*	12 oz/350 g *plain flour*
½ tsp *ground mace*	3 tsp *baking powder*
¼ tsp *ground cloves*	½ tsp *salt*
1 tsp *grated orange rind*	Up to 2½ fl oz/75 ml *warm water*

Cream the butter and sugar together particularly well. Once light coloured and fluffy, add in the spices and orange rind then beat in the eggs one at a time. Stir in the carrot and the nuts. Fold in the sifted dry ingredients and the water to obtain a good cake batter consistency. Do not beat in the flour and water but mix gently – if using an electric mixer use lowest speed possible.

This mixture will fill three greased and floured sandwich tins or a roasting tray, similarly prepared (see above for proportions and sizes). Bake in a preheated 350°F/180°C/Gas 4 oven about 25 minutes for the layers and 35-40 minutes for the square cake. Allow to cool in the pan slightly before loosening the edges and turning out onto a rack.

You can eat this cake just as it is but it is often served with an icing made from cream cheese.

CREAM CHEESE FROSTING

4 oz/115 g *butter, softened*	Approx 10-12 oz/275-350 g *icing sugar*
8 oz/225 g *cream cheese (packaged)*	Up to 1 tsp *vanilla essence*

Combine all ingredients in a mixing bowl and mix smoothly to a spreading consistency. Some chopped nuts or some grated orange can also be added. Use to stick together the sandwich layers or to smooth over the top of the square cake. I like to sprinkle with a whisper of cinnamon or nutmeg.

BUTCH CARROT CAKE

Makes a 9-10 in/22.5-25 cm diameter cake

3 *eggs*
¼ pt/150 ml *cooking oil,*
   be generous
1 lb/450 g *Barbados or*
   dark brown sugar
2 tsp *vanilla essence*
8 oz/225 g *wholemeal or white*
   flour

½ tsp *salt*
2 heaped tsp *baking powder*
2 tsp *ground cinnamon*
1 tsp *ground nutmeg*
12 oz/350 g *grated carrot*
3 oz/85 g *desiccated coconut*
8 oz/225 g *canned crushed*
   pineapple

The eggs must be beaten really well until thick and pallid. Add the oil, sugar and vanilla, and beat well until sugar is dissolved. Mix the flour, salt, baking powder and spices together and fold evenly into the mixture. Stir in the carrot and coconut then drain the crushed pineapple and stir in the fruit only. Ensure the mixture is as even as possible then pour into a greased nonstick baking tin that is 9-10 in/22.5-25 cm diameter and quite deep. If you do not have a nonstick pan it might be as well to line the tin with greaseproof paper.

   Bake for 1½-2 hours in a preheated 350°F/180°C/Gas 4 oven. It is a very moist cake so be certain it is cooked before taking it out of the oven. You cannot really overcook it, but if the top is badly burning put a little foil loosely over it until the centre of the cake is done. Do not turn out of the tin for at least 30 minutes and delay eating for several days if you can. Doesn't really need much to go with it other than restraint; but you could make an icing with the syrup from the can of pineapples.

CHOCOLATE CAKES

It is a brave man who publishes yet more chocolate cake recipes, particularly when so many delicatessens now sell excellent rich and dark ones by the slice. I think these three recipes are different enough to merit the interest of any genuine chocoholic and the variations I suggest are your key to fascinating new flavour combinations. Have you had chocolate cake with a chocolate-banana icing? A chocolate cake flavoured with rose-water and baked with geranium leaves? A spiced chocolate cake with chestnut icing? Read on, and you will have.

EGGLESS CHOCOLATE CAKE

This popular recipe from New Zealand makes a richly coloured moist cake. Children thoroughly enjoy making – and eating – it!

To make a 7-8 in/17.5-20 cm cake or a 8-9 in/20-22.5 cm ring

1 lb/450 g *self-raising flour*	6 oz/175 g *butter*
2 oz/50 g *cocoa powder*	2 tbsp *cider vinegar*
½ tsp *salt*	¼ pt/150 ml *water*
14 oz/400 g *sugar*	½ pt/300 ml *milk*

Even if you have nonstick baking pans, it is as well to butter them for this recipe and to make a layer of buttered paper or of a butter wrapper on the bottom. Having prepared the baking tin, sift the flour, cocoa and salt together then stir in the sugar. Melt the butter in a saucepan, remove from the heat and add the vinegar, water and milk.

Add the liquid ingredients to the dry ones and mix thoroughly without whisking, whipping, or in any way overworking the batter, which should be very smooth and rather wet.

Put into the tin and bake in a preheated 350°F/180°C/Gas 4 oven for 1 hour. Leave in the tin for 15-20 minutes before turning out. This cake keeps very well and doesn't need an icing. The original recipe calls for all water rather then milk and water but I think this always gives a rather steamed flavour – you may like that and if so, or if you have no milk and need to bake a cake, go ahead. If you prefer icing, then try one of those given after the next recipe.

REALLY RICH CHOCOLATE CAKE

This really is the answer to those who yearn for ever darker, ever richer chocolate cakes. In fact it is hardly like a cake at all, for it is flat and rather like a mousse in the middle – alarming if your recipe book hasn't told you to expect it! Although I prefer my cakes to be singletons, there is a case for baking this in two tins as you will get a marginally lighter result.

For 1 × deep 8 in/20 cm tin or 2 × 8 in/20 cm sandwich tin

Cocoa powder (see method)	5 *large eggs, separated*
6 oz/175 g *dark unsweetened chocolate*	3 oz/85 g *ground almonds or walnuts*
6 oz/175 g *unsalted French butter*	2 oz/50 g *plain flour*
6 oz/175 g *caster sugar*	*Flavouring* (see *Options*)

Grease and dust with cocoa powder one deep tin or two sandwich tins and set to one side.

Melt the chocolate over hot but not boiling water and stir constantly. Break up the butter, add and stir until incorporated, still keeping the heat only as high as needed to melt the butter slowly – high heat will stiffen the mixture and the endeavour will be doomed. Once the chocolate and butter are blended, remove the bowl from the water and stir in the sugar until totally dissolved then let that all cool to room temperature.

Beat in the egg yolks one by one, then the nuts and the flour. Now choose your flavouring and add that.

Whisk up the whites until firm but not dry and fold them into the flavoured chocolate batter. Ladle the mixture into the tin or tins and bake immediately in a preheated 350°F/180°C/Gas 4 oven until the sides just begin to shrink from the tins. It will take about 25 minutes for the sandwich tins and perhaps 40 minutes for a single tin. If you want, you might put the mixture into a larger one, say a 10 in/25 cm tin, in which case the thinner layer of mixture would take only 30-35 minutes to bake to the right degree – remember it should be moist in the middle.

Let the cake rest in the pan a good 10 minutes then turn out onto a cooling rack.

I like it just as it is, naked temptation. But you can fill or glaze it a number of ways.

Options The most common flavouring would be brandy and 1-2 tablespoons would be right – you should only just be able to taste it in the mixture before baking, but black rum, Calvados or Crème de Menthe would all be fabulous, too. Vanilla essence is something that can be used by itself or in tandem with a spirit, especially with rum. I have seen an American recipe which uses whisky, but I can't think it would be as good as the above. A medium or cream sherry would be though!

The most startling flavouring is rose-water – startling both because it is unexpected and because it is unexpectedly good. You need about 2 tablespoons and, for more drama, line the baking tin with rose geranium leaves, which add a little extra perfume but an astonishing perfumed flavour when you bite into them. It is such a remarkable coup to use rose geranium leaves, that I suggest you merely flavour the cake with vanilla to dramatize their effect even more.

If you make a sandwich cake it may be filled with any sharp jam, and apricot is probably the best. If you reduce some jam over heat and put it through a sieve and pour that over the cake, it will act like a glaze when set. You can put icing over that or leave it as it is. Blackcurrant jam and raspberry jam are excellent in chocolate cake.

Chocolate icings come in all shapes and sizes.

Butter Icing
To each 8 oz/225 g of icing sugar, use 3 oz/85 g softened butter and at least 1 heaped tablespoon cocoa powder. A few drops of vanilla essence is always good and you will need about 3 dessert-spoons of another liquid to bind the icing together. Water is fine, but you could use the spirit you have used in the mixture. If you have made a plainly flavoured cake, rose-water is one of the most fascinating flavours for your icing. But do taste and ensure that the chocolate flavour is strong enough; nothing is worse than weakness in chocolate. A butter icing might be too rich for this cake so it may be better to settle for one of the following.

Cream Chocolate Icing
This is made simply and expensively by melting together 2 tablespoons of double cream to each 1 oz/25 g of dark chocolate. Let it cool until thickening then spread over like a glaze.

Glacé Icing
Simplest of all is to flavour icing sugar highly with cocoa powder then to mix with some warm liquid to a thick creamy consistency. For 8 oz/225 g of sugar you will need no more than 4 dessertspoons usually.

ALLSPICE CHOCOLATE CAKE WITH CHESTNUT ICING

This recipe uses both cinnamon from the Old World and the most important New World spice – allspice. It is invaluable, to me, tasting like a mixture of cinnamon, nutmeg and cloves.

Allspice used to be known as Jamaica pepper or pimento, and is a natural companion to chocolate

For a deep 8 in/20 cm square tin

6 oz/175 g *butter*
6 oz/175 g *sugar*
3 *eggs*
1 tsp *vanilla essence*
8 oz/225 g *self-raising flour*

4 tbsp *cocoa powder*
1 tsp *ground allspice*
1 tsp *ground cinnamon*
Approx ¼ pt/150 ml *milk*

Icing

3 oz/85 g *butter*
4 oz/115 g *chestnut purée*

12 oz/350 g *icing sugar*

Butter the cake tin and dust it with cocoa powder rather than with flour. Cream together the butter and sugar very well, then beat in the eggs one by one. Mix in the vanilla.

Sift together the flour, cocoa and spices and mix in gently. Stir in milk to form a soft, 'dropping' consistency then gently pour into the prepared tin.

Bake in a preheated 350°F/180°C/Gas 4 oven for 60 minutes or so, depending on the size and type of tin you have used. Leave in tin for 10 minutes then turn out to cool on a wire rack.

To make the icing, mix together the butter and chestnut purée. This can be plain chestnut purée or the very rich vanilla flavoured variety. Mix in the icing sugar evenly then spread over the top and sides of the cake. Let the icing set crisply and, just before serving, dust with a fine cloud of equal quantities of ground cinnamon and allspice.

Options   Some black rum in the chestnut icing would give even more of the flavour of the New World to this cake.

Of course, any of the icing recipes given previously would be excellent too. But one of the most stunning icings to make for a chocolate cake is made by mixing butter icing with mashed banana and butter. It is best to be generous with this sort of icing, so start with a whole packet of icing sugar, the 3 oz/85 g of softened butter, a couple of tablespoons of cocoa powder and one or two ripe bananas, depending on size. Mix in a food processor.

CHEESECAKES

Nowadays, women's magazines, delicatessens and wine bars hardly seem able to exist without regularly featuring cheese-cakes. Name a flavour and someone has invented a cheesecake of it – coffee, chocolate, mandarin, black cherry, Grand Marnier, apple, mint, fudge, toffee . . . . Australia is specially good at inventing new ones of the gelatine variety but I don't think editors should publish recipes that include packaged cheese, instant coffee powder and canned mandarins mixed together. Surely our friends and families deserve something better than that?

The cheesecake is largely regarded in Great Britain as something rather fast and foreign, the sort of thing you buy from delicatessens or eat in a restaurant. Yet in the days when every household expected to make soft cheeses and curds at home, cheesecakes were common fare throughout the kingdom; some were sweet and rich, some were savoury, some had pastry cases, some were only for the rich, some sustained the poor. Once the housewife and cook began to rely on the corner shop, there was no longer much soft cheese to be had and home-made cheese-cakes disappeared from most tables.

Supermarkets and refrigeration now mean soft cheeses are again nationally available to almost everybody, thus there is good reason why the British cheesecake tradition should be well and truly revived. Frankly, there is nothing to it.

THE BISCUIT BASE

Just in case you don't know how to do it, I'll start by giving you a recipe for the biscuit base that is so popular. Digestive, wheat-meal or graham biscuits are all good, but I think crunchy ginger biscuits are much better for most recipes.

The proportions I find work best are about 1½ oz/40 g butter to approximately 8 oz/225 g biscuits. While the butter is melting, put the biscuits in a folded tea towel and crush them with a rolling pin. Slide the crumbs into the butter and mix well with a fork. Press firmly into your springform base, taking great care to get a good firm edge – in fact the outside should be thicker than the middle, so build it up a little all round. That's all there is to it. Ginger biscuits or any of the wholemeal types benefit from the addition of a generous helping of ground cinnamon.

TYPES OF CHEESE SUITABLE

There is no proper soft cheese for cheesecakes. Any of them may be used, including those you buy already mixed with fruit, especially the pineapple version.

The differences you might find when making a choice between cottage cheese, curd cheese, cream cheese and such commercial types as Philadelphia, are those of price, texture, fat and moisture content; the first is up to you and lumps in cottage cheese can be sieved out. Varying moisture contents are basic to soft cheese and unavoidable, and when converting a recipe from the relatively dry cottage cheese to a soft fresh moist cream cheese, add a little extra binder in the form of an extra egg.

You can diminish the richness of some cheesecakes either by using a lower fat cheese or by using milk instead of cream in the mixture. You can even mix two soft cheeses together for the sake of economy or less cholesterol – say, cottage cheese and cream cheese in any proportion you like. Each variation will change the final result a little, but not so much that most people will notice or care.

There is, or was, a British cheesecake notable for containing no cheese at all! Usually made in pastry-lined patty shapes, these cheesecakes are a stock item in the cake and home-cookery shops that proliferate in Australia and New Zealand. Nowadays they are generally a yellow sponge mixture baked in puff pastry cases with a dollop of raspberry jam between the two.

FLAVOURINGS

There is almost nothing that cannot flavour a cheesecake. Lemon and orange, vanilla and almond are the basics and most other flavours are probably better for being combined with one of these, especially lemon or vanilla.

Variations need only to bear in mind two things:
(a) that the flavour of your additive is concentrated enough to be detectable when added to the mixture and cooked; and
(b) that if it is liquid, such as a fruit purée, it does not alter the unbaked texture so much that it will not set. It is best to use very concentrated flavours or dry ingredients, such as toasted chopped nuts, concentrated essences or liqueurs.

Some popular ideas are coffee essence or coffee powder, or to make mocha flavour, a combination of cocoa powder and instant coffee – excellent with rum, of course, or one of the Caribbean coffee liqueurs, Tia Maria or Kahlua.

Finely chopped preserved ginger is marvellous combined with a lemon flavour and topped with halved pears.

A toasted hazelnut cheesecake might be finished with a chocolate flavoured, soured cream topping or scattered with hazelnut praline.

TOPPINGS

There are two popular ways to top a cheesecake. The first is with baked soured cream, the other is with a thickened purée of fruit which sets to a greater or lesser degree depending upon how sloppy you wish to be. Or you can use both.

Soured cream topping

This can be put onto any baked cheesecake you wish. It is essential on the Philadelphia cheesecake, and the simple, vanilla flavoured version can be successfully put atop any other flavour.

The method is to take a ½ pint/300 ml of soured cream (two small cartons do nicely) plus up to 2 oz/50 g of sugar and a teaspoon or so of flavouring. This is spread on top of the baked cheesecake and then cooked for just 10 minutes in a very hot oven – 475°F/240°C/Gas 9. As soon as it comes from the oven it is best to put it into the refrigerator as this prevents cracking, but I know a lot of people will not want to do this, for fear of upsetting the temperature of the refrigerator.

Vanilla is the usual flavouring but most cheesecakes would be equally happy if pure almond essence were to be substituted. Of course you could use any flavouring essence but it seems a shame to use these artificial devices. Better to use liqueurs, for instance, to get orange, mint or other flavours. Or grate in some lime peel, stir in some cocoa or coffee powder, or chopped toasted coconut or hazelnuts. By flavouring a soured cream topping interestingly and then covering that with a fruit concoction some very interesting things indeed can happen.

Fruit toppings

Essentially all you need to know about thickened fruit toppings for cheesecake is that you need around 2 tablespoons of arrowroot or cornflour to thicken liquid that varies between ¼ and ½ a pint/150 and 300 ml, and that usually you need to add a little more sugar to most syrups from canned fruits.

Cherry topping

This is by far the most popular topping and is good quite plain or with added flavourings. You simply drain the liquid from a can of pitted red cherries – usually about 1 lb/450 g – and make this up to a generous ¼ pint/150 ml. Mix in about 4 oz/115 g sugar plus a teaspoon of lemon juice then stir in 2 tablespoons of arrowroot or cornstarch. Heat, stirring all the time until boiling then simmer for about 5 minutes or until the floury taste disappears. Take off heat and mix in the cherries. You may like to add a drop or two of food colouring but I prefer to leave it pale.

For black cherries, which are sweeter than red ones, you will need less sugar, perhaps only 2 oz/50 g.

Let the mixture cool and start to thicken before you put it on to the cake then chill it thoroughly.

Both cherry toppings are nice with finely grated or shredded orange peel, with a sprinkle of cinnamon and pinch of cloves. Some Kirsch or Maraschino is good with the red cherries, black rum or brandy with the black ones.

Pineapple topping

Drain the liquid from an 8 oz/225 g can of crushed pineapple then add pineapple juice, orange juice, gin or water to make it up to a scant ¼ pint/150 ml. Add in 2 oz/50 g sugar, brown or white, plus 1 tablespoon of arrowroot or cornflour. Heat and thicken until clear and cooked. Mix in the drained pineapple. The whole recipe can be doubled. Some coconut liqueur or some black rum and a scattering of toasted coconut would make a pina colada flavour topping.

Canned mangoes, peaches, apricots, blueberries, blackcurrants, pawpaw – even fruit salad – can be thickened in this manner and used to top a cheesecake. Grate some fresh lime peel over anything remotely tropical. Fresh fruits such as raspberries and strawberries are better mixed into thinned sweetened cream and spread on at the last moment.

Fruit glazes

These are terribly simple and perfectly delicious. Make them the same way you would a glaze for ham or a cake, that is you boil 1 lb/450 g of jam or fruit jelly over medium heat until reduced by at least a third, but on no account let it burn. Force through a sieve to remove any lumps, pips etc., then pour onto cool cheesecake immediately. You can use any jam you like but the sharpness of apricot is particularly good.

You may add spice to apricot, peach or nectarine jams, grate orange rind into any flavour and, naturally, add liqueurs or brandy. But be exceptionally careful when testing the flavour, for hot jam is terribly dangerous and gives really awful burns. Raspberry or strawberry with orange rind and/or orange liqueur are superb.

To be quite certain you like the effect start by using just 8 oz/225 g jam or jelly or give a very thin coating and add more if you like.

These jam glazes are very useful for setting whole fresh or canned fruit in a pattern on top of a cheesecake. For instance an apricot glaze would perfectly complement and anchor a ring of fresh sharon fruit slices (a crisp persimmon-type fruit from Israel). Raspberry is great for pears and, of course, it is never wrong to use fresh and preserved fruit of the same kind together – peach jam on fresh peaches, blackcurrant jam on fresh blackcurrants and so on.

CREAMED LEMON CHEESE

The following two recipes are for uncooked cheesecakes *without* bases, although you can of course put them on something tasty.

Serves 6

1½ lb/675 g *fresh cream or curd cheese*	8 oz/225 g *caster sugar*
4 *eggs, separated*	2 *lemons*
	¼ pt/150 ml *double cream*

Mix the cheese with the yolks of the eggs and caster sugar. Wash and grate the rinds of the lemons, beat the cream until thick and add both to the cheese. If you would like to add some lemon juice, more sugar or even more cream, now is the time to do it. Then whisk up the whites of the eggs until firm but not dry, and gently incorporate them into the cheese mixture. Serve chilled in glass coupes with a couple of crystallized violets.

This mixture can also be put onto a sponge base with an interleaving of excellent raspberry jam, piled into a blind-baked flan case or served as a sauce for something like an orange cake.

FROMAGE À L'IMPÉRATRICE

Serves 4-6

4 oz/115 g *raisins*	*Vanilla essence*
Rum, warmed	¼ pt/150 ml *double cream*
1 lb/450 g *fresh cream cheese*	*Glacé fruit*
4 oz/115 g *caster sugar*	

First soak the raisins in enough warm rum to cover them and let them swell up. Then beat the well-drained fresh cream cheese smooth with the sugar and some vanilla essence. Fold in the whipped double cream (use more if you like). Now add the swollen raisins plus some sliced glacé fruit which you have cut in small pieces – cherries and apricots are best, and a little angelica looks pretty. Some chopped toasted almonds are an excellent addition, too. This can also be frozen and served more like an ice cream, but then I should add a little liqueur.

NO-COOK CHEESECAKE

There is no need to use gelatine in an uncooked cheesecake. This makes quite a thin cheesecake but is rather rich, and thus I like to serve it accompanied by fruit rather than all by itself. You can always double up to make a thicker one. Perfect for fruit toppings.

For an 8-9 in/20-22.5 cm tin with ginger biscuit base

8 oz/225 g *cream cheese*	*Grated nutmeg*
½ *lemon*	*Fruit (see method)*
At least 2 tbsp *caster sugar*	

Mash up the cream cheese, and add the finely grated rind and juice of the half lemon plus the caster sugar – more if you have a sweet tooth. Check for flavour then spread onto the thin ginger biscuit base and dust it with nutmeg, an essential. Chill at least 1 hour and then serve it accompanied by whatever you like.

Options   Here are some of the things *I* like: the pulp of two or three passionfruit spread over the top; fresh or defrosted raspberries lightly crushed and mixed with a little orange juice or liqueur; sliced strawberries lightly mashed in whipped cream; a little gooseberry purée. For something more tropical, you might consider using the juice and peel of a lime instead of the lemon. It's frightfully good and goes naturally well with other tropical goodies like fresh pineapple or mango or pawpaw, even those out of a can.

Some whipped cream worked into the mixture or arranged on top will extend this cheesecake admirably. See also the earlier sections on flavourings and toppings.

JOHN TOVEY'S CHOCOLATE MINT CHEESECAKE

Like so many of John Tovey's recipes, this is seminal and can be varied ad infinitum, according to whatever liqueur you have in the cupboard. Most liqueur flavoured cheesecakes would be good with a layer of thin, dark, unminted chocolate pieces in the middle, especially those that taste orangey.

For a 10 in/25 cm springform tin with digestive biscuit base

3 tbsp *Crème de Menthe*	2 oz/50 g *caster sugar*
1 envelope *gelatine*	½ pt/300 ml *whipping or*
3 *eggs, separated*	*double cream*
9 oz/250 g *cream cheese*	4 oz/115 g *chocolate mint crisps*

Put Crème de Menthe into a saucepan, sprinkle the gelatine over and leave to one side. Whisk up the egg yolks then beat in the cream cheese, sugar and cream. Warm the gelatine very gently until melted, then pour into the mixture through a warm sieve and mix in well.

Whisk the egg whites until firm but not dry and fold them into the mixture. Crush the mint crisps (they must not have a creamy filling).

Ladle half the mixture into the springform. Add the crushed mints, leaving a few for decoration, then spoon in the remaining cheese mixture. Sprinkle the last of the mints over the top. Leave to set and served chilled but not iced.

Options   Use plain chocolate digestive biscuits for the base. Lightly dust the completed cake with sweetened cocoa powder.

YOGHURT CHEESECAKE

For an 8 in/20 cm springform tin with biscuit crumb base

4 rounded tsp *gelatine powder*	3 *eggs, separated*
¼ pt/150 ml *hot water*	*Salt*
12 oz/350 g *cream cheese*	10 oz/275 g *caster sugar*
5 oz/150 g *natural yoghurt*	½ pt/300 ml *double or*
1 tbsp *lemon juice*	*whipping cream*

Dissolve the gelatine in the hot water. Beat the cheese, yoghurt and lemon juice together until smooth. Combine egg yolks, a pinch of salt and 6 oz/175 g of the sugar and stir over low heat (or over hot water if you are nervous) until thick – beware of curdling. Add gelatine solution. When cool add cheese mixture. Whisk the egg whites until stiff but not dry, gradually adding the remaining sugar. Whip the cream. Fold the cream and then the egg whites into the cheese mixture. Pile quickly into the case and refrigerate

Options   For a fruity version use a carton of fruit yoghurt and decorate the top with the same fruit. You might leave out the yoghurt altogether, replacing it with more cream or 4 oz/115 g more cheese, or add one of the toppings or flavourings given earlier.

PHILADELPHIA CHEESECAKE

This terribly smooth and rich cheesecake can be made with other than the branded cream cheese of its name, but this version is a classic. The special interest is the use of soured cream as a dressing, to complete the cake.

For a 9 in/22.5 cm springform tin with biscuit base

1 lb/450 g *Philadelphia cream cheese*	4 oz/115 g *sugar*
	1 tsp *vanilla essence*
2 *eggs*	

Topping

½ pt/300 ml *soured cream*	1 tsp *vanilla essence*
2 oz/50 g *sugar*	

Preheat the oven to 375°F/190°C/Gas 5

Beat the filling ingredients together until very smooth, adding extra sugar or vanilla if you wish. Pour into the base and bake for 20 minutes. Remove from oven and let cool for 15 minutes. Turn the oven up to 475°F/240°C/Gas 9. Then blend together the topping ingredients. Smooth over the cake then bake for just 10 minutes. Cool, then chill very well before serving.

This is ideal as the base for sharp fruit toppings, but does very well just as it is.

LOW FAT CARROT CHEESECAKE

This answers the modern requirement of many people for food with a lower fat content by using the ancient technique of including carrots to give lightness, richness and flavour to baking.

For an 8 in/20 cm springform tin with ginger biscuit base

1 lb/450 g *carrots, trimmed*	1 tsp *ground cinnamon*
½ pt/300 ml *orange juice*	½ tsp *ground nutmeg*
1 lb/450 g *cottage or curd cheese*	½ tsp *ground ginger*
3 tbsp *flour*	3 *eggs*
1 tbsp *sugar*	

Wash and trim the carrots but do not peel them unless they are genuinely in distress. Slice thinly or grate then cook in the orange juice until well softened and able to be puréed – at least 20 minutes probably.

Make a purée of the carrots, including all the orange juice, then beat the cheese into that. If you are using cottage cheese, force it through a sieve first to remove the lumps. Other soft cheese should be whisked a little in case there are hidden lumps. Add all the remaining ingredients and mix very well. If you don't you will get white lumps, which doesn't look very good.

Ladle this mixture gently into the prepared springform and bake for 1 hour at 350°F/180°C/Gas 4. Leave to cool completely before eating. I think it is better if left to mature overnight and it is nice lightly chilled rather than warm or iced.

Options If cholesterol is not a worry to you, you can make this with cream cheese, but with such added richness you may like to add a few teaspoons of strained lemon juice.

A sharp apricot-jam glaze, with or without some spice or some brandy, would make this very party-like.

KÄSEKUCHE

This recipe was found in New York but originally came from Germany. Unusually it uses cottage cheese, but curd or cream cheese, or some economical or palate-pleasing combination, may also be used.

For a 9 in/22.5 cm springform tin with biscuit base

4 *eggs*	8 fl oz/225 ml *double cream*
6 oz/175 g *caster sugar*	1½ lb/675 g *cottage cheese*
A pinch of salt	2 oz/50 g *plain flour*
1 *medium lemon, grated rind of*	1-2 tsp *vanilla essence*

Beat the eggs (room temperature, please) and sugar until very thick, light and smooth. Add the other ingredients one after the other, beating all the while. Beat until quite smooth. Poor gently into the biscuit-lined tin and bake for 1 hour at 350°F/180°C/Gas 4. Turn off the heat and leave in oven with door half open until only just warm; this helps prevent splitting but sadly not always.

Options   Made with cream cheese and orange juice and rind it is startlingly good and surprisingly light as with the following recipe. Using sour cream instead of sweet cream is also nice, and a sprinkle of freshly grated nutmeg or crushed cardamom does wonders. A ginger biscuit or pastry base makes this specially special.

ISRAELI JAFFA-ORANGE CHEESECAKE

This recipe is interesting for several reasons – it uses yellow cornmeal to give a lighter texture, it has no base and it's incredibly simple. I'm told that it's equally good and even more unusual made with grapefruit.

For an 8 × 12 in/20 × 30 cm baking pan

1½ lb/675 g *cottage cheese*	4 oz/115 g *white flour*
4 *eggs*	¾ pt/425 ml *milk*
At least 6 oz/175 g *sugar*	*Vanilla essence*
2 oz/50 g *fine yellow cornmeal*	1 *orange, grated rind and juice*
(*polenta*)	2 oz/50 g *butter, melted*

Cream the cheese, eggs and sugar together then add all the other ingredients except the butter. Mix smoothly but don't overdo it.

Check for flavour; since you have enough orange juice for flavour, I think the rind of half a good-sized orange is enough, for this will be strengthened as the cake is cooked and the zest oils are released. If you think the mixture too orangey or too sweet, add lemon juice or lemon peel. In fact it's not a bad idea anyway as lemon acts on orange like salt does on other foods, making it better than the original.

Now stir in half the melted butter and pour the other half in to coat the baking pan. Put in the cheesecake mixture and bake at 350°F/180°C/Gas 4 for 1½ hours until nicely browned. Serve lukewarm with soured cream.

Options   You could put a nice shortcrust in the pan first if you like and use cornflour instead of yellow cornmeal.

SOURED CREAM CHEESECAKE

Rich and expensive; so although it originally came to me with the common base of crushed biscuits held together with melted butter, I think it is worth the effort to give it a base of excellent shortcrust pastry which you will first have to bake blind. While this base is still hot, spread it with some raspberry or strawberry jam which will seal the pastry and prevent it getting soft too quickly after the cheesecake mixture has been put into it and baked. It should be made in a lightly greased 9 in/22.5 cm springform pan.

5 *eggs, separated*	1 *small lemon, juice of*
4 oz/115 g *sugar*	1 oz/25 g *flour*
1 lb/450 g *cream cheese*	*Vanilla essence*
16 fl oz/450 ml *soured cream*	

Beat the egg yolks with the sugar until pale and light. Add the rest of the ingredients slowly and then fold in the egg whites, which have been beaten until stiff but not dry. Pour gently into pan (you can sprinkle some buttered crumbs around the edge if you like) and bake at 325°F/160°C/Gas 3 for 1 hour. Then turn off the heat and leave for 1 hour *without opening the door*. Then remove and cool completely before serving, perhaps slightly chilling first.

Its rich flavour and texture go extra well with fresh sharp fruit. This is also good made with orange rather than lemon and using rose-petal jam is another delicious variation.

14 Fruit, Ice Creams and Sorbets

Big heavy puddings are fairly unfashionable these days, and most of the grander restaurants prefer to base their last courses on fruit. In particular sorbets and ice creams of exotic fruits are served, usually a selection of two or three on a sauce, which is invariably raspberry based.

This direction is a boon for the home entertainer and delicatessen customer, for most of them will offer a range of pure dairy ice creams and fascinating sorbets that can be kept on hand or bought at the last moment. The trick of serving a sorbet on a bed of raspberry of other fruit purée has saved many a busy entertainer and looks and tastes far better than the small amount of effort required.

If you want to do more than just this, the delicatessen offers you amazing opportunities. These are but a few of the most successful and simple. The addition of some fabulous biscuits from France, some real butter shortbread from Scotland or an unusual liqueur from anywhere will make most of the recipes in this selection high on your list for repeat performances.

RASPBERRY COULIS

Amongst the few indispensable items in any good shop's deep freeze are frozen raspberries. Although they defrost exceptionally well, they are not always good enough to serve as is, unless as decoration on a pavlova or some other creamy dessert. Far better make a strained purée, flavour it nicely, and use that to make a stunning difference to almost everything.

Never listen to the admonishments of those who insist that purées of raspberries, blackberries and other soft fruits be poached or in any way cooked. The freshness of flavour and the balance of acid and sugar are both totally destroyed. The usual packaging of raspberries is in 8 oz/225 g packs, but you can adjust this recipe according to what you find. Of course, if you have fresh raspberries it will be even better.

Serves 4-12 depending on use

---

8 oz/225 g *raspberries,*   3-4 oz/85-115 g *caster sugar*
        frozen or fresh
Always put 10-12 raspberries aside to use as garnish.

It is certainly easier to make the initial purée of raspberries if you have a liquidizer or a good processor, but they aerate the sauce and lessen its brilliant colour. As you must remove the pips anyway it is not much more bother to force the fruit directly through a sieve. The most efficient way to do this is with a soup ladle, rather than the tiny edge of a wooden spoon. Flavour the purée with sugar and stir well until dissolved. This is perfectly usable as is, but can be made even more exotic. My favourite additions and variations are:

Rose-water   2 or 3 teaspoons of triple-distilled rose-water makes a classic and sensual combination that is the best of all dressings for perfect strawberries.

Orange Juice   The juice of half an orange and a teaspoon of grated rind.

Orange Liqueurs   Grand Marnier, Cointreau, etc.

Raspberry Liqueurs   When using this, cut down on the sugar initially; if you go wrong, add a squeeze of lemon juice.

Raspberry Eau-de-vie   The clear, sharp non-sweetened raspberry brandy adds a haunting flavour which is specially welcome when the coulis is to be served with something rich and full-flavoured, such as mangoes or really ripe peaches or pears.

Crème de Cassis   The rich sweet essence of blackcurrants marries exceptionally well with raspberries in anything creamy. Serve with a fresh mint leaf or two, as well.

Strawberries and Raspberries

A good raspbery coulis is a superb sauce for virtually any other fruit, especially soft fruits. You cannot go wrong with strawberries and raspberries. Line the base of a small dish with sponge fingers or macaroons. Top with 1 lb/450 g strawberries mixed with the full measure of a flavoured raspberry coulis, top with more sponge fingers and sprinkle those with the same flavour you added to the raspberries – rose-water, orange juice, etc. Chill for several hours before serving with thin, cold cream.

Pears and Raspberries
The affinity of pears and raspberries is little known but quite remarkable. A perfectly ripe pear, peeled and halved, bathed in lemon juice then served cut-side down in a pool of raspberry coulis is a sight and flavour to be cherished. If you like, or have, some poached pears, these would be equally good, particularly if poached with vanilla.

Coulis finished with framboise eau-de-vie is superb when served as a bed for a sharp pear sorbet, either as a pudding or as a palate cleanser in the middle of a long meal.

Mangoes and Raspberries
The combination works almost any way you care to think. The most glamorous, and one which will stretch a large mango between three people, is to bake some feuilletés of puff pastry 4-5 in/10-12.5 cm long and 1-2 in/2.5-5 cm wide. Cut these in half when cool, remove any uncooked pastry. Slice the cheeks from large mangoes (one mango for every three guests), peel them and slice into strips. Lightly toss in orange juice or lime juice. Arrange the mango pieces evenly between the pastry feuilletés and place in the middle of small serving plates. Spoon raspberry coulis carefully onto one side only of the plates, so that it justs reaches the halfway point of both ends of the pastry. On the other side gently pour the finest thick cream you are able to find – unpasteurized Jersey cream is what to look for. Dot three raspberries evenly on top of the cream then serve carefully.

If you forgot to glaze the pastry with an egg yolk, sprinkle each construction with a little caster sugar before serving.

If you can arrange it, it would be very clever to have the pastry warm and the sauce, fruit and cream just lightly chilled.

Cheese and Raspberries
Soft cheeses, quarks and crème fraîche are perfect foils for raspberry coulis of any flavour (but rose-water is best). Simply serve each guest a generous amount of whatever you can buy

and pass around a jug of raspberry sauce. For a little more luxury, have each serving sitting in a little puddle of cream or topped by some sweetened whipped cream. Ensure that the cheese and coulis are very cold or this will be very cloying, especially on the sort of hot day on which it should be served. Garnish with a leaf of rose geranium.

Cream and Raspberries

Nothing is simpler to make or serve than a raspberry cream, which is what most books call raspberry fool. Whip up ½ pint/300 ml double cream with a few drops of vanilla then fold in most of your coulis mixture, leaving the effect rather marbled. If you have another carton of raspberries, crush them very lightly and fold them through, too. Serve alone or with meringues and a splash of the liqueur or flavouring in the coulis. Top with the remaining coulis. A raspberry cream is sensational when slices of very ripe peach are folded into the mixture.

With or without peaches, coarsely crumble some meringues and fold those into your raspberry cream. If you are really in trouble, and need to extend your pudding to cater for extra guests, the meringue trick can be continued almost ad infinitum. Otherwise, slice up the cake you have for that *other* occasion and top with your raspberry cream-peach-meringue mixture.

BLACKBERRY COULIS

Frozen and fresh blackberries are much more available these days because of cultivation, and the cultivated ones retain a fair measure of the attractive acidity of the wild blackberry. You make a coulis of blackberries exactly as for raspberries, either force them directly through a sieve or liquidize them first and then sieve. Remember to retain a dozen for garnish.

You will need rather more sugar than for raspberries; for 8 oz/225 g fruit expect to use up 6 oz/175 g of sugar, but check carefully as you go.

The best support flavouring I have found is apricot brandy, of all things, and you will need 3 or 4 tablespoons on average. Use this sauce in almost every way you would the raspberry variety.

KIWI FRUIT WITH BLACKBERRY AND APRICOT BRANDY COULIS

Serves 4

1 recipe for *blackberry coulis* *(see above)*	4-6 *kiwi fruit*
	2-3 *fresh limes*
3 or 4 tbsp *apricot brandy*	

Make the blackberry coulis, flavour with apricot brandy and chill well. Peel the kiwi fruit and cut lengthwise into segments rather than into those boring rings. Bathe them in freshly squeezed lime juice but do not do this more than 30 minutes before serving as they will bleach and mush up. If the kiwi fruit are big and fat, which they should be, each can be cut into eight segments, which is right for one serving. Otherwise you will need more kiwi fruit and have to cut them into only six pieces.

When it is time to serve, sauce the bottom of four plates with the coulis, then arrange the kiwi fruit segments like the spokes of a wheel. Put a couple of reserved blackberries in the centre then lightly scrape a little lime peel over the lot.

BLACKBERRY SYLLABUB

The classic syllabub of wine-sweetened cream is terribly rich and thus not the sort of dessert beloved by the mainstream of opinion nowadays. This syllabub though has the advantages of being light and sharp and filled with fruit purée so you can pretend it is doing you good.

From the cook's point of view it is no trouble at all; prepare the basic mixture early in the afternoon or even the night before and whip it up just before dinner, or lunch.

Remember to keep back some blackberries for garnishing.

Serves 6-8

8 oz/225 g *blackberries*	½ *lemon, grated rind of*
¼ pt/150 ml *Amontillado sherry* *(or see method)*	1 *orange, grated rind of*
	3 oz/85 g *sugar*
2 tbsp *brandy*	¾ pt/425 ml *double cream*

Put the blackberries, which can be in their frozen state if that is how you bought them, into a bowl with the sherry or wine, brandy, lemon and orange rinds and sugar (if you have no Amontillado sherry, then use an equal amount of a dry sherry or of a dry white wine). Leave to marinate for as long as it suits you – 4 hours in a warmish place is the minimal time. Turn a few times during the first hour to help the sugar dissolve.

Reserve some of the marinated fruit then force the rest of the mixture through a sieve using the back of a soup ladle to save energy and to speed up the process. Once everything possible has been passed through, pour in the cream and beat until it stands in soft peaks.

Spoon the syllabub directly into tall serving glasses and chill thoroughly. Add the reserved fruit as decoration. Serve with thin ginger or almond biscuits.

Options A grander presentation is to first put a couple of blackberries in the bottom of each tall glass and to cover them with an extra dessertspoon or so of brandy and then to spoon in the syllabub. Top with a twist of orange peel or some freshly grated peel and the biscuits you have chosen.

If you have made some blackberry gin I imagine only greatness would result from using that instead of brandy, both in the initial mix and in the bottom of the glass. Do write and tell!

This is equally successful using raspberries, fresh or frozen. Either flavour of syllabub might be used atop the other fruit or on strawberries.

MY ICE CREAM

There are as many ways of making ice cream as there are flavours. The simplest is made by folding a fruit purée or a syrup into whipped double cream, something prohibited to many of us these days simply because of the expense. Otherwise an egg custard is called for, which is wonderful, but requires skill and patience.

This ice cream uses sweetened condensed milk, of all things, but really is a triumph of the first order. It is so simple and so amazingly cheap in comparison to others that you will scarcely believe the rich end result. You don't even have to beat it halfway through freezing – although it will improve the texture even more if you do. Remember to let ice cream soften in the refrigerator before serving or you will not truly appreciate the flavours.

Makes about 4 to 6 small servings

6 fl oz/175 ml *sweetened condensed milk, chilled*	¼ pt/150 ml *double cream, chilled*

Having turned your freezer down to its lowest temperature, turn the condensed milk into a chilled bowl and beat it until thickened. Pour in the cream and keep beating until the mixture has more or less doubled. Then fold in your chosen flavourings; the following are the ones I tested and I heartily recommend each one.

Apple and Cinnamon
Fold in ½ pint/300 ml slightly sweetened apple purée together with about 2 dessertspoons lemon juice and at least ½ teaspoon ground cinnamon. Turn into containers and freeze. Leave at least 24 hours in the freezer before serving, as the flavour develops. Some raisins which have been soaked in rum or orange juice would transform this into Apple Strudel Ice Cream.

Guava and Fresh Lime
Strain the juice from a 14½ oz/410 g can of guavas and reserve; purée the guavas and strain. Fold the purée into the basic mixture together with 1-2 dessertspoons freshly squeezed lime juice. Freeze. Serve with a little of the syrup from the can poured over the top and some freshly grated lime peel.

Apricot and Orange
Soak 8 oz/225 g dried apricots overnight in water to cover. Strain off and reserve the liquid. Purée the apricots then sieve directly into the cream/condensed milk mixture. Add 4 dessertspoons of lemon juice, 2 dessertspoons brandy and 2 teaspoons of freshly grated orange rind. Freeze.

Meanwhile reduce the soaking liquid to half its quantity together with a dessertspoon of sugar. Once chilled, flavour lightly with a little more brandy or an orange liqueur, and pour over each serving. This ice cream looks even better if scattered with chopped pistachio nuts.

Victoria Plum and Ginger

Drain the liquid from a 20 oz/550 g can of Victoria plums and reserve. Remove the stones. Liquidize the fruit and fold that purée into the basic mixture together with 4 dessertspoons lemon juice and 1-1½ teaspoons ground ginger.

To serve, reduce the liquid from the can to just ¼ pint/150 ml and chill well. Pour a little over each serving.

Banana

Mash three very ripe bananas with 5 drops of vanilla or rum essence and a squeeze of lemon or lime juice. You might substitute the pulp of 1 or 2 passionfruit for one of the bananas.

Citrus Curd Ice Cream

Even more simple is to fold whipped double cream into lemon curd, and to freeze that; unimaginably good if you have orange curd. I should fold ½ pint/300 ml cream into 1 lb/450 g of curd then adjust the curd content for a stronger or sweeter flavour.

CHESTNUT AND NUT ICE CREAM

I was told this idea originally came from Mauritius, presumably because of its French connections, and because the French make what are probably the best chestnut products of all.

8 oz/225 g *unsalted French butter*	1 tbsp *vanilla essence*
8 oz/225 g *caster sugar*	1 tbsp *brandy or rum*
1 lb/450 g *unsweetened chestnut purée*	4 *eggs*
8 oz/225 g *ground almonds or hazelnuts*	½ pt/300 ml *double cream (optional)*

Cream the butter and sugar particularly well until there is not a hint of graininess and the mixture is very pale. Add the chestnut purée, the finely ground nuts, vanilla and brandy or rum. Plain ground almonds are very nice but, if you roast hazelnuts until golden then grind those, the toasted nuttiness is a distinct improvement in my view. Be careful not to roast them so much that they develop a bitterness; provided you grind them finely enough, you do not need to remove the skins.

Separate the eggs and blend the yolks into the mixture. Whisk the egg whites then fold in gently. If you want also to add cream, which lightens the mixture, whip it and fold it in, before the egg whites.

This does not need to be beaten during freezing but should be frozen in a mould or bowl from which it can be turned out for maximum presentation effect – and at this price you want to get every bit of value from it.

Decorate with a fruit sauce or with fresh fruit. The ideal is marrons glacés in brandy syrup, but sharp soft fruit, a chilled purée of fresh black cherries and black rum, puréed plums with cinnamon and brandy, apricot and orange purée with a touch of mint essence, or just good old chocolate sauce would all finish the construction perfectly.

CANNED FRUIT SORBETS

The advent of more and more deep freezer capacity and a far better choice of fresh fruit throughout the year has seen a gradual waning of the popularity of canned fruits. Useful as they are, and delicious as many are, they simply don't taste the same as the real or the frozen type, mainly as a result of the high temperature at which they must be cooked to ensure they will last.

Nonetheless, the majority of them are not actually awful (except for strawberries, kiwi fruit and passionfruit, which simply are not suited to the process of canning), and in an emergency can make pretty exciting sorbets in a matter of hours.

Two canned fruits stand out as the basis for sorbets – lychees, and a rather special type of pawpaw or, as some would call them, papayas. The type to look for has many names, including mountain pawpaw, babaco and naranchi. The main differences are in flavour and in what part of the fruit you eat. The flavour is a truly heady mixture of honey, passionfruit and pawpaw. But unlike the fruit you may know, you do not eat the middle (which is seedy), but the fleshy skin. In fact when you open the can they look exactly the same as yellow or white peppers, pale, pointed and eviscerated. You will not easily find them but when you do, buy several cans. The initial scent when you open the can is so highly perfumed it can put many off, but this is not the way to eat them. They must be well chilled and that is why a sorbet made from them is so wonderful.

The technique for making any sorbet from canned fruits is the same whatever you use. Drain the fruits, liquidize and sieve carefully. For something like lychees, you need to do this several times to get maximum yield. Meanwhile reduce the syrup over heat until it is about half its original capacity, but do not let it caramelize. Mix the two together. Chill and then freeze, stirring from time to time.

Once the mixture is frozen at the edges and mushy in the centre, whisk it well until smooth and evenly textured. Then fold in the beaten white of an egg, which makes the texture smoother, increases the volume and ensures the sorbet will melt more slowly when you serve it. If you have an ice cream and sorbet maker, the egg white may be put in at the start of the freezing process.

Let the sorbet soften slightly before serving; sorbets should not be served hard and ice cold or the subtleties of flavour are lost.

Here are some ideas:

Lychee and rose-water sorbet (by the way, several of the great chefs of London agree with me that canned lychees make better sorbet than fresh ones); mountain pawpaw with some lime juice; pears with Maraschino, Kirsch or Poire William (the first, although more unexpected, is the most delicious) – a little vanilla goes well in this, too; apricots with orange peel or with chopped preserved ginger – try a dash of Crème de Menthe or some chopped fresh mint, too; peaches with chopped, toasted hazelnuts, which should only be added after the initial freezing; Victoria plums with nothing but a squeeze of lemon juice; greengages with tiny chunks of dried apricot and perhaps a touch of some eau-de-vie or Mirabelle; fruit salad – I've not tried it but I think a can of fruit salad, especially a superior tropical fruit salad, would make a really scrumptious sorbet.

And one more – don't overlook apples or apple purée, the basis of extraordinary sorbets, especially if made into an apple strudel sorbet with the same flavourings as my Apple Strudel Ice Cream.

TEA CREAMS, ICES AND SORBETS

When I was asked to help recreate a Victorian gala buffet for the National Trust at the stunning pleasure gardens of Claremont in Surrey, I accepted with haste. The evening was a triumph for everyone, blessed with one of the hot, still, balmy nights so typical of the summer of 1983. Hundreds of those who came had dressed in Victorian costume. They were entertained by bag-pipers and a steam organ. Men rode penny-farthing cycles, children played with hoops. You really could believe you were at a Victorian garden party and nothing was allowed to shatter the image.

I served a choice of creams made from Rose Tea, Formosa Oolong, Earl Grey and Red Cherry Tea. Eaten with summer's soft fruits to the sound of Handel's 'Music for the Royal Fireworks' while under a canopy of the most exuberant and thrilling pyrotechnical display seen in this country, they were the final key to being truly in another time and place.

Although you can use most quality teas for making chilled and iced desserts, the best will be made from one of the most useful of the relatively new products on the market – fruit flavoured teas. They are usually made from a basic tea impregnated with the essence of a fruit, but some, such as jasmine, rose or spiced-orange tea will actually have dried flowers or peel included. The range is quite phenomonal, over thirty when last I checked. You'll find mango and passionfruit, peach and blackcurrant, apple, cherry – even wild strawberry.

They make wonderfully refreshing and interesting drinks, and are perfect for iced drinks. But nothing matches the novelty and thrill of creams, ice creams or sorbets made from them. My favourite so far is Fortnum and Mason's Wild Strawberry Tea; but every one I have tried is worthwhile and every one can be used for any of the following three recipes.

You will usually find that your tea flavoured liquid will contain specks of tea leaves, and tea dust will spoil the look of the final pudding. I strain everything through muslin to be sure.

TEA CREAM

Serves 4-12 depending on accompaniments

1 oz/25 g *tea leaves, dry*
½ pt/300 ml *milk, boiling*
5 oz/150 g *sugar*

1 envelope *gelatine*
½ pt/300 ml *double or whipping cream*

Cover the tea with the boiling milk and let stand 7-9 minutes for a large leaved tea, 5-7 for medium tea. More ordinary teas can be used for this – the ones with the smaller leaves – and they will need to brew for 3-5 minutes. (Frankly the results will not be all that good.) Strain off the milk and make it back to ½ pint/300 ml with cold milk or water. Dissolve the sugar in this.

Spoon out 5 or 6 tablespoons of the mixture into a small saucepan, sprinkle on the gelatine and melt over very gentle heat until totally dissolved. Strain through a very fine sieve back into the milky tea and stir well. Strain through muslin. Once this mixture is cool, but before it starts to set, whip the chilled cream until firm and peaky then fold the two together. You must work fairly quickly as the cold cream will encourage the gelatine to set. Turn into a mould which has been rinsed with water or very lightly brushed with a vegetable oil and chill well to set firmly.

Serve alone, with fruit, or with one of the other tea desserts which follow.

TEA ICE CREAM

½ pt/300 ml *milk*
1 oz/25 g *tea leaves, dry*
5 oz/150 g *sugar*
1 level dessertsp *cornflour or arrowroot*

2 *egg yolks*
A pinch of salt
½ pt/300 ml *whipping or double cream*

Boil the milk and pour over the tea leaves, stir and let stand 7-9 minutes for large leaves, 5-7 for medium. Strain the milk tea off then make up the volume of liquid back to the original with a little more cold milk. Strain through muslin. Mix the sugar, cornflour or arrowroot, yolks and salt together in a saucepan and whisk in the flavoured milk. Heat, stirring, until thickened and simmer very gently for at least 5 minutes until the starchy flavour has gone.

Strain to ensure there is no suspicion of lumpiness, then leave to cool with clingfilm on its surface until at room temperature but before starting to set solidly.

Whip the cream and fold evenly but lightly into the custard. Freeze. You can give it a good whisking when half frozen if you like, which will further lighten the texture, but do not overdo it.

These tea ice creams are surprisingly highly flavoured and thus only a small serving is very satisfying. Naturally enough they mix with virtually any other fruit flavoured pudding or with fresh fruit itself.

For important occasions, when you have time for some elaborate preparation, you might consider serving each guest a dessert consisting of a portion of three different cold-tea puddings – a tea cream, a tea sorbet and a tea ice cream.

TEA SORBET

Whether you make these with a China tea, a Ceylon, Darjeeling or Assam tea, they are always refreshing and enjoyed. But if you make them with one of the fruit flavoured teas they become quite sensational. At the risk of repeating myself, the Wild Strawberry Tea version is one of the best things you will ever taste.

---

1 pt/575 ml *boiling water*	*Lemon juice (optional)*
1 oz/25 g *tea leaves, dry weight*	1 or 2 *egg whites*
Up to 5 oz/150 g *sugar*	

Pour the boiling water onto the leaves and let stand 7 minutes if the leaves are big, 5 minutes if they are medium-sized. The teas which have very small leaves are too rigorous of flavour to be used. Strain the tea well then make back up to 1 pint/575 ml with cold water.

Add all the sugar now or use just some of it and wait until the liquid is cool before finally committing yourself to how sweet it should be. Remember that very cold food tastes much less sweet than when it is warm. A little lemon juice might be added also but this is usually only needed if you are using a fairly plain or uninteresting tea.

When the liquid is cool put it into a suitable container and place this in the freezer. Once it is set at the edges but mushy in the centre, beat it well until even consistency. Then whisk up the egg whites until firm but not dry and fold them in. Freeze.

Let soften considerably (in the refrigerator) before serving.

Options   Fruit juices are excellent partners to cold tea. Thus you might make a sorbet of tea and pineapple juice, a particularly splendid combination, by soaking the tea leaves in just ½ pint/300 ml of boiling water and making up the full volume with unsweetened pineapple juice. An amount of mint added to the tea leaves would also be good. Apple also blends well with tea and if you are unable to buy an apple flavoured tea, then use half tea and half unsweetened apple juice as above.

The varieties at your fingertips mean you can match your sorbets to your diners, to your dinners or to the seasons. For instance, you may like to serve a jasmine tea sorbet after Chinese food, perhaps in partnership with a lychee sorbet.

Index